PRAISE FOR TONY PERROTTET

Pagan Holiday: On the Trail of Ancient Roman Tourists

"A terrifically funny writer . . . this history-cum-travelogue is as enjoyable as it is informative and twice as quirky."
—*Boston Globe*

"An appealing mix of the zany and the arcane . . . [Perrottet's] insistence on seeing what the ancients saw, no matter the filth, decay, and craven commercialism obscuring most ancient sites, becomes a terrific running gag."
—*New York Times Book Review*

"Brilliantly researched and beautifully written."
—*Rocky Mountain News*

The Naked Olympics: The True Story of the Ancient Games

"It's so great to have a truly funny (and poetic) writer putting the lurid colors back on the pale marble, where they belong. . . . It's full of the get-a-load-of-this factor—those juicy, vivid stories you can't wait to tell your friends. To my mind, that quality is the distinguishing trait of great nonfiction."
—Teller of Penn and Teller,
Las Vegas entertainer (and onetime Latin teacher)

ALSO BY TONY PERROTTET

Off the Deep End:
Travels in Forgotten Frontiers

Pagan Holiday:
On the Trail of Ancient Roman Tourists
(originally published as Route 66 A.D.*)*

The Naked Olympics:
The True Story of the Ancient Games

Napoleon's Privates:
2,500 Years of History Unzipped

· THE ·

Sinner's Grand Tour

A JOURNEY THROUGH THE
HISTORICAL UNDERBELLY OF EUROPE

Tony Perrottet

BROADWAY PAPERBACKS
NEW YORK

914
PERROTTET, T

BROADWAY

Copyright © 2011 by Tony Perrottet

All rights reserved.
Published in the United States by Broadway Paperbacks,
an imprint of the Crown Publishing Group,
a division of Random House, Inc., New York.
www.crownpublishing.com

BROADWAY PAPERBACKS and its logo,
a letter B bisected on the diagonal,
are trademarks of Random House, Inc.

All photos, unless otherwise credited, are from the author's collection.

Library of Congress Cataloging-in-Publication Data
Perrottet, Tony.
The sinner's grand tour : a journey through the historical underbelly of
Europe / Tony Perrottet.—1st ed.
p. cm.
1. Sex and history—Europe, Western—Anecdotes. 2. Grand tours
(Education)—Anecdotes. 3. Perrottet, Tony—Travel—Europe,
Western—Anecdotes. I. Title.
HQ18.E8.P47 2011
914.04—dc22   2011001256

ISBN 978-0-307-59218-7
eISBN 978-0-307-59219-4

Printed in the United States of America

Book design by Jennifer Daddio / Bookmark Design & Media Inc.
Cover design by Dan Rembert/Jim Massey
Cover photograph of The Three Graces by
Antonio Canova/© Araldo de Luca/CORBIS

1 3 5 7 9 10 8 6 4 2

First Edition

For Lesley and the boys

CONTENTS

· THE ·
Sinner's Grand Tour

The desire to possess that which is forbidden is as strong in the man as the child, in the wise as the foolish.

—Henry Spencer Ashbee,
The Index of Prohibited Books (1877)

THE DEVIL'S
TRAVEL BUREAU

It was a classic summer's day in London—the city was enveloped by veils of dismal rain—and as I skulked through the lonely back streets of Bloomsbury, I began to feel like Dr. Jekyll before a binge. Decent folk who passed me by seemed to hasten their step, ducking beneath their umbrellas when they glimpsed my wild eyes.

It was as if they could sense my furtive mission. I was on my way to the British Museum, where I planned to locate the dreaded Secretum, the world's most extensive cache of historical erotica, and then wallow in its shameful contents.

In the high Victorian age, with Oscar Wilde in the defendant box, fig leafs on every statue and moral watchdogs on every corner, many a guilty-looking gentleman would have trodden this same path to London's most hallowed institution. But instead of admiring the respectable exhibits, these discerning types would have slipped through the crowds to meet a museum official, the Keeper of the Secretum. Letters of introduction were presented, written by trustees or college dons, and then the visitor (who might have been accompanied, on rare occasions, by a female companion or two) would be ushered down a dark stairway to the North Basement, to wait for a door to be unlocked.

As the blue flames of the gas lamps spluttered to life, shelves full of writhing limbs emerged from the darkness—naked lovers carved in marble, satyrs in gold leaf on parchment, bronze phalluses of astonishing proportions. For the delectation of the chosen few, the Secretum offered an array of historical artifacts that were considered too obscene for public display. Cultures that the Victorians could barely dream of were here, brazenly enjoying themselves in every possible manner.

It must have seemed like a shrine to forbidden pleasure.

The Secretum was created in 1866, at the height of the era's sexual hysteria, to protect the public from the moral perils of history. The year before, 434 ancient phallic objects had been donated by a freethinking doctor named George Witt, who had made his fortune in Australia from banking. Dr. Witt was convinced that all world religions had begun with phallus worship, and had gathered around him a clique of wealthy phallus collectors who supported his thesis. While accepting the bequest, the British Museum trustees voted to allocate a special room where the Witt Collection could be examined in suitable privacy. The room was quickly supplemented with "obscene" treasures from all historical periods. British archaeologists and academics had long been returning from their journeys around the world with shocking depictions of guilt-free sex. By the 1890s, the Museum Secretum, Secret Museum, boasted over 1,100 wicked objects.

Today, we can get a detailed idea of the chamber's contents from the Secretum Acquisitions Register, a leather-bound tome where each new arrival was carefully noted. Preserved in

The Egyptian Room, official façade of the British Museum when the Secretum was offering forbidden treats to select visitors, shown around 1890. (© Lesley Thelander)

the museum archives, the Register makes entertaining reading. The word *ithyphallic* ("erect penis") appears in every second listing, with the pages often enlivened by thumbnail sketches. But it is the breadth of the collection that is most arresting. The Secretum held an eye-popping variety of Greco-Roman art, including a graphic sculpture of the god Pan fornicating with a she-goat; a medieval chastity belt; lewd engravings from Renaissance Venice; eighteenth-century porn from the oeuvre of the Marquis de Sade; ribald documents from Georgian British sex clubs; and much more. In short, the cream of Europe's erotica had been gathered in one thrillingly dingy chamber.

Naturally, the Secretum earned an underground, if highbrow, cachet. But despite its fame amongst the cognoscenti, it was so risqué that very few scholars felt comfortable describing their emotions in print; the records that survive are reserved, stiff-upper-lip complaints about the poor lighting or stale air. Still, we can imagine the enthusiasm of enlightened visitors to be similar to that of Henry James, who examined a portfolio of Lord Byron's graphic letters and sketches with his friend the novelist John Buchan. Buchan recalled in his memoir, "The thing nearly made me sick, but my colleague (James) never turned a hair. His only words for some special vileness were 'singular'—'most curious'—'nauseating perhaps, but how quite inexpressibly significant.'"

In 1912, the Secretum collection was divided up and moved to a series of locked backroom cupboards. Although new pieces, including two-hundred-year-old condoms, were still being added as late as 1953, the official attitude changed during the permissive 1960s. Items were slowly redistributed to their rightful places in the museum, and even the name Secretum fell from use. In 2001, the curator David Gaimster identified the last resting place of its vestiges as Cupboard 55 in the Department of Europe and Prehistory, and published an article with several photographs showing a few last saucy treats, which he regarded as a "time capsule" of misguided Victorian attitudes to censorship.

Today, although the museum doesn't overadvertise the fact, the entire storage collection is available to the public for "object identification" by appointment on Tuesday afternoons. So when I was in London, I made an appointment to visit Cupboard 55.

Finally, the museum was looming above me, like a haunted temple in the rain. I jostled past noisy tour groups and entered the polished halls of the King's Library. With a set of e-mailed instructions in my top pocket, my imagination was now racing like a schoolboy's. Perhaps just pulling a certain book from the shelf would open a secret panel, revealing a mahogany-lined

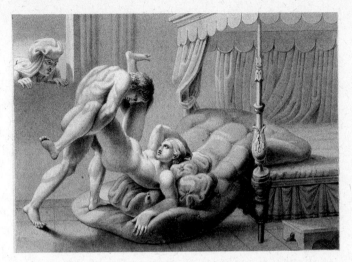

Copy of Renaissance Venetian pornography from I Modi, *or* The Positions, *safely locked up in the Secretum during the Victorian age. (© Trustees of the British Museum)*

parlor managed by tuxedoed servants. The reality of my visit was a little less Merchant Ivory. In the appointed room, I muttered my name into an intercom, and a door clicked open to reveal a shabby, abandoned hallway coated in hospital-gray paint. A pallid secretary appeared and led me up some echoing stairs to the storage areas. The walls were cracked and chipped, the windows opaque with grime.

I was getting excited.

Waiting for me was a curator, Liz Gatti, a fashionable sylph with an understated nose piercing. She was an incongruous figure, like an emissary from Marc Jacobs somehow lost in *Bleak House.*

"We get a lot of inquiries about the Secretum," she began, as I signed the visitor's book. "But I'm afraid you'll be disappointed. There's hardly anything left."

"Oh, I'll have a peek anyway," I said with what I hoped was proper aplomb.

We followed a corridor that was now lined with antique wooden cabinetry, each marked with a bronze number plaque, until we stopped in front of Cupboard 55. This was it, the dreaded Secretum's last known resting place.

"No whiff of brimstone," I joked.

Ms. Gatti looked at me askance, then pulled out a wad of keys.

I held my breath as she creaked open the aged hinges, as if it were a vampire's casket. Squinting in the semi-darkness, I made out rows of peculiar items that looked a bit like dreidels.

"Egad," I muttered, mystified. They *were* dreidels.

"Everything really has been moved about," Liz sighed. "Today we use the cupboard to house Judaica."

This was deflating and bewildering news: the last items from Cupboard 55 had been redistributed in 2005.

"But is there nothing here from the former Secretum?" I pleaded.

"Well, actually . . ." she said hesitantly, fingering the keys. "A few bits and bobs."

That was when she cracked open the adjoining door— Cupboard 54.

And there, neatly cushioned in a silk-lined wooden box, was a selection of candy-colored wax phalluses from eighteenth-century Italy. Liz explained that they had been donated by the avid phallus hunter Sir William Hamilton, British envoy to Naples during the Napoleonic Wars, who found them being used as fertility offerings in a village church and liberated them for Britain. (His busy career as a collector in Italy was overshadowed by the scandalous fact that his wife, Lady Hamilton, ran off with Lord Nelson). On the shelf below, a clinically white, acid-free Styrofoam sheet held items from the Witt Collection: Rows of ancient Roman phallic jewelry, crafted from coral, amber, and glass and now laid out like colorful insects in an entomology case. Amulets depicted lovers indulging in a range of athletic coital positions. One strange statuette showed a winged dwarf with a monstrous organ. Of course, phallic objects were carried every day as good luck charms in ancient Rome and are no longer off-limits. But today, filed away in this cobwebbed corner, they felt like the last buried link to that Victorian hysteria.

My eyes ran over the wealth of oddities—badges worn by medieval pilgrims, depicting the female genitals; a tobacco-pipe-stopper from the Tudor age, showing a knickerless woman pulling up her skirt—before settling on the last display. Lovingly laid out on a felt base were four eighteenth-century condoms,

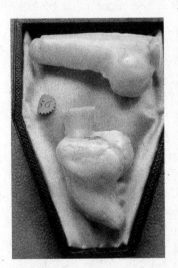 

Items from the former Secretum: Left, wax phalluses from southern Italy. Right, 18ᵗʰ century condom made from animal membrane. (Both © Trustees of the British Museum)

which had been discovered in the pages of a 1783 British self-help book, *The Guide to Health, Beauty, Riches and Honour*. These pioneer contraceptives were handcrafted from animal intestines. They were like works of art, intentionally pretty, tied at the open end by little pink ribbons of silk. They had survived in mint condition, all the way from the era of Casanova.

I was in historian's heaven.

REPROBATES ABROAD

With its breakthroughs in rail and sea transportation, the Victorian age also marked the birth of modern travel, and it would have been a stolid visitor indeed for whom the Secretum did not inspire wanderlust. If such peculiar wonders lurked here in London, how much more could be found in the outside world?

Those last remnants of the cache had the same inspiring effect on me. The British Museum was only the first stop in a personal Grand Tour I'd planned across Europe, in search of forbidden historical fruit. Today, the entire continent is still littered with secret boudoirs, perverse relics, and ancient dungeons, many of which, I was convinced, could be found.

In a way, this was a trip I'd been plotting since I was a teenager. I attended one of the last hard-line Irish Catholic high schools in Sydney, where the records of history were hardly less sanitized than they were for Victorians. In this orthodox world view, the ancient Greeks were lofty philosophers, Renaissance popes were cultured patrons of the arts, Georgian aristocrats were demure scientists and scholars, and all those Edwardian writers who moved to Capri were just interested in the scenery.

Even as an adolescent, I suspected there was more to it than that. And in recent years, the academic world has been deluged with research that focuses on the human, daily details of history, overturning the sterile view of the past. Whole volumes are now penned on the gay clubs of belle époque Paris or Weimar Berlin. The Marquis de Sade is more famous than any Catholic saint, and a lesbian nun in Renaissance Venice has as many biographies as Britney Spears.

Now, as I rushed through the dark streets of London, my mind was filled with images of history's most riotous fleshpots. I was going to hunt down the physical evidence of all those subversive texts. What if I found the truth behind Europe's most fabled lost wonders—the elaborate love-making "thrones" used in nineteenth-century French brothels, for example, or the pornographic chambers in the Vatican?

I arrived back at my hotel—it was called the Goodenough Club, which sounded like the sort of place Ebenezer Scrooge might put up his mother-in-law—but stopped short outside my room, frozen by the sound of bloodcurdling screams from within. It had almost slipped my mind that I wasn't taking this journey of discovery alone.

The moment I turned the handle, reality came crashing back. The floor was ankle-deep with clothes, toys, colored markers, plastic bottles and half-eaten food. It looked as though a horde of Pictish barbarians had ransacked the place. It was hard to believe the damage had been done by just two kids, aged ten and four. Now Henry and Sam were jumping off the beds like ecstatic ninjas. My wife, Lesley, looked shell-shocked. Any attempt to calm the boys had only inflamed their jet-lagged frenzy.

Les told me the management had been calling with complaints. Apparently the people downstairs thought a second blitz had begun. It was no use explaining that these kids were fresh off the plane from New York, a cross between Botticelli cherubs and Spielbergian children of the corn.

Instead, I explained to Lesley how I'd just examined a goat-intestine prophylactic. She nodded distractedly. "Do they deliver pizza in London?"

Les was very understanding when I'd first broached the idea of this trip back home in Manhattan.

"So it's a young man's erotic journey from Milan to Minsk?"

"What?"

"It sounds great. But I'm coming too. And so are the kids."

I'd clutched my map of Europe, with my route carefully zigzagged in red marker, and began to stammer out the many logical objections to the idea. Dragging both the boys around Europe would be—what was *le mot juste*?—excruciating. We'd be better off going up the Empire State Building and tearing up $100 bills.

"Well, we can't stay here!"

She did have a point. We were staring down the barrel of another brutal New York summer. The city would soon be stewing in its own fetid juices, and the boys would be ricocheting around the walls like Ping-Pong balls. Leaving the three of them in our tiny apartment would resemble some sinister Nazi experiment.

I pulled out my trump card: "You know, the material I'm researching is not exactly *kid-friendly*. . ."

But even as I said the words, I knew it was a lost cause. In today's uncensored era, Henry, at age ten, had probably seen more sexual imagery than I had by age thirty-five—and that's just from watching *The Simpsons*. He shrugged it all off with one furrowed eyebrow. And growing up in the East Village isn't the most protected environment on earth. His best friend's dad is a celebrated New York pornographer. Visiting the brothels of Old Paris or Pompeii is simply an historical approach to sex ed.

Sam, meanwhile, was only four years old, so would be less interested in randy Roman satyrs than the flavors of Italian gelato.

Before I knew it, our "family vacation" was settled. I tried to be philosophical: If nothing else, the next generation would have a broader view of the past than I did.

But now, in London, as I surveyed the wreckage of our first hotel room, the wisdom of the plan was difficult to recall. We were supposed to be traveling for three months, to the most sophisticated corners of Europe, on singular missions that were as delicate as an eighteenth-century timepiece. *How, precisely, was I going to stay sane?*

At least I could take refuge in my feverish visions of history. To paraphrase Virginia Woolf, every gentleman needs a Secretum of his own.

Chapter One

HELLFIRE HOLIDAYS

The Great British Sex Club Tour

We'd only been traveling for a week when I told Lesley I'd been fondling another woman's pubic hair.

Her eyes lit up. "Cool," she said. "Whose?"

A buxom British aristocrat's, I said. Quite possibly a Marchioness. A high class prostitute, at the very least.

We were climbing along the ramparts of St. Andrews castle in Scotland, buffeted by a fierce sea wind. Seagulls hovered above us as Henry and Sam flung themselves about the ruined walls, thrashing one another with the wooden swords we'd bought them in the ubiquitous museum gift store. It was a terrifying sight: Cherubs gone berserk.

Naturally, Les pressed me for details.

"Well, it wasn't the most romantic setting . . ."

In fact, I'd had the encounter in a fluorescent-white room in the Museum of St. Andrews University, where a curator had handed me a pair of latex gloves to protect their treasured relics from my bodily oils. The item looked like a typical antique silver snuff box, oval in shape and delicately engraved. It was

Locket containing the pubic hairs (under parchment) of a royal mistress, circa 1822. (Reproduced courtesy of the University of St. Andrews.)

only when I popped the lock that I discovered its true curiosity value.

Inside, a delicate piece of parchment concealed a tightly packed clump of hair, now turned silver, although I thought I detected a tinge of remaining ginger. These, the parchment explained in florid script, were in fact the pubic hairs trimmed from "the mons Veneris [mound of Venus] of a Royal Courtesan of King George IV."

This all-too-personal connection to the past had me breaking out in a sweat; now you wouldn't see *that* in *Antiques Roadshow.* And the snuff box had been just the foreplay, I enthused to Les. The museum had archived a whole cache of raunchy curios that had somehow survived from what must qualify as the kinkiest sex club in European history, the oddly named Beggar's Benison. To me, it was the most vivid reminder so far that the fun-loving Georgian era could be more brazen than today. Such intimate curls, snipped from one's amorous conquests, were a popular form of souvenir; lovers exchanged them as tokens of affection, and rakes wore them like cockades in their hats as tokens of potency.

In this particular case, the famously randy George IV had become a member of the Beggar's Benison while he was still a dandyish young prince in cravat and lace cuffs. Years later, while visiting Edinburgh as king in 1822, he provided this token to the club as a gesture for old times' sake. It's impossible to know from whom the curls truly originated, but his consort at the time was Elizabeth, the Marchioness of Conyngham, a feisty and alluring gold digger ("beautiful, shrewd, greedy, voluptuous," rejoiced one historian) who listed the future Czar Nicholas I among her many paramours.

For me, this was more thrilling than finding King Arthur's helmet. It was for moments like this, I told myself, that tourism in Britain is alive and well. And this was even before I saw the erotic toasting glasses or the pewter masturbation props.

SEXY BEASTS

Les was relieved that my hunt for lewd relics was finally showing some success; the road to Lady Conyngham's unmentionables had not been an easy one. Back in London, she had even suggested we skip Scotland entirely, thereby avoiding the gloomy veils of rain that sweep down from the North Sea. But I'd insisted that any self-respecting tour of historical sin has to commence in the phantasmagoric wonderland of sex that was Georgian Britain, the era from 1714 to 1837.

Few historians have described that golden age without a tangible pang of nostalgia. Long before the unbridled heyday of Mick Jagger and Austin Powers, debauchery proliferated up and down these sodden islands, fueled by prodigious amounts of alcohol and reckless moral abandon. "There was a gusto about 18th century vice unmatched before or since," writes Fergus Linnane in wistful tones in his *London: the Wicked City.* The ruling classes led by decadent example, as a fabulous influx of wealth from the budding empire provided them with the freedom to indulge their every fantasy without restraint. To modern eyes, the most striking feature of that crescendo of abandon is the proliferation of sex clubs. Today, they are generally referred to as Hellfire clubs, after one licentious group that operated in London in 1721. (The evocative term is still used by the dozens of s&m clubs in operation around the world; one Hellfire Club operated in New York's Meatpacking District beginning in the 1970s.) The British had long displayed a passion for bibulous societies—visiting foreigners would marvel at the plethora of clubs for artists, writers, scientists, beef eaters, bird-watchers—so clubs for carnal pleasure were a natural addition. Many of their rites were shaped by the era's newfound curiosity in science and world religions, not to mention the pleasant Enlightenment ideal that sex could be pursued for pleasure rather than procreation.

Although Georgian club activities have long been swathed in legend and rumor, historians agree that the most respectable intellectuals of the age cavorted alongside its most profligate rakes. They were joined by the era's liberated women, including successful actresses, opera singers, and the rebellious daughters of noble families who had been married at an early age to philanderers or dullards. Each club developed its own unique formalities and rituals. Members often wore outrageous fancy dress and used special regalia, which could take the form of wicked drinking vessels or medals; in one, voting ballots would go into a wooden box modeled on an inverted human torso, with yea or nay votes going into respective orifices. Meetings were held in the private wings of taverns, where, after a high-cholesterol buffet—beef, more beef, eel pie, and peaches in port—there would be ribald toasts, readings from pornography, and visits from comely young "posture molls" who were paid to pose suggestively on a table, the Georgian version of lap dancers. Special rooms were generally provided so members could retire with companions, and even ladies of fashion might unwind with handsome rent boys. Afterward, the more energetic gents might continue carousing in upscale commercial venues such as Miss Falkland's Temple of Love on St. James Square, where one could sip champagne in damask-lined parlors before using the "elastick beds," spring-loaded to provide new heights of pleasure, much like the vibrating beds of Vegas hotels.

At first, one could only find such adventurous clubs in London. There was a women-only club on Jermyn Street offering discreet lesbian encounters, the Mollies Club that welcomed gay members, and the Flagellant's Club, for those who favored a little birching (a habit so popular that it was known in brothels throughout the Continent as "the English vice"). But as the eighteenth century progressed, even more creative sex clubs began to emerge in the remoter corners of Britain, where the most peculiar rituals could be conducted away from prying eyes.

Sadly, in the prudish Victorian era, most traces of the Hellfire clubs were scratched from the historical record. The horrified grandchildren of the rakes burned many of the most embarrassing letters and club artifacts. In modern London, even the locations of their meeting places have mostly been erased or transformed. But I was delighted to discover that the Victorian purges did not reach the remotest corners of the British countryside. In fact, the homes of two legendary Hell-fire clubs could still be tracked down today. In no time, I'd mapped out a road trip that was based not on ye olde castles and countryside but the hidden remains of Britain's wildest partygoers.

Les was thrilled by the news that I had hired a car for a road trip. Oxford, perhaps? Bath? Stonehenge? She had a cousin somewhere in Somerset. . . .

"Nope." I pointed triumphantly to our first stop on the map. "West Wycombe!"

SODOM-ON-THAMES

The tiny village of West Wycombe in Buckinghamshire would be typical of any rural English outpost, except for one compelling twist: It was home in the 1750s and '60s to a blasphemous club which went by the innocuous name of the Order of the Friars of Saint Francis of Wycombe. It was the brainchild of the era's most colorful rake, Sir Francis Dashwood, patron of the arts, humanitarian landowner, and shameless debauchee. ("Rapist, sodomite," condemns one historian. "Gentleman, scholar," notes another.) Membership of the order included some of the highest peers of the British realm, who, according to popular tradition, indulged in sacrilegious orgies, human sacrifice, and devil worship. Modern scholars discount the more rabid rumors of Satanism. But legends about the brotherhood have been embellished through the generations, inspiring a string of

Victorian pornographic novels, pop culture films such as the 1961 Peter Cushing movie *The Hellfire Club,* and cult episodes of *The Avengers.* A version of the sinister club even turns up in Stanley Kubrick's *Eyes Wide Shut,* when Tom Cruise stumbles onto a remote rural manor filled with masked aristocrats indulging in unspeakable acts.

To untangle the sordid truth about the club, I first needed to find a base to stay in West Wycombe—and these days, the most terrifying thing about the village may be the Tripadvisor guest reviews of its sole hotel, the George and Dragon pub.

"A real letdown!"

"Skip it!"

"Oh dear!"

"Never again!"

"One to avoid."

But we couldn't avoid it. Apart from its being the only accommodation, the George and Dragon was the perfect historical setting—a three-hundred-year-old carriage inn that lurks in the very shadow of the Dashwood family estate. So I decided to prepare Les for the worst by giving her a printout of the reviews to look over as we drove along the M5. ("Boy, how disappointing!" "Food and service was a joke!" "Take earplugs!")

She was quiet for a while, pondering the horror that lay ahead. "How many nights are we staying?" she finally asked.

"Oh, three, maybe five. Remember, we're researching sordid Georgian history. We don't want a Holiday Inn with kitchenettes."

"As long as it's not *too* squalid. Remember what we agreed regarding the boys. No food poisoning. No vermin."

Henry chimed in from the back seat. "Does it have a pool?"

He hadn't traveled a lot in Europe. "It'll have beds."

"Oh, man."

Sam, thankfully, had passed out in his booster seat.

I explained that West Wycombe was an essential stop on any self-respecting Hellfire journey. Sir Francis Dashwood's tenth-generation descendent, Sir Edward, was alive and well in the ancestral mansion. He was even operating the family's secret tunnels as a tourist attraction called the Hellfire Caves. If we stayed in the village, I reasoned, I could surely pay him a visit.

West Wycombe turned out to be little more than a cluster of miniature dwellings buried like a frightened hedgehog in the rolling green countryside. The George and Dragon seemed innocent enough at first, with whitewashed walls and exposed beams typical of its days as a coaching inn, and a cobbled driveway worn with ruts. I stooped under a low doorway and

West Wycombe Park, an enclave of Italian taste designed by the most notorious debauchee of 18th century Britain, Sir Francis Dashwood.

entered the darkened pub, savoring the whiff of ancient beer soaked into decaying carpet. A couple of orange bulbs gave off less light than candles.

"Hello," croaked a voice from the gloom. "Fancy a pint, mate?"

I looked at my watch—10:00 a.m. Well, might as well ingratiate ourselves.

Two figures were hunched at the bar like gargoyles, with tobacco-yellow skin, greasy long hair, and eighteenth-century dentistry; one of them turned out to be the cook. Well, nobody can say that traveling in rural England isn't exotic. Just a few miles from the bright lights of modern London, the Hogarthian stock was hardly diluted. In hushed tones, they told me stories of Sir Edward, the modern scion, who lives on the splendid estate but once came into the pub. "He's a regular bloke," they said. "He *drinks,* you know."

Henry watched wide-eyed from a corner booth, looking like a ripe candidate for kidnapping to Fagan's lair. Sam was playing with the silver condiment tray, quietly mixing teaspoons of sugar to the salt then spreading it over the table.

As I lugged our bags up the stairs, the George and Dragon creaked and groaned as if it were alive. The room was a bit frayed and airless, perhaps, but not quite the desperate rat hole depicted by the reviews. From our window, I could see the tiny hilltop church, instantly recognizable for a very strange addition to its architecture. A gilded wooden sphere the size of a weather balloon was mounted on top of its steeple, gleaming in the sun like a *Dr. Who* device or antique Orgasmatron. In 1763, Sir Francis himself had devised this ball so that he and a few friends could sit inside it, knee-to-knee, and enjoy panoramic views of his estate. Sounds harmless enough, but these were not your average rural views. According to village lore,

Sir Francis Dashwood's golden ball, the Georgian era's strangest party venue, mounted on St. Lawrence's Church, West Wycombe.

Dashwood had invited the vicar up to his new golden orb to enjoy the vista. The man of the cloth was horrified to discover that Dashwood's garden had been landscaped to mimic the female form, with two hills topped with pink flowering shrubs at one end and a tightly cropped triangle of forest at the other. On a prearranged signal, fountains erupted at each of the garden's erogenous zones, causing the vicar to collapse in shock. He was only revived with "strong liquor."

In the hallway, I picked up the black rotary phone the size of a bread box and dialed Sir Edward's office. A secretary with a fine accent explained that the squire was away for the day "on business" but would be returning to his estate soon.

"Business," I thought—a code word for mischief if ever there was one.

Back in the bar, I found Henry examining a small engraving of a maiden about to be ravished by an energetic monk.

"Dad, is he one of the club people?"

It was time to visit the boiled lolly shop.

"Come on, creatures!" I said, using one of my fond names for the boys, although it drew an appalled expression from the publican's wife.

"They're not creatures," she said. "They're human beings!"

I also liked to call them Thing One and Thing Two but decided not to explain.

The order's notorious clubhouse was the medieval abbey of Medmenham (pronounced Med-num). It is now a private mansion, but you can see it on the opposite bank of the Thames by hiking for a mere two hours through brambles and cowpats. In 1750, when he was an up-and-coming, thirty-two-year-old member of Parliament, Sir Francis Dashwood renovated the abandoned ruins into a private rumpus room for theatrical and carnal misbehavior. Members included fellow scions of the British government, such as the Earl of Sandwich and radical John Wilkes, and it was visited by celebrities like the writer Laurence Sterne, artist William Hogarth, and Benjamin Franklin, who became Dashwood's close friend. From the few surviving reports of members and guests, there is no doubt that a dozen randy "apostles" would gather in monks' robes for twice monthly bacchanals beneath the Abbey's stained-glass windows and erotic frescoes. Women of fashion would travel from London to join the frolics dressed as nuns, and saucy local "nymphs" were paid to lie naked on his altar so the monks could lick holy wine from their navels—a mere aperitif before

Medmenham Abbey, scene of depraved Hellfire club meetings in the mid-18th century.

the real festivities began. But the precise nature of the ensuing entertainment has been a matter of feverish speculation by scholars ever since.

In 1765, after fifteen years of club life, the highest-ranking members of the order fell out over politics. Dashwood retreated from his abbey to an even more secret venue. An old chalk mine existed in the hillside of West Wycombe, so Sir Francis had workers expand the tunnels into an elaborate network of passageways and caverns going down three hundred feet. The torch-lit underworld evoked the pagan catacombs of Rome, with alcoves to house suggestive statues and even a bridge built over a subterranean stream, dubbed the Styx. Benjamin Franklin was impressed with the effect when he stayed with Dashwood in 1772: "His Lordship's imagery, puzzling and whimsical as it may seem, is as much evident above the earth as below it," he wrote. Long after the club activity ended, local school children and Victorian tourists would explore the site by candlelight. Then, in 1951, the Dashwood family realized the caves could be a genuine money spinner. They cleared the fallen debris and opened the tunnels as the Hellfire Caves. Publicity was unwittingly provided by the local vicar, who denounced the unholy project from his pulpit and complained to the *Daily Mirror* that "my tummy wobbles like a jelly every time I pass the entrance."

Today, the Hellfire Caves qualify as West Wycombe's only tourist attraction. In the leafy hill above the village, the entrance is still framed by Dashwood's original flint-work facade that evoked the nave of a Gothic church. We paid our entrance fee at the gift store, and ventured gingerly into the cave's dark maw, where a sign soberly warns that "sufferers of dizzy spells, faints, blackouts and loss of balance should not enter." The clammy air seeped down our collars as we followed the sepulchral corridors, peered into eerily lit niches that had been decorated with mannequins in period dress. Although this was supposed to be a family-friendly attraction, the modern Dashwoods couldn't resist a few naughty references. Les distracted Henry from reading a plaque with the juicy "Nun's Poem," in which a young initiate confesses to a ménage à trois with an abbot, to an induced abortion, and to "Sapphic pleasures" with her fellow convent girls.

The highlight is the cavernous Banqueting Hall, with four cozy little Monks' Cells radiating from its perimeter, each containing moss-covered statues. The piped-in voice of one of the Dashwoods announced in plummy tones that these cells were once furnished and "used by the club members for privacy with their ladies." It then added that the Hellfire Caves are now available for hire—"a unique and atmospheric venue for any dinner party or disco." The chill air made this prospect

Ghostly statue within the "monks' cells," Hellfire Caves.

seem dubious, but an attendant, who was fixing a light, assured me that they'd just had 220 people down for a birthday party. "There are some amazing sound effects in the tunnels," he said. "Security is excellent: You don't get gatecrashers down here, and no matter how much noise you make, you don't disturb the neighbors. It even gets *warm* during parties. It's amazing what body heat can do!"

Back at the George and Dragon pub, a few other lost souls gathered for dinner. We crouched together in a foggy window seat, gnawing on mutton chops washed down with porter ale. Henry drew pictures of vampires for some reason, which attracted concerned looks from the elderly publican. When I mentioned that we were in Buckinghamshire to hunt down relics of the sordid Hellfire Clubs, he raised one blood-shot eye.

"Quite the family trip, then," he said, dipping into a fresh pint.

SEX AND SENSIBILITY

I had yet to meet Lord Dashwood—the twelfth baronet, that is, Sir Edward. After all, who else could clear up the enduring mysteries of the Hellfire Club? The next morning, when I hoisted the black rotary phone again, the secretary explained that, why, yes actually, Sir Edward would be happy for me to drop by for a chat.

"Really?" I asked, not quite believing it. But before she could change her mind, I dropped Les and the boys by the church mausoleum—there was an exciting urn that contained the withered heart of a Hellfire Club member—and drove off to meet the lord of the manor.

At the forbidding iron gates of West Wycombe Park, I punched in a security code, and they creaked open to reveal a tree-lined carriage path stretching into the distance. In Sir Francis's day, the estate had been scattered with erotic "follies," which remained so notorious in the early 1800s that Jane Austen included sly allusions to them in *Sense and Sensibility*. (Even her use of the name Dashwood for her characters, argues Janine Barchas of the University of Texas, created "an uneasy atmosphere of wealth, infamy, and illicit sexuality.") As I strolled along, I tried to spot any wicked relics in the shrubberies. The air was fragrant with freshly cut grass; a lake stretched to the left, with swans regally cruising beneath a statue of Neptune. Thoroughbred horses gamboled on the sea of green, and a vast Italianate mansion hovered on the crowning hilltop.

Dazed by the feudal idyll, I must have become disoriented on the paths and ended up in the forest, until a man in a white four-wheel drive vehicle pulled up beside me.

"Are you Sir Edward?" I asked.

"Wish I was!" the warden guffawed before pointing me in the right direction.

I finally found the master sitting behind a desk in the estate office near the stables. This modern descendent of the wicked old rake had the affable, professional demeanor of a village accountant, reminding me a little of the British actor-playwright Alan Bennett. He was in his mid-forties, bespectacled, and casual in khakis and a crimson polo shirt. This Lord Dashwood is a quiet family man; instead of deflowering local virgins, he spends his time managing the family's five thousand acres of farmland. Still, I couldn't help but rejoice at meeting the direct descendent, who might provide clues to the true club activities.

Over tea and biscuits, Sir Edward was quick to defend his ancestor's reputation, arguing that the popular concentration on his sex life does him an injustice.

"Sir Francis wasn't crazy," he insisted. "He was just a tremendous, larger-than-life character. And he had bloody good fun. He traveled a hell of a lot. He supported the arts. He developed the first semaphore system." (The golden ball on the church steeple wasn't just for boozing—apparently Dashwood used mirrors to flash coded messages as far as Oxford, about twenty miles away.) "He looked after his villagers in quite an enlightened way. There were so many facets to his life, which is probably why he got on so well with Benjamin Franklin.

But, yes, he was also very self-indulgent—a bit like Richard Branson today."

And the order? "Oh, it was a good, fun men's club," Sir Edward said. "Yes, they all dressed up and drank a hell of a lot, and, yes, there were women involved. But look at the men themselves. They were very erudite; they loved the classics, astronomy, and astrology. They weren't into black magic. The charges of Satanism are rubbish. But they *were* interested in exotic philosophies. Eastern mysteries fascinated them."

Of course, he added mischievously, the aura of sexual depravity has always been excellent for business. In fact, if it weren't for the devilish eighteenth-century reprobate, the Dashwood family would be in dire financial straits. It was hard to believe now, but two generations ago, West Wycombe Park was bankrupt, Sir Edward admitted. The mansion was a wreck, with most of its period furniture auctioned off and many of its faux-finished walls whitewashed. But in the 1950s, income from the Hellfire Caves helped fund a recovery. Sir Edward's father had renovated the house; he even tracked down many of the original household artworks and furniture. A deal was cut with the National Trust to allow paying visitors, many of whom are lured by the Hellfire Club's dastardly reputation, into the lower floors of the mansion. Today, the estate is a popular film location for period costume dramas and it certainly isn't turning down any ghost-hunting TV shows where psychics with infrared cameras overnight inside the caves, trying to capture tormented souls on film. "It brings in the crowds," Sir Edward shrugged.

So had any of the club artifacts survived? I asked. Were there any relics left hidden beneath the floorboards, any of the robes, skull cups, or corrupted sermon books?

Sir Edward shook his head sadly. "The nineteenth-century

Dashwoods were less enthusiastic about the club," he said. "Any relics have vanished."

Afterward, I visited the Dashwoods' Palladian mansion, a kaleidoscope of Italian marble, chandeliers, classical busts, and tapestries. The dining room boasted portraits of Sir Francis himself waving tipsily in Ottoman garb and one of his female cronies, the luscious actress Fanny Murray, exposing her left breast with an insouciant smile. In the estate grounds, I finally found Sir Francis's Temple of Venus, where a grotto's entrance and curved walls were designed to evoke a vagina and a pair of spread legs. The entrance is still guarded by a statue of Mercury, the god who guides travelers on safe journeys and who, incidentally, taught humankind to masturbate.

It had started to rain, so I slipped inside the damp crevice

The view from the cave beneath the Temple of Venus, one of the "erotic follies" on the Dashwood estate.

and sat on a marble block. It was not a bad place to take stock of the evidence on the Order of St. Francis.

In the end, historians are left to piece together what really happened at the order from the few fragmentary and dubious sources—the club cellar book, which listed liquor consumption, and reports from former members and guests, including scurrilous verse by the poet Charles Churchill. But here in the womb of the estate, it wasn't hard to imagine the club at its prime. On warm summer nights, guests would arrive at the abbey via luxury gondola, alight on the docks and wander through the torch-lit garden, glimpsing statues with suggestive inscriptions in Latin amid the foliage. Once inside, they would be met by the twelve hooded "apostles" in their long white habits and the chief voluptuary, Sir Francis, whose red robe was trimmed with rabbit fur. According to a 1779 account purporting to be by a female guest, *Nocturnal Revels*, each friar was allowed to invite "a Lady of cheerful disposition, to improve the general hilarity." The aristocratic "nuns" wore masks until all the males had arrived, so that they could leave unrecognized if an acquaintance—or husband—was among the guests. In a candlelit dining room where a grand mantelpiece was inscribed with the words FAY CE QUE VOULDRAS (a quote from Rabelais, "Do As You Please"), a long table was resplendent with polished silver, crystal, and "food of a most exquisite kind and in gargantuan proportions." There were plentiful mockeries of Catholicism and the Papacy. A satiric grace was recited in Latin, and fine claret was then drunk from cups that had been fashioned from human skulls. The latest pornography was read from volumes bound as sermon books. Scraps of food were tossed to the club mascot, a baboon dressed as a priest. But further details will always be vague. In the late 1800s, a Buckinghamshire historian named Thomas Langley tracked down Sir Francis's elderly housekeeper at Medmenham and quizzed her on the specifics of club meetings. Apparently he was so horrified by her stories that he decided they "might as well be buried in oblivion."

The killjoy.

"Where to next, Dad?" Henry asked as we packed up the car. I sensed a certain relief that the George and Dragon would be behind us. "Somewhere warm, right?"

He seemed to think that if we just hit the road we could end up in Hawaii. I cleared my throat nervously. "Well . . . not exactly."

The most perverse and resilient Hellfire Club of all actually thrived in a land more often associated with bagpipes and offal than riotous pleasures of the flesh. Founded in 1732, the Beggar's Benison lasted in Scotland for over a century, to 1836. By a stroke of good fortune, the original club minutes have been passed down through the ages, so there is no doubt that its meetings were little short of bizarre. Even more exciting to me, there were indications that the twisted club relics had also survived.

Before leaving New York, I'd found a thin volume privately printed in Edinburgh in 1892. The frontispiece warned that the text was "Solely Intended for Antiquaries"—Victorian-speak for dirty-minded connoisseurs—and it included shadowy photographs of some quite disturbing Benison memorabilia. I pored over nineteenth-century travel guidebooks to Scotland for clues to their whereabouts. In one 1860 opus, *The Fife Coast from Queensbury to Fifeness,* the author, Henry Fairnie, alluded to the Beggar's Benison's celebrations that were carried out "with the want of refinement characteristic of the age." Most important, he refers to a cache of artifacts "still in existence at Anstruther. . . ."

"Where?" Les asked.

"Anstruther. The original home of the Beggar's Benison. It's a fishing village north of Edinburgh. They met in a tavern there—and it still exists!"

We pored over a map. Anstruther was located on the East Neuk of Fife, by the Firth of Forth, which sounded like somewhere Bilbo Baggins might hang out.

The newspaper showed the weather forecast in Scotland— rain, rain, rain, sometimes heavy, sometimes light—but I tried to remain upbeat, playing up the Gothic atmosphere. It was in these soggy recesses of the British Isles, I explained, that the darkest secrets were best preserved. History somehow congealed in the damp.

What's more, I swore that we could get there in just a couple of days, if we drove nonstop, that is. Henry groaned and buried his face in his hands.

LIFTING THE KILT

Fifty miles north of Edinburgh, Fife's windswept cliffs seem carved by a giant bread knife. Back in the eighteenth century, this whole coastline was a gloomy expanse of coal pits and salt pans, where villagers eked out a harsh life pickling herrings or smuggling whiskey. The East Neuk still isn't exactly picnic territory today. Following the lead of the Scots, we bought fish and chips and ate them sitting in the car in the rain, staring out to sea. Les pressed her nose to the window: "Ooh, there's some lovely filth down here, Dennis."

The Tripadvisor reviews of the Smuggler's Inn in Anstruther made the George and Dragon sound like the Plaza.

"The pits!"

"Dirty and shabby . . ."

"Sleep in your car! You'll be more comfortable!"

"An absolute disgrace . . ."

"Carpets are stained, rooms smell . . ."

"Aweful!" [*sic*]

I was sure it must be another exaggeration. "Let's hit the road!" I cried, with all the panache of Chevy Chase in a National Lampoon movie, and put on the Proclaimers CD for the fifth time that day.

The tide was out when we arrived in Anstruther, leaving a lush layer of pungent seaweed. Trawlers lay on their sides like beached whales, and a forlorn web of nets was drying on the stone walls. Every so often, tiny rays of sunlight peeked through the gray clouds just long enough to remind us of what we were missing. I left the gang beachcombing. They have a mania for the beach glass in any country, and in Anstruther there was treasure everywhere, as if shipwrecks had been depositing the stuff for centuries. I happily went off on my own obsessive hunt, followed by cawing gulls.

Nobody was peddling Hellfire Club history in Anstruther. In a salt-encrusted museum devoted to fishing, the village's local historian, Christine Keay, gave an involuntary shudder when I mentioned the Beggar's Benison. "Every now and then, some artifact will resurface at auction in Edinburgh or London, and there will be a flurry of interest in the club," she said. "But, no, we're not promoting it as a tourist attraction."

And the relics? She didn't think there was anything left in Anstruther.

I slogged back across the seaweed to inspect the foundations of Castle Dreel, where the club held its first meeting in 1732. The group's enigmatic name—which in full was The Most Ancient and Puissant Order of the Beggar's Benison and Maryland—was born of a story about King James V. While traveling in Scotland incognito, he asked a local wench, "a buxom gaberlunzie [beggar] lass," to carry him across a river on her back. Rewarded with a gold coin, the delighted woman offered the king her blessing: "May prick or purse never fail you." (In today's terms, may you never be in need of cash or Viagra.) This beggar's *benison*—that is, blessing—became the club credo.

But club members found Castle Dreel too decrepit even in 1732, so its gatherings were moved to a discreet neighboring tavern, today called the Smuggler's Inn.

Anstruther, home of the Beggar's Benison self-abuse club, with the remains of Castle Dreel visible to the left.

With its back entrance down stone steps to a slimy canal once used for contraband deliveries, it was a contender for Robert Louis Stevenson's *Kidnapped*. If anything, the panicked Tripadvisor reviews had understated the aura of decay. Like most pubs of its age, every wall had the skewed angles of a German Expressionist film set. A half dozen moth-eaten drunks swaying back and forth at the bar, like bachelor sea lions who had left their pride in defeat to spend their last days huddled together, breaking wind. The scent of sour bile added to the mix indicated a truly committed boozer's venue.

Undaunted, I traipsed upstairs and found a weather-beaten little housekeeper. She looked at me as if I were insane.

"You want a room?" she asked. "Here?"

The rotund owner, who was gnawing on potato chips in his office, looked me up and down suspiciously, as if he knew just what I was up to.

"Take your pick, mate," he said, jerking his thumb toward the empty rooms in the rear of the establishment. I chose two small chambers with ocean views—that is, across the village graveyard.

"There's something sick about this place," Les whispered, when we'd all gathered in the family lounge upstairs, which was designed like Captain Hook's cabin. "Not just seedy—sick. It has a really weird vibe."

The urchins, sensing our unease, huddled together as if they might be dragged off for sacrifice.

"Just one night," I promised.

We urgently needed a distraction. In a darkened annex, which had exposed stone walls from the original eighteenth-century tavern, I noticed the housekeeper was helping a technician set up a karaoke system. I asked her about the gentleman's club and she paused long enough to tell me that a historian had once visited here and asked the same thing. This room was the oldest part of the pub, so it must have been here that any gatherings had occurred.

I ordered some drinks and we settled into a booth to absorb the rich historical atmosphere. Maybe the Smuggler's Inn wouldn't be so bad.

Then we heard a series of thuds from the direction of the tight spiral staircase.

"Will you look at that," I heard one of the drunks from the bar downstairs. "That kid fell all the way down the stairs."

I dashed down to find Sam waddling around the bar as if nothing had happened. Luckily, the steps were covered with the thickest, and the dirtiest, shag pile carpet in Britain. But the fall had upset the drinkers, and they continued to murmur over their pints grimly, making me feel as paternally responsible as Homer Simpson.

Back upstairs, we wedged Sam into the booth and tried to stay cheerful. Random squawks of feedback emitted from the karaoke machine for another hour or so, until the technician gave up and had a drink.

If a traveler had managed to peep through a keyhole at an actual Beggar's Benison meeting here 275 years ago, he or she would have witnessed a disconcerting pageant, the likes of which *Masterpiece Theatre* has so far been in no hurry to depict.

Thanks to the survival of the minutes, we can reconstruct the club meeting that took place on the night of November 30, 1737—St. Andrew's Day. In miserable weather (the minutes read: "Tempest"—which must have been quite something to have been worth noting in Scotland), twenty-four members, all male, gathered in the firelit room. They represented a cross-section of educated provincial society, from landed gentlemen, doctors, and lawyers to humble customs clerks, and included older men and young, single men and married. Everyone was wearing olive green silk sashes and a string of club medals. On a table in the center of the room, a pair of pink-cheeked posture molls hired from the local village ("aged 18 and 19") struck acrobatic poses in the nude, while members inspected the "Secrets of Nature" with a clinical eye. Touching the talent was strictly forbidden; if anyone was overcome by desire or booze and broke this club rule, he would be thrown outside into the rainy alley. (Sometimes the girls themselves caused a ruckus, as happened at a 1734 meeting. One Betty Wilson, age fifteen, turned out to be "a bad model and very unpleasant," and had to be escorted from the inn.)

First came the initiation rites. A club official produced a large pewter plate, called the Test Platter, placed it on an altar, and folded a white napkin upon it. At the blowing of a horn, three new members were led in from a small room where they had been sequestered, trousers down. Perhaps due to sheer anticipation, combined with glimpses of the naked posture girls, these initiates had already achieved a priapic frenzy. Or perhaps, like modern sperm clinics, the waiting room was conveniently supplied with the club's erotic literature. In any case, the trio advanced to the platter and went to work with enthusiasm until they produced "a horned spoonful." The three flushed initiates were then presented with a special club diploma decorated with the naked figures of Adam and Eve, and handed phallic-shaped drinking vessels, called prick glasses, charged with fine port wine. A toast was offered to "Firm Erection, fine Insertion, Excellent distillation, no Contamination." The prick glasses turned out to be jokes; when the new members tried to drink, port spurted down their chins and shirts.

The club sovereign then reverently produced the most legendary of the Benison props—a wig that was supposedly made from the pubic hairs of King Charles II's many mistresses, and would imbue the wearer with sexual potency. He put this astonishing item on his head to raucous toasts and cheering. He then ordered the other members to relieve their tensions in the Test Platter. ("All frigged," observe the minutes.)

As the waves lashed the castle ruins and rain hammered the dark tavern windows, festivities continued. An extract from *Fanny Hill,* a pornographic novel then circulating in manuscript, was read. A doctor lectured on the latest research in gynecology. New club rules were submitted for a vote. And there was much, much drinking.

"Broke up at 3 o'clock a.m.," conclude the minutes.

Surely someone at the Smuggler's Inn knew about all this? I realized with a shudder that I would have to interview some of the characters in the public bar. By nightfall, the boozing had escalated, with drunks howling outside in the lane, slurred arguments and doors slamming within. After a dinner of fried potato scallops, I tucked the boys into bed, gave Les some earplugs, and crept downstairs.

The same half dozen boozers were still there. But instead of staring at the countertop, they now had their eyes fixed on the barmaid—a local student whose ample figure was squeezed into tight jeans and low-necked blouse, a serving wench Boswell would have fallen for.

When I mentioned that I was researching eighteenth-century history in Anstruther, she shrugged with indifference.

"I do medieval," she said. "Not interested in anything later than ninth century."

"Actually, I'm researching a masturbation club that met in this pub in the 1700s. . . ." I asked if she'd ever heard of the Beggar's Benison.

"No, mate—but you've got my attention."

As I proceeded to describe the Benison's colorful rites, two figures at the bar unexpectedly creaked to life. It turned out that one of them had found an old book about the club at a flea market. (It seemed to be the same 1892 volume, "Solely Intended for Antiquaries," I'd seen in New York.) And the other had been interested enough to buy an academic treatise on Scotland's Enlightenment societies. They even went on to lament that most of the young folks in Anstruther had forgotten their rich cultural heritage.

"A couple of years ago, some young lads started a rock band here in town called the Beggar's Benison," one remembered fondly. "They had heard about it, and knew it was sort of *naughty-sexy,* maybe a bit shocking to get some attention. They put up posters for their first gig all over. Then I tipped them off as to what the club was *really* about. They ran around all red-faced, tearing down their posters. Wasn't exactly the image the poor bastards were after, being associated with a bunch of *wankers.*"

"Still," the other mused, "at least those Benison buggers had some peace. They had somewhere to go with their mates." He reminisced about how his father used to disappear to the pub for hours every Friday night, until his wife would fetch him.

"Always a bit embarrassing," he sighed. "To get *fetched.*"

The barmaid leaned forward to pour another round of beer, revealing her majestic décolletage. Conversation froze as everyone admired the Secrets of Nature. Talk picked up again when she turned away. This happened over and again, like clockwork. It seemed to encourage the pace of drinking.

As the classic Beggar's Benison stories were recounted, I detected a perverse Scottish pride in the club. Wankers though they were, the Anstruther members were also true rebels. They were against the Kirk, or Church of Scotland, which repressed every whisper of sexual freedom and forced, for example, adulterers and fornicators to stand in sackcloth and be publicly pilloried. (Several radical ministers were actually active members of the club over the years, including one Bishop Daniel Low—although he became ashamed of his role in the self-abuse rites and asked in his dotage for his name to be removed from the records. This required, apparently, fifty deletions.) They were against the English, especially their taxes, and many were involved in smuggling. (Scotland's parliament had been dissolved in 1707, surrendering ultimate power to Westminster.) Even the club's ritual masturbation was an act of defiance against the anti-onanism texts coming out of London, which argued that self-abuse was a grave medical danger that could lead to blindness and consumption in the young.

Why, they were Scottish nationalist heroes, in their way. Chapters of the Benison were reported wherever Scottish men went—in London, New York, Canada, even India and outback Australia. It was one of the country's greatest exports.

As the night drew on, the Scottish accents grew thicker, and I realized that I'd understood about five words in the last two hours. Worse, the Benison fans clearly weren't going to let me leave. They even threatened to start buying me drinks—an all but unheard-of event in Scotland. True, the Smuggler's Inn was probably as close as I would ever get to the legendary taverns of the eighteenth century, but enough was enough. All this male bonding, with braying laughs and spraying spittle, was just too much for me.

I was about to lie down on the floor and pretend I'd passed out when I felt a tap on my shoulder. "Tone. Ah . . . *Tone*."

Eureka! It was Les.

"Sorry, but I think you'd better come upstairs," she muttered. "The boys are freaking out." Apparently the creaking floors, slamming doors, and sound of the gales outside were the stuff of nightmares—not to mention the terrors of the shared bathroom.

I drained my glass and feigned resignation.

"You bin fetched, mate!" one of my new pals roared with triumph.

"Yeah, he's bin fetched, he's bin fetched!" the others laughed.

"It's true," I muttered, as I bowed out of the pub. Just as well. This Hellfire research was getting to be hell on the liver.

The next morning, with the beer still sloshing around inside me, I slunk downstairs to face a "full Scottish breakfast," of fried eggs, fried potatoes, fried bacon, and fried sausages.

"Fancy some fried bread with that, love?" the housekeeper asked.

I realized I still hadn't had any luck finding the fabled relics. When I cornered the pub's owner, he confirmed that he had no secret cupboard of self-abuse props.

So if they weren't in Anstruther, where were they?

The mystery began to clear when I finally got a call through to historian David Stevenson, who, apart from many other talents, must qualify as the world's leading expert on Scottish masturbation cults. Professor emeritus in Scottish history at the University of St. Andrews and author of the seminal work, *The Beggar's Benison: Sex Clubs of Enlightenment Scotland and Their Rituals,* he had recently retired and fallen off the academic grid. But once I had tracked him down, he was only too happy to share his arcane knowledge and suggested I drop over to his house by the Firth of Forth.

Mrs. Stevenson was waiting for me at the front door.

"So you're one of those strange people interested in the Beggar's Benison, are you?" she asked immediately, with disapproval.

"I am," I confessed sheepishly. And reminded her that her husband was the world authority.

"Well, I hope that's not what they write in his obituary," she said. What about his work on the Scottish Covenanters, the Scottish Counter-Revolution or the Scottish Freemasons? All overshadowed by the bloody Benison. She gave an ironic, seen-it-all-before sigh. "Now you're on to 'men's business.' I'll leave you alone."

Settling into the plaid sofa, I eagerly plunged into sex club lore.

"I first heard of the Benison forty years ago, when I was a student in Edinburgh," said Stevenson, a soft-spoken, grandfatherly figure with a silver beard, wearing the increasingly rare combination of socks and sandals. "One or two scholars had touched on it, but they didn't want to get their fingers dirty. It was all very hush-hush, so I started making some inquiries beneath the covers."

After the Beggar's Benison was disbanded in 1836—the year Queen Victoria ascended to the throne, symbolically enough—its obscene memorabilia had been inherited by its last surviving member in Anstruther, Matthew F. Connolly. (That was where the 1860 travel guide book author, Henry Fairnie, had seen them.) In 1865, Connolly gave the relics to, of all people, a Glasgow church minister, who valiantly rejected periodic suggestions that they be burned. In fact, he cooperated in letting many of them be photographed for the 1892 volume on the club. In 1897, they were given to a curator at the Kelvingrove Museum, but they were too volatile to become part of the collection.

"It's a miracle they survived at all," Stevenson said. "I'm sure there were many more clubs of this nature, but their relics were destroyed, so we know nothing about them."

Finally, we have to thank a retired Scottish army officer, Colonel Robert Maxwell Canch Kavanagh, whose twin passions in life were military camouflage and self-abuse clubs, for salvaging them from the dustbin of history. In 1921, Kavanagh purchased the cache directly from the elderly curator, for an undisclosed sum, and it became part of his private collection. He also tracked down the prize piece of club regalia, King Charles II's pubic hair wig. A true devotee, Kavanagh then tried to revive the Benison in Edinburgh, without success. "Male bonding rituals had rather changed," Stevenson said.

But had the fabled trove stayed in Scotland? I asked urgently. I had read one wild report that they had ended up in the United States in the 1980s—a plausible enough notion, given that so many offbeat European curios, such as Napoléon's severed penis and Beethoven's ear bones, had found loving homes on American shores.

"Oh, the Benison items never left these bonny shores," Stevenson assured me. "In fact, they're only a few miles away. I'll get you an appointment."

GENTLEMEN, CHARGE YOUR
INDECENT DRINKING VESSELS

History is a polite business at St. Andrews. Golf fans flock here to stay in lace-curtained B and Bs and try their luck on Scotland's most venerable course; even the town ruins are manicured like putting greens. At the hallowed University of St. Andrews, the guardians of the Benison items dilly-dallied on my appointment for a couple of days. ("Of course, every request to see the *Club Collection* has to be approved," one college staff member told me. "We have to be careful. We don't want the media to announce, 'University where Prince William went to college has rooms full of porn!'") By the time everything was confirmed, the heavens were shining on my mission. At 10:00 a.m., I dashed through the flower-filled cloisters (yes, the same ones that Prince William once dashed through!), under the medieval arches to the university museum repository—a tragically stark modern building opposite the police station. A receptionist showed me to an anonymous room, painted a clinical white, as if I were about to give evidence or be strip-searched. But the door opened and two young female curators entered carrying heavy cardboard boxes, marked BBWCC, Beggar's Benison and Wig Club Collection.

With a cheery greeting, they snapped on white latex gloves and began to lay the treasured contents on the table, carefully unwrapping each item from archival paper and acid-free bubble wrap.

This was it, I marveled—the strangest fragments of British history, which after a century's use and abuse at the Smuggler's Inn in Anstruther, had ended up here.

"These pieces are a bit notorious here at the museum,"

confessed Jessica, the more senior of the two curators, who was wearing a crisp white blouse. It wasn't hard to see why. One phallus after another, fashioned from glass and metal, was carefully revealed. These were followed by a colorful array of sashes, bowls, platters, and medals engraved with lewd, vaguely hallucinogenic images, like lighthouses modeled on penises and roosters with penis heads. Some were engraved with shapes known as "vulviform," but the male organ certainly got top billing.

I picked up the Test Platter, the receptacle for the Benison members' seed, and read the inscription, THE WAY OF A MAN WITH A MAID. There was a clumsy engraving of an erection with a purse hanging from it and the date, 1732.

It looked as though it had been carefully washed.

There were two of the so-called prick glasses, each about nine inches long. They were made from blown glass and had

The "Test Platter," focus of the Beggar's Benison's self-abuse rituals. (Reproduced courtesy of the University of St. Andrews.)

seen rough handling; each had a cracked gonad. Perhaps their fragility was what inspired the other, longer version of the phallic drinking cups, crafted from metal. There was also the silver horn used to summon initiates in Anstruther, engraved with the phrase "My breath is strange," from the Book of Job. (The full quote is "My breath is strange to my wife," from Job 19:17.) And a rather nice porcelain punch bowl.

"It's an accident that the university has ended up with this collection," said Jessica. "If it were offered to the museum today, we wouldn't accept it. The items really have nothing to do with our mission, which is to chronicle the history of the university. But now we have them, we have to look after them!"

The university doesn't exactly celebrate its sexy stash; in fact, the Beggar's Benison and Wig Club Collection relics have never been publicly displayed.

"St. Andrews is a family tourist spot," said the assistant curator, Amy, who was wearing pink earrings and pigtails. "There was some thought of exhibiting a few of the tamer items, but

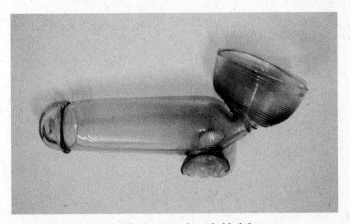

Beggar's Benison "prick glass," used in ribald club toasts.
(Reproduced courtesy of the University of St. Andrews.)

it was vetoed. I mean, how do you explain what they were used for in a G-rated way?"

But what of the fabled wig, the notorious club mascot, supposedly woven from the pubic hairs of King Charles II's mistresses?

They revealed a wooden wig box. Like a game-show host, Amy creaked open its door to reveal the wig stand, a wooden head with a protruding chin and nose. Someone had painted on eyes, unfortunately crossed. The effect was ghoulish.

But the wig itself was missing.

"At some stage, the wig went astray," Amy said mournfully. "When the museum received the club relics, there was no trace of it."

The adventures of the wig turned out to be the most extraordinary part of this twisted Scottish epic. According to club lore, its provenance can be traced back to 1651, when hedonistic Charles II visited Fife and was treated to riotous drinking parties. After his return to London, he sent the wig of pubic hairs as a gift to his dissolute friends, its significant size making it a symbol of royal virility. (Practical details of the souvenir's creation—woven? glued?—are lost in the mists of time.) In 1732, the headpiece was presented to the Beggar's Benison in Anstruther and for decades worn in club ceremonies to tap into its talismanic power. Then, in 1775, a tragic schism struck the Scottish club world. Lord Moray, a descendent of the wig's original keeper, ran off with the prize and started his own breakaway society in Edinburgh—the Wig Club. Instead of ritual self-abuse, initiates to the new club were obliged to kiss the pubic relic and contribute hair from their own mistresses' nether regions to embellish its thinning mane.

It was as compensation for this sorry loss that King George IV, who had become an honorary member of the Beggar's Benison four decades earlier, presented the club with the locket of his own mistress's pubic hairs in an elegant silver snuff box in 1822. Benison tradition holds that he greeted the sovereign at the Leith docks on his highly publicized official visit and pressed it into his eager hands. The tuft was intended to be the embryo, as it were, of a new and revitalized wig, although the idea never got off the ground. At least nobody stole it, as I found out this wonderful morning, when I got to examine the royal gift in the club cache. The records say that King George

The Wig Club's box and stand—minus the dreaded wig itself. (Reproduced courtesy of the University of St. Andrews.)

was given in return several prick glasses to take home to the royal palace—"to his intense delight."

Perhaps this was reason enough for royal concern over where Prince William would study. The press might at any point take a leering interest in the trail of royal debauchery. "You know the British tabloids." Jessica shrugged.

Hmmm, the royal connections were everywhere, I mused to myself. Who could have possibly stolen such a treasure?

In the underground archive of the university library, with anemic PhD students blinking at their laptops, I sifted through original Beggar's Benison diplomas and piles of scribbled correspondence until I found a crumbling, leather-bound volume— the Minutes of the Knights Companion of the Wig, starting with the first meeting on March 6, 1775. The ornate cover features a gilt drawing of the stolen pubic headpiece—even more wild, florid and curly than I had imagined, like an exuberant head of broccoli.

I tried to track the wig's progress since the last meeting of the club in 1826. According to his notes, it had been perfectly intact when the indefatigable Colonel Kavanagh had gotten hold of the Wig Club artifacts in the 1920s. It appears to have gone astray at some point in the 1930s. In 1938, when American historian Louis C. Jones of Columbia University hunted it down for a book on Georgian clubs, he received the report that the wig was being preserved "in a lawyer's office in Leith . . . although which lawyer's office [Jones writes] this author did not discover."

Here ends the trail. But I couldn't stop thinking about this last detail. Could it be that the sacred relic was somehow still sitting in a solicitor's filing cabinet?

But Les grew irritable when I suggested a detour to Leith.

And even I had to accept that I couldn't scour every legal office in town. Henry and Sam were now in open rebellion. They'd had quite enough of seedy provincial backwaters, deranged publicans, and icy rain. They wanted swimming pools, sushi, and videogames—thinking for some reason that all this could be had on the Continent—but would settle for spring mattresses, clean towels, and a door that locked. We ended up in a generic Edinburgh hotel, and I had to admit it was nice to have a shower that didn't spit flakes of rust on your head.

Our northern tour was winding down, and, as British comics say, it's always a relief to get the first leg over. The boys were gazing in catatonic bliss at the first TV they'd seen in two weeks. "Spongebob, Chowder," Henry murmured holding his knees and rocking back and forth.

Meanwhile, on the hotel computer, I had found Leith's only online magazine, where I could place a classified ad about the wig. Perhaps someone had heard stories from a grandparent, or even knew where the relic was but had remained silent out of embarrassment? I immediately got a line back from the editor of *Leith Links*. "This seems to be far, far too interesting to ignore," he wrote, with evident patriotic pride. He suggested that I write a report on the wig's peregrinations, which a few days later appeared under the promising title, "The Case of the Missing Wig."

Is Scotland's Strangest Relic Still Hidden in Leith? ran the headline. An Ongoing Investigation by Our New York Correspondent. Up top was a fetching cartoon of a bald King Charles II asking, "Have you seen my wig?" I concluded with a rousing call to arms for all Scottish history lovers: "Could the wig—no doubt the worse for wear—still be somewhere in the musty cupboards of a Leith solicitor's office? . . . Anyone with any information on the item's whereabouts, please drop a line. . . ."

The next morning, I called David Stevenson, to tell him about my media blitz. He wasn't optimistic. "I imagine some poor young legal clerk put his hand into a filing cabinet one day and discovered this festering ball of hair. Probably let out a shriek and threw it straight into the fire."

Chapter Two

PARIS TO THE GUTTER

"Erotic Archaeology" of the Belle Époque

To get a fresh view of any overly romanticized city, I like to follow an out-of-date guidebook—out-of-date, preferably, by a century or more. By celebrating forgotten avenues and long-gone eateries, these yellowing editions manage to conjure the past as a tangible world, teeming with activity and life. You can almost hear the horse traffic, smell the flower markets, taste the roast quail.

So in the case of Paris, the City of Eternal Love, I chose a suitably specialized reference—a prostitute guide from 1883.

THE PRETTY WOMEN OF PARIS

Their Names and Addresses,
Qualities and Faults,
being a Complete Directory or
Guide to Pleasure
for Visitors to the Gay City.

Not quite as practical as the latest Rough Guide, perhaps, but an effective distraction from the modern world nonetheless.

The Belle Époque, the "beautiful era" from 1880 to 1914, when Paris established itself as the world capital of illicit pleasure, may qualify as Europe's most beloved golden age. Romantic movies like *Moulin Rouge!* with their cast of handsome rogues, mad painters, and golden-hearted ladies of the night, ensure that its reputation continues to smolder, as do the parade of Impressionist blockbuster art shows. At the time, Paris blazed even more brightly as a beacon of permissiveness. It was universally acclaimed the most stylish city in the Western world, with the finest restaurants, most avant-garde writers, most brilliant entertainments—and sin, lashings of sin, elegantly prepared.

Sex, and most particularly the sex trade, was simply *classier* in Paris. "There may be other towns. . . as voluptuous as Paris," conceded one English visitor of the 1880s, "but none where love and pleasure are practiced with more exquisite refinement."

For travelers arriving from benighted Anglo-Saxon lands, the city was a delightful assault on the senses. Stepping from the railway platform, they felt transported to an endless springtime: the air was more fragrant, the breezes warmer, the streets more alive. Paris pulsated with theaters, dance halls, and brasseries with their distinctive zinc-topped bars—over thirty thousand drinking spots, three times more than New York and six times more than London—all exuding a palpable sexual energy. Even the poorest Parisian girls wore their clothes with coquettish flair, visitors raved. The flower girls in their near-transparent summer dresses, were "fearfully fascinating," wrote the English poet Arthur Symons, who vis-

ited in 1890, "faces so eager and wild, so wicked and so innocent, so impure and so pure; ripe red lips that might suck
the soul out of you; mouths so amorous and at the same time
so full of laughter . . ." The city was the ultimate escape, an
enclave of erotic fantasy far from judging eyes, and its freedoms were not only reserved for men. High-society women
from Moscow to Minneapolis were drawn to its parlors, where
adultery was an avid sport, like moths to the flame. At dawn,
they would be seen quietly leaving the fashionable mansions
of the Champs-Élysée and stepping into waiting carriages,
their elaborate undergarments rolled into a convenient ball.
Gay visitors employed only slightly more discretion, heading
to the marble-laden bathhouses around the Luxembourg Gardens to meet handsome students eager for cash. Local bon
vivant Marcel Proust himself favored the Hôtel de Saïd near
the markets, where off-duty legionnaires gathered for R & R.
The most exclusive lesbian club was called Les Rieuses, the
Merry Women, hosted weekly by a trio of Parisian actresses in
a private candlelit mansion.

But Paris's true fame is owed to its prostitutes, known as
les cocottes or *les horizontales*. The rest of the world marveled
at the brazenness of their trade, which had been regulated
since Napoléon's day to control the spread of venereal disease. By the belle époque, there were 150 licensed brothels
in central Paris alone, where girls were given twice-weekly
medical inspections, an unheard-of precaution in Britain or
the United States at the time. They were known as *maisons
closes*, closed houses, because their green window shutters remained bolted at all hours of the day. Some of these houses
became international legends for their luxury and decor. The
most upscale were designed by famous French artists, and offered nightly *tableaux vivants*, living paintings, with creative

Paris's most illustrious "fantasy brothel," Le Chabanais, photographed around 1900. Top: the grotto-style entrance. Bottom: the Louis XV room. (Courtesy Galerie Au Bonheur du Jour, www.aubonheurdujour.net)

themes like "the naval officers on leave," "the wife wakes up," or "the crazed nun."

A step down in the market were the licensed streetwalkers, who would retire to government-approved hotels, where furnished rooms were available for an hour or a night. In the 1880s, there were approximately thirty thousand "public girls," so that wherever men wandered in the city, whispers would emanate from the shadows, *Couchez avec?* Many foreign visitors, rather than viewing the trade as the last resort of women who had been abandoned or widowed, celebrated it as another example of Gallic good taste. "Are they not winsome, as fresh as rosebuds fresh gathered?" mooned one English traveler of the ready supply of French girls, adding that in the Latin Quarter, "for a five-franc piece, you can have your will of her." That was eighty-five U.S. cents—about $40 today. On the Right Bank, he warned, the rate was twice that.

But while the romantic view of the Parisian *cocotte* flourished—gay, carefree, enjoying her work—the reality was, not surprisingly, very different. In the darker recesses of the city, the going rate in budget brothels was a mere one franc ($7.50 today). Nicknamed *maisons d'abattage*, "slaughterhouses," these were places where men took a numbered ticket and lined up outside the doors, and a worker would endure up to 60 *passes* a day. At this desperate bottom end of the market, any girl who did not register within the system was at the mercy of the dreaded Police de Moeurs, Morality Police, which hunted down unlicensed prostitutes. Abuses were rampant. After midnight, agents would block off whole streets in the working class districts and launch themselves into the crowds with terrifying shouts. According to historian Jill Harsin in *Policing Prostitution in Nineteenth-Century Paris,* the scenes were reminiscent of Nazi roundups in the ghettos.

Cheap hotels would be locked and searched room to room for "clandestine whores." Many innocents, invariably poor, were dragged to the women's prison of Saint-Lazare by mistake, before the notorious system was finally toned down in 1904.

The most legendary class of *fille de joie* operated on a level far above the state-regulated brothels and the grubby fingers of the Morality Police—the top-class courtesans of the belle époque, *les grandes cocottes*. These were the true princesses of the Parisian demimonde. Many had risen from poverty to become the lovers of financiers and politicians, princes and millionaires, and through their beauty and connections were able to shape their own lives. A lucky few amassed personal fortunes, their incomes bolstered by lavish gifts of fine clothing, jewelry, even whole mansions and country villas, before their charms faded. The painter Auguste Renoir, in the biography by his son Jean, *My Father Renoir,* refers respectfully to the courtesans' strength of character and keen intelligence, which made them excellent companions in any social circle.

It was to help outsiders navigate this exotic world, with its own codes and manners, that my guidebook *The Pretty Women of Paris* was written in 1883.

This slender opus has long enjoyed an underground cachet among academics for its wealth of colorful detail. Although anonymous, it was evidently composed by a well-to-do expatriate in Paris who was intent on assisting his countrymen, with 169 copies privately printed in 1883 (four of them on "syphilitic-green paper" for the personal use of the Parisian chief of police, the author cheekily claims in his preface). Today, *Pretty Women* is extremely rare, with only three known survivals. One of them happens to be in the New York Public Library, kept safely under lock and key in the Rare Books Division, so before I left, I made an appointment to peruse it. (Mysteriously, it is part of the Arents Collection of Tobacco). The librarian winked at me over his spectacles as he handed over the text bound in discreet gray paper: "Looks *interesting. . . .*"

It was—a keyhole peek into the bedrooms of 1883. The two hundred or so women are listed alphabetically by name and address, with each one given an extensive description in the florid style of the era. Admittedly, it's hardly high literature. The author strays into the crass vernacular of the horse track, praising "a well-nourished frame," "teeth white and strong" and "ruby gums that are a sure sign of health." The comely Berthe Legrand, of 70 Rue des Martyrs, has "teeth like a terrier," but the mere movement of her hips stimulates men's desires, the author enthuses, "like the vapor of cooked meat on the olfactory nerves of a hungry man." But there is also a wealth of anecdote and gossip that allows the women's outsize personalities to shine through the overheated prose, allowing me to recreate the ambiance of the city during its erotic apogee. What's more, *Pretty Women* includes specific addresses for the finest clubs, nightspots and private boudoirs. All this would—I hoped—lead me to the belle époque's liveliest secrets.

THE CHUNNEL OF LOVE

As the Eurostar whisked us under the English Channel, with the promise of sunnier times ahead, I reasoned to Les that there was a point to all that dismal northern weather: We would now experience the same euphoria travelers felt in the 1880s when they escaped stodgy Britain for salubrious

France. I realized I had to redeem myself after the bleak parade of moldy Anglo lodgings. The boys were starting to resemble pallid Dickensian waifs, refusing point blank to eat another egg.

I wanted a great hotel for us in Paris, so I began looking for a former brothel. This wasn't difficult: In fact, it's probably harder to find a hotel there that *wasn't* a former brothel. But then I found something even better: the Hotel Édouard 7, former pied-à-terre of the most notorious lecher of the belle époque.

In his profligate youth, the Prince of Wales—Britain's future King Edward VII—was a celebrity in Paris, thanks to his Gargantuan appetites for both food and sex. Perpetually availed of champagne and cigars, his girth filled out by five high-protein meals a day, he would receive a standing ovation at the theater whenever he appeared with a comely new paramour on his arm. "Bertie" (also nicknamed Edward the Caresser by the English) had plenty of free time to play: He remained the gadabout heir to the throne until age fifty-nine, thanks to the epic sixty-four-year reign of his mother, Queen Victoria. When he was finally crowned in 1901, he arranged for a special box for all his mistresses to attend the ceremony, much to the chagrin of his wife, Alexandra.

From 1877, Bertie kept an apartment in a building on the Avenue de l'Opéra, an address he relished because it was the Right Bank's upscale epicenter of vice, then dubbed the clitoris of Paris. He gave it up twenty-seven years later when he became king, and the building changed hands several times before it became a hotel. But it has carried on the Parisian tradition of admiration for the prince, naming each suite after his many celebrated consorts, including actress Sarah Bernhardt, opera singer Nelly Melba, American socialite Jennie Churchill (mother of Winston Churchill), and courtesan Alice Keppel (great-grandmother of Camilla Parker-Bowles, second wife of Prince Charles).

Even today, legends of Edward's appetites still filter through Paris. One in particular stands out. According to *Maisons Closes*, the classic study of Paris brothels written in 1958 by an eccentric antiquarian calling himself Romi (real name Robert Miquel), the prince grew so obese in middle age that he commissioned the construction of a *fauteuil d'amour*—a "sex chair"—to be kept in his favorite brothel. This bizarre device was said to have allowed him to have sex with two prostitutes at once without crushing them with his enormous bulk.

The chair's provenance could be traced until 1951, when, sadly, it disappeared into the hands of private collectors.

When we arrived at the Hotel Édouard 7, the immaculately groomed doorman smiled at us knowingly, as if we were

Avenue de l'Opéra, heart of the Right Bank's up-market vice in the belle époque.

on an illicit tryst—rather strange, considering we had two ram-
bunctious urchins in tow. Les remained suspicious as we were
led through the gleaming foyer, past a bronze bust of the portly
prince, and up the elevator to the fifth floor, where Bertie had
his apartment. Our room was designed in "belle époque *mod-
erne*"—the same rich velvet upholstery, but with sleek enamel
picture frames instead of the traditional ornate gold. There
was even a balcony over the wide Avenue de l'Opéra, leading to
the Palais Garnier. Completed in 1875, this famous boulevard
was a key element in Baron Haussmann's nineteenth-century
transformation of Paris from a medieval warren into the visu-
ally coherent Ville Lumière, City of Light, we know today—a
vast stage set for the pursuit of the good life. It wasn't hard to
imagine the chic crowds flashing their diamonds beneath gas
chandeliers, their faces bathed in prismatic light. Unlike other
European opera houses, the Paris Opéra was privately funded,
and rich male "subscribers" were allowed access backstage.
After the performance, they would trawl the cluttered dress-
ing rooms, hung with costumes and silk petticoats. ("It was
common knowledge," writes historian Charles Bernheimer,
"that dancers at the Opera were chosen more for their sex appeal than for their talent . . .")

Like Prince Bertie, I was well pleased with my Parisian
address. Gazing through the fluttering curtains, I could imagine that nothing had changed in Paris since Monet rented his
first studio—at least if you closed the double-glazed windows
against the traffic.

The Pretty Women of Paris paints a lively picture of this brilliant district and the beautiful women who ruled it. Poring
over its pages, we can learn a great deal about the individual

courtesans, including the names of their pets, the number of their illegitimate children, and the color of their thoroughbred horses. We can also gain more substantial insights into how belle époque society worked, learning, for example, how these women began their extraordinary careers. Many burst into the Parisian high-society scene via the stage, where a poor but attractive girl might get her big break. The wealthy actress Lucie Davray, a favorite at the Opéra in 1883, had been a teenage flower seller during the siege of Paris when she was plucked from a crowd to perform a play for the troops and was discovered by a lecherous agent. Others were more entrepreneurial. Marie Estradère earned a name for herself at a government soiree; instead of mingling, she retired to a bedroom and gave the politicians "manual relief" for five francs. Another self-promoter, Hautense Daubinesco, became a regular in the most exclusive social pages of the French press thanks to her pro bono work with journalists. The eccentricities of each courtesan seemed to function as niche advertising. Mathilde Lassens liked to make love while her maid played a barrel organ in the next room. Lee d'Asco filled her mansion with animals, including a tame bear, and on one occasion, as if more notoriety were needed, she ascended in a hot-air balloon dressed as a man wearing a revolver. After tossing her clothes to well-wishers below, she returned to the ground stark naked.

Pretty Women also depicts the courtesans' opulent, if precarious, lifestyle. Then as now, dealing with client requests could be a delicate business. We discover that Leonie de Clómenil kept a solid silver chamber pot and floor mirrors to entertain her many bathroom fetishists. Henriette Chavaroff had a regular engagement with a rich Spaniard who liked to see her kill a live rooster with a knife. And Marthe Dalbet would show off the small scar on her neck inflicted by a jealous "idiot lover" who attacked her with sulfuric acid, then jumped to his death from the window in remorse. For some, the risks were richly rewarded. At age twenty-nine, Gabrielle Elluini was credited with a fortune of £100,000, roughly $20 million today. She turned down the proposals of aristocrats to marry a dashing young actor, then spend her days painting and hosting right-wing political meetings. A belle from the American South who called herself Mrs. Jackson married a French count and lived in luxury worthy of Marie Antoinette.

Few of the women who flit across *Pretty Women*'s pages are remembered in history books. An exception is La Valtesse de la Bigne, born Louise Delabigne, who became the lover of Emperor Napoléon III and influenced his diplomatic decisions. Her regal beauty and wit put her on a par with the hetaerae, courtesans of ancient Greece—the author opines—despite the fact that by 1883 she was "suspiciously near forty." Blessed with sky-blue eyes and cascading auburn hair, Louise had made her start as an artist's model whose bevy of famous lovers, including Manet and Courbet, earned her the nickname Painter's Union. She eventually married an indulgent Turkish banker and established herself in a palace filled with priceless artifacts, including a giant bed of gilded bronze. La Valtesse kept to her artistic roots by hosting a literary salon every Monday night, which was frequented by male admirers including Flaubert, Guy de Maupassant, and the Goncourt brothers. The meticulous author Émile Zola also attended while researching his famous novel about a courtesan, *Nana,* whom many believe to be based on La Valtesse. Zola's depiction is the moralistic counterpart to *Pretty Women.* Nana is beautiful but vacuous and self-absorbed, and the unwitting agent of a new social revolution. Like some "diseased insect," she rises from the gutters of Paris to wreak revenge on the aristocracy, infecting men's bodies, destroying their spirits, and leeching their wealth, before she slides back into the cesspit in which she was born. La Valtesse was at first offended—Zola used details from her house, even her bed, as the model for Nana's—but was reportedly bemused by his focus on the character's brute sexual appeal to men. "As if a woman so stupid could succeed in this life," she scoffed. "To triumph, one must establish relationships at a higher level."

PARIS ON $25,000 A DAY

"D-a-a-a-d, can we go up the Eiffel Tower today?"

Sam woke up with the same question ever since he saw the structure explode with fireworks on Bastille Day. Les was under the impression that the Louvre might be worth a look. But I explained that the famous sites of Paris had to be avoided at all cost. Summer was no time for riding *bateaux mouches* along the Seine. The crowds, the ticket lines, the souvenir vendors . . . the experience would be deathly. Instead, I steered them on my alternative itinerary. Observed the right way, Paris was a palimpsest of erotica.

At first blush, finding actual physical traces of the louche past is a masochistic pursuit. For the last century, Parisians have traded on nostalgia for the belle époque, and restaurants that survive from the era have usually undergone a dozen renovations and even offer floor shows for tourists. With their red vinyl banquettes, faux-brass lamps, and irritable waiters in white aprons, they are closer to Pepé Le Pew cartoons than period reality. Worse, Paris has also undergone a transformation in its very atmosphere and reputation. The legal brothels of Paris were all closed in 1946, and the city was "cleaned up" by postwar conservatives. It is now Europe's bourgeois capital par excellence, well-to-do and rather smug. There is nothing of the sensual frisson in the streets of, say, Rio de Janeiro, Havana, or Barcelona. In fact, most of central Paris is about as provocative as the Upper East Side. Historic playgrounds like the Palais Royale now feel like a minimalist art event. In short, Parisians' strongest passions are reserved for their shoes.

It takes a combination of perseverance and creativity to locate the era's sacred sites. *Pretty Women* in hand, I first tracked down the Maison Dorée, or Golden House, on 20 Boulevard des Italiens, the busiest café hunting ground of aspiring courtesans in 1883—now a bank. Across the street once stood the Café Anglais, whose respectable facade hid the notorious Grand Seize Room. It was here that the Chilean belle Isabelle Féraud agreed to settle a wager by a young man that he could extract a flower from her nether regions "without injuring the blossoms." She chose a gardenia and reclined upon a table as admirers crowded about. "A roar of applause greeted the saucy scamp as he lifted his flushed face," wrote one eyewitness, and revealed the intact flower between his teeth, like some perverse ancestor of Gomez Addams. Señorita Isabelle apparently took his triumph in stride. She went about with a golden key to her bedroom dangling on her watch chain, to provoke spur-of-the-moment offers. One besotted youth had given her £1,000 for a night, roughly $25,000 in today's currency, and was later seen wandering Paris with no boots.

Lapérouse, a romantic restaurant that still operates on Le Quai des Grands-Augustins, once maintained private rooms for gentlemen to discreetly ply courtesans with champagne, delicacies, and expensive gifts. Against all logic, we decided to dine there en famille. Luckily, Les traveled well prepared: She'd purchased two boy's suits from H&M before we left New

The courtesans' mirror in the private rooms of Lapérouse restaurant.

York, specifically so we could venture into swank Parisian eateries without snide looks from other diners. In fact, as we took our plush seats for the prix fixe lunch, they looked like infant Beatles on tour. We tried to order nineteenth-century style, although it was hard to share escargots with linked elbows when the boys were gurgling in horror. To my relief, the phalanx of hovering waiters intimidated them into staying in their seats and keeping their grossed-out mewling to a minimum.

The main dining room of Lapérouse is now inspired kitsch, with art nouveau mirrors on every wall, but the tuxedoed maitre d' took us upstairs to visit the original cozy *chambres particuliers,* which survive in the attic under softly lit chandeliers. The antique mirrors were clouded with etched marks. Apparently, the ladies would test their diamond gifts by scratching them along the glass, to make sure they weren't being duped.

Afterward, we scoured the stalls of used-book vendors by the Seine, the *bouquinistes,* who for centuries had sold works "to be read with one hand," unavailable in the rest of Europe, along with risqué souvenirs like translucent lingerie embroidered with the words *Prenez-Moi,* Take Me. In 1883, literature fans would visit the Enfer, or Hell section, of the Bibliothèque Nationale, where nine hundred pornographic books were kept in a restricted reading room (it was discontinued in the 1960s), or seek out the specialist collectors often referred to as erotobibliomaniacs. The esteemed "Auguste Lesoue. . .f" claimed to have thirty thousand volumes and eighteen thousand etchings in his library, and an elderly colonel of the Russian Imperial Guard, Prince Alexandre Galitzin, had published an underground guide to erotica, *Catalogue of the Secret Cabinet of Prince G**** in Bruxelles.* Of course, there was also the perverted Frederick Hankey, a retired English officer who had one of the filthiest libraries in Europe. He boasted of attending public executions in order to arouse his passions and fantasized about binding his books in human skin. (The Goncourt brothers, the great Parisian chroniclers of the demimonde, described him as "a madman, a monster, one of those men who live on the edge of the abyss.")

Then there was Montmartre. It is difficult to picture today, but in 1883 the quarter was still a rustic hillock with barnyard animals in the streets, although it had plentiful cheap bars frequented by writers, artists, and their free-living models, who draped themselves revealingly over chairs, sipping absinthe and smoking cigarettes sweetened by opium. Travelers loved to slum at cabarets like the Chat Noir, which offered witty stage spectacles combining themes of sex and death, and of course can-can dancers performing their jaw-dropping routines. I paid my respects at 75 Rue des Martyrs, site of the Japanese Divan, where the modern striptease was invented in 1894 by one Blanche Cavelli with a show called "Yvette's Bedtime." Today, it's still a lounge club, the Divan du Monde, although all traces of the oriental decor have vanished.

Unfortunately, the pleading for the Eiffel Tower didn't stop. "*D-a-a-d* . . ." I had been determined not to sully my mission with such a tawdry tourist activity, but finally I buckled. After waiting in line for ninety minutes, a lightning storm enveloped the spire, and all visits were abruptly ended. On the second attempt, we were better prepared. We took a bottle of wine, some Brie and baguettes, so we could at least enjoy a picnic while waiting to buy the tickets. Unseemly perhaps, but soon the exhausted, hungry, and painfully sober Spaniards around us were looking on in envy as we merrily approached the ticket booth. The French have finally cottoned on to the true needs of travelers: At the summit, we discovered a champagne bar that dispensed plastic flutes for a mere $20 each.

Now, with Paris at night stretched out before us, I had to admit this wasn't such a bad idea after all. Back on earth, we lolled on the moonlit grass, fell off the carousels, and searched in vain for a public restroom. A typical night out for family debauchees.

MIDNIGHT IN THE SEX MUSEUM

The next evening, after reading *Asterix the Gaul* to the boys for the twelfth time, I decided to venture out alone and see what might happen if I visited one of the addresses in *Pretty Women*. The very first listing under A was Jeanne Abadie at No. 80, Boulevard de Clichy. Mademoiselle Abadie was "a dashing, well-dressed person of about twenty-seven, who looks very well by gaslight, in spite of her false teeth." She had been brought up in the wings of a theater, where she caught the eye of the rich boulevardiers. Her personality was "rough and fiery," the author warns, but "her tariff is moderate."

The address was in the heart of Pigalle, now the center of Parisian sleaze. So as Les curled up with a good book, I slipped out into the night.

"Don't get *too* carried away with this research," Les muttered, without looking up.

I emerged from the Métro at Place Pigalle, a name once heavy with romance. In 1883, bohemians were hanging out at the Café de la Nouvelle-Athène, where Degas had painted *The Absinthe Drinkers,* and Parisians were hailing Manet's colorful depiction of local nightlife, *The Bar in the Folies-Bergère.* (Less romantically, Manet died that same year from tertiary syphilis contracted in his misspent youth.) But the vibe in Pigalle these days is tragically more like Times Square 1983, with the Boulevard de Clichy now lined with neon-lit sex shops, peep shows, and scrums of Germans out on stag nights. Still, I dutifully began following the numbers, looking for Mademoiselle Abadie's old haunt at No. 80. It turned out that the very next door, No. 82, is the all-too-famous Moulin Rouge. It was opened in 1889, and in Mademoiselle Abadie's day was a more humble music hall. Tonight, guards with loudspeakers were herding throngs of tourists into lines behind velvet ropes. No. 78 was an erotic supermarket. But where was No. 80?

It was then I noticed, a couple of doors down at No. 72, the Musée de l'Érotisme, the Museum of Eroticism. The modern world has seen a flurry of successful institutions in this field, but they are clinical and uninspiring places. Surely this one would tap into the rich tapestry of Parisian sensuality. It was open daily until 2:00 a.m., appropriately, so I eagerly handed over my admission to the gaunt attendant dressed as a Goth.

At midnight, the museum was deserted, except for a few

giggling couples. I carried around my notebook and scribbled furiously, trying hard to look scholarly. The exhibition began without much promise. Spread over seven floors, most of the collection seemed to be cheap souvenirs from Japan. But the displays were more inspired on the level devoted to Paris, with original nineteenth-century photos of bordello scenes, street-walkers, cross-dressers. Projected on a wall were blue movies from the early 1900s, which would be shown in the waiting rooms of brothels "to excite the appetites." They were the direct descendents of the *tableaux vivants* of the belle époque *maisons closes*. One involved two "nuns" cavorting with a puppy, with the girls looking at the camera and laughing.

Parisian low life was obviously still going strong right through the 1930s, the heyday of Henry Miller and Anaïs Nin. How could the postwar brothel closures have so completely destroyed the culture?

The museum's co-owner, Alan Plumey, was still in his office. Wiry and unshaven, edging for a cigarette, he looked like he had just spent a wild night on the tiles. Plumey had started this museum in the early 1990s, he said, inspired by the success of Europe's first sex museums in Amsterdam and Berlin. He had chosen the Pigalle location with hesitation. "I dislike the avenue, it's rather horrible," he admitted. "But unfortunately, Pigalle has the history. The name is internationally famous. Ten million tourists a year now come here. We catch a few of them."

I asked him what had ended the epic saga of Parisian debauchery. To illustrate, Plumey took me to one of his favorite exhibits, a handwritten ledger of accounts from the Second World War, where a Parisian prostitute carefully listed the schedule and income from her dealings with German military officers. It was a busy roster.

"Horizontal collaboration," he grinned wolfishly.

Prostitutes were the scapegoats of the Occupation, he explained. No sooner had the Germans taken over Paris in 1940 than working girls were obliged to take them on as clients. The luxury *maisons closes* were converted into brothels for Nazi officers and did a roaring trade, to the disgust of French men, who were already feeling emasculated by the nation's abject military collapse. It's still something of a sore point in France: When historian Patrick Buisson revealed in his 2009 book, *1940–45, Erotic Years,* that some Parisian prostitutes even preferred the German conquerors for their personal cleanliness, good looks, and hard currency, it caused a scandal. In contrast to the image of heroic resistance, many single French women—and married women whose husbands had been killed, wounded, or were POWs—were also forced to sleep with the enemy for cash or black-market goods. But it was the prostitutes who drew French rage after the Liberation in 1944, their hair clipped and sometimes marched naked through the streets by howling crowds.

A popular French heroine named Marthe Richard—a former aviator, First World War spy, and supposed resistance figure—was chosen by conservative French politicians to lead a campaign to close the bordellos. In the spring of 1946, urged on by the strictly Catholic Yvonne de Gaulle, the municipal council of Paris passed legislation to end 150 years of tolerance. One brothel madame tartly noted that she recognized many of her best clients voting for the ban: "I suppose all the poor guys were afraid to be roasted by their wives when they got home if they'd voted against it." It was the end of an era. Before long, most of the brothels were turned into residences for students. Naturally, the move didn't end the sex trade, but removed its glamour. It also made the plight of women forced into prostitution much worse. Around 1,500 brothel workers either ended up on the streets or had to set up illegal houses in the suburbs. Prostitution in Paris became much the same as in London, Moscow, or Cleveland—a marginalized profession, more vulnerable to disease and street violence. By the 1950s, many Parisians recognized that the ban was a failure. Police records proved that the self-righteous Marthe Richard was a fraud, a former prostitute herself who had changed her name, fabricated her heroic history as a spy, and spent the first years of the Occupation in pro-Nazi Vichy procuring women for German officers. She went on record as regretting her campaign to close the brothels, and in her sixties she went on the Paris stage—ironically enough, playing a madam.

But the extirpation of the city's sinful golden age was complete, Plumey mourned. "Nothing remains of that time. Only a few facades. You can go to the site of Le One Two Two"—a famously elegant *maison close* from the 1930s on 122 Rue de Provence, a favorite of Humphrey Bogart and Cary Grant— "it's now a union office, the National Federation of Leather and Hide Workers. It's comic," he added bitterly. "Comic!"

"Any relics of the famous brothels?" I persisted.

"Historians have asked me three thousand times if there are brothel artifacts," he scoffed, exasperated. "There is nothing in Paris! Nothing!"

By the time I left, bracing myself for the generic sleaze of Pigalle, Plumey was decidedly maudlin. "Today, the erotic in Paris is dead. Vanished! If you want an erotic ambience, go to Bangkok, São Paolo, Budapest. There is nothing left in Paris but nostalgia." He smiled ruefully. "This whole city is just a museum of eroticism."

Outside, thinking once again of the winsome Mademoiselle Abadie, I stopped in front of an open doorway. The sign said La Diva, and if the sequence was right, it must be No. 80. Purple neon announced: THÉATRE, SHOW PRIVÉ, TABLE DANCE, LAP DANCE. Could this have been *chez Jeanne* back in 1885? I peered for a second too long, and the doorman demanded 20 euros to enter. I sighed. *Well, hopefully it would be tax deductible.*

I was led into a dark, odoriferous bar, where a topless African girl was grinding a pole to throbbing music. The half dozen males in the audience, sitting at separate tables, shifted their blank gaze to me as I tried to hide in a private booth. Another African girl, wearing a golden Jazz Age dress, materialized by my side.

"Hello, would you like a drink?"

"Oh, no, that's OK," I gurgled suavely.

"Do you mind if *I* have a drink?"

Egad—I could imagine being extorted a fortune by the bouncers for her glass of "champagne" when I tried to leave. I hedged.

She countered: "Where are you from?"—clearly the routine conversation starter. "Which do you prefer, New York or Paris?"

I burbled that I was actually a historian, here because I'd read in an old guide that this had been a courtesan's home 130 years ago. . . .

"Really?" she asked. "You read that in a book?"

"Yes."

"In New York or Paris?"

"Well, New York."

"And which do you prefer, New York or Paris?"

LAST FANTASY IN PARIS

So much for human remains. In its last pages, *Pretty Women* had included an appendix listing the classiest brothels in the Paris of 1883. Although known only by their street addresses, they were once notorious enclaves of Parisian luxury safely operating inside palatial buildings. Surely *something* survived. And sure enough, just around the corner from our hotel lay 12 Rue Chabanais—which was, my guidebook raved, quite simply "the finest bagnio [bathhouse, a nickname for bordello] in the world."

If Paris was an island of fantasy within Europe, Le Chabanais, as Parisians affectionately referred to it, was its most creative expression. Each of the bordello's thirty rooms was decorated in a different theme, creating a Disneyland of the erotic arts. It was opened in 1878 by a rich former courtesan,

12, Rue Chabanais today—a century ago, the most legendary bordello in Europe.

"Madam Kelly," who allegedly spent over 1,700,000 francs on the interior design, $12.75 million in today's terms, and was soon attracting Europe's wealthiest financiers, politicians, dukes, and stars of the stage.

So I wandered down Rue Chabanais, now a quiet lane behind the Louvre. The antique facade at No. 12 was still intact—a slender, eight-story building sporting a fresh coat of matte beige. Back in 1883, Le Chabanais' exterior had also been kept plain to deter the riffraff. But as soon as the door was opened, a magical world was revealed. The bordello's vestibule was designed as an underground grotto, complete with artificial rock walls and flowing waterfalls. The porter, an African in Moorish garb, stood below a sign declaring in English, WELCOME TO THE CHABANAIS, THE HOUSE OF ALL NATIONS.

Today we can recreate a visit from a surviving floor plan, vintage photographs, and the brothel's own small green souvenir books, which were handed out at top cafés as advertising. Clients were led to the first floor, the Pompeii Room, where scantily clad ladies were reclining on Roman couches beneath sixteen elegant vignettes by—who else?—Henri de Toulouse-Lautrec, depicting male and female centaurs involved in sensual acts. Le Chabanais was one of the artist's favorite retreats, where he spent long hours studying the casual moments when the girls were off work and simply enjoying one another's company. It was on this floor that the financial business was discreetly transacted. No money could change hands upstairs, so clients would purchase *jetons,* or tokens, from the madam in advance, to trade for drinks and services. The minimum was 100 francs—around $750 in today's currency. Absolute discretion was guaranteed, which is what made Le Chabanais a favorite with foreign dignitaries on tour. The sojourn was routinely described on their itineraries as a "visit to the president of the Senate"—a code that apparently backfired when the Queen of Spain actually *did* ask to meet the president of the Senate and was taken to the brothel, causing a minor diplomatic scandal.

From this point, clients only had to choose their fantasy. There was the Hindu Room, the Turkish Chamber, the Louis XV Salon. The Venetian Room, evoking the Italian Renaissance, had a giant bed in the shape of a seashell. In the Japanese Salon, six divans were arranged in a circle around an incense burner, with decor so sublime that it won first prize in Paris's 1900 International Exposition (itself a sign of just how tolerated prostitution was at the time). There was an Eskimo Chamber with an igloo, and even a Pirate Chamber, with portholes against which sea water would be thrown by workers.

It came as no surprise to me that Le Chabanais was a firm favorite with the Prince of Wales. For a start, it was easy waddling distance from his Right Bank apartment. His preferred fetish was the Hindu Room, and it was here that he installed his two creative custom-made props. The first was an enormous bathtub crafted from gleaming red copper. It was cast in the shape of a ship, with a melon-breasted siren on the prow. The prince is believed to have filled it with Mumm champagne on warm summer nights.

The other creation was his *fauteuil d'amour*—his love throne, or sex chair. By the 1890s, his girth was forty-eight inches, but the machine's tall handles enabled him to lower himself without doing the poor girl any serious damage. The inventive device became notorious in Paris. It remained in Le Chabanais after the prince's death in 1910, and the brothel owners even proudly displayed it when they began offering guided tours in the 1920s—during the day, when the girls were sleeping. The American newspaperman Walter Annenberg went on this particular tour in 1926. "They took you around the bedrooms like Tussaud's waxworks," he later recalled, "and told you about the clients."

King Edward's sex chair, which Annenberg described as a type of hoist, was the highlight: "(The prince) stepped in there as if he were going into a stall."

When I rang the buzzer at No. 12, a balding doorman in a canary yellow sweater let me in. Of course, he said with a knowing smile, this used to be Le Chabanais, the most successful brothel in all of Europe. Today, it was an office building. The fantasy rooms had all been stripped long ago. But the original marble staircase was still there in the foyer, as well as the wrought-iron doors of the brothel's two elevators—working in separate directions, to avoid embarrassing meetings. Their finely wrought grilles depicted a mother bird valiantly protecting her chicks from an approaching serpent.

I asked about the fate of the brothel's contents. "You should ask Madame Canet," he shrugged, pointing across the street. "She's the erotic archaeologist."

The memory of so much sin could not be washed away so easily on Rue Chabanais. Directly opposite No. 12 lay a boutique called *Au Bonheur du Jour,* which, the doorman proudly informed me, was the only commercial gallery of historical erotica still operating in all of Paris, owned by a former dancer named Nicole Canet. (The gallery name, "Daytime Delight," refers, slyly, to the joys of stolen afternoon trysts.)

OK, I thought, *this is just the specialist I need.*

I found Madame Canet unwinding at the back of her gallery. The erotoarchaeolgist was in her fifties, her wafer-thin frame fastidiously attired in a designer sundress and silk scarf. Surrounded by male nude photographs, with the piercing mascara-lined eyes of a silent film actress, she was the picture of Parisian elegance.

But I quickly learned that Madame was not having a good day.

"I'm tired!" she declared, clutching a bowl of herbal tea. "I'm not on form at all. Last night, I ate too quickly—a Chinese meal. Now I'm not well! To run a gallery like this, it's too much for one person. I hang all of the exhibitions myself, I deal with the public. . . . Oh, I should never have opened this boutique! It's really too much alone."

I offered my condolences, while delicately steering the conversation toward her glass cases of alluring nineteenth-century relics. She had started collecting historical items when she first moved to Paris from Burgundy several years ago. When she stopped dancing professionally, she began selling full-time. "I love to go back in time and play detective," she said. "I need to discover things that aren't in public circulation, things that need a certain expertise to identify and to authenticate. The erotic creations of the nineteenth century, for example, have a different sensibility, a different feel, a different emotion. Pornographic images were much more shocking in those days, and it was very dangerous to carry in your pocket, for example, postcards of naked men."

Madame Canet had opened her boutique in 1999—"of course, now I regret it!"—but had not deliberately chosen it for its proximity to Le Chabanais.

"It was an accident, in fact. I found the listing in the newspaper," she said. "But, you know, I wonder if there really is such a thing as coincidence. When I staged an exhibition on *les maisons closes*, the location received huge publicity. Thirty thousand people came, the lines were extending down in the street. But I sold nothing! The French don't buy erotica. They treat my store like a museum, and won't even buy a €2 postcard. My best customers are Germans, Swiss, Americans."

She narrowed her eyes at me. "And you, do you collect?"

"I'm just a writer!" I confessed. "I can't afford it." She looked at me accusingly.

To change the subject, I asked about the Parisian nostalgia for the *maisons closes*.

"Oh, the sex trade has been so transformed today, it is so crass and vulgar. Back then, it *was* more glamorous, more mysterious. But the only women who achieved true independence were the top courtesans, who lived like goddesses. There were many low-category brothels in belle époque Paris that were sordid—really sordid. And even in the most expensive brothels like Le Chabanais, there was only a facade of luxury. . . ."

The women were virtual prisoners, Madame Canet explained. They signed a legal contract stipulating that their living expenses would be deducted from their earnings, including their food, heating, laundry, candles, hairdressing, cigarettes, and opiates. Girls even had to rent their beds, their sheets, and new clothes—a fashionable dress went for 2 francs a month, a pair of stockings 6 sous. Few emerged with a profit. For all its swank, Le Chabanais was no better. Just above the Hindu Room, with its crystal glasses and goose-down mattresses, thirty-six women were sleeping in twenty-two narrow iron beds in the attic. Inspectors found these workers' accommodations to be as squalid as a slum tenement, with tin basins full of dirty water, wallpaper falling in strips off the wall, wood stoves and rickety tables covered with make-up jars and coffee grounds. Only slivers of daylight would ever penetrate the permanently closed window shutters, ensuring a rank and un-healthy atmosphere. The girls were allowed outside only once every two weeks, in the company of the madam. "Who could withstand this claustration during the day, this eternal false illumination of the nights, this imprisonment prolonged for a week, two weeks, a month?" asked the French social cam-paigner Louis Fiaux in 1892. His exposé of brothel life, *Les Maisons de Tolérance,* was so detailed that it, too, became a collector's item among French pornography lovers. A scandal occurred one hot July 14, during the Bastille Day festivities, when the suffocating girls crept out to join a public dance in their diaphanous chemises. According to one report, the crowd's "stupefaction" at the rouged women changed to "en-trancing delight" when the girls began "high-kicking of the most unblushing kind, considering that knickers are unknown in a brothel."

Not quite all of the brothel props had disappeared. Among Madame Canet's triumphs of erotic archaeology was a *porte-jetons,* a gentleman's bamboo cane, designed to hold twenty brothel tokens inside the handle; iron dog collars used for nineteenth-century S&m pursuits ("Businessmen spent their days being so unreasonable to workers, they wanted to be punished at night!"); even the rhino horn–handled whip of La Valtesse de la Bigne, the legendary courtesan, elegantly inscribed with the letters V and B in pink.

When I asked what her favorite discovery had been, Ni-cole leaped to her feet.

"There was a very large contraption, beautifully sewn from crimson dyed leather," she said. "The man put his face into a mask, and planted his feet down *here,*" she said, positioning herself to demonstrate. "He was tied in at the waist, you know? The penis was *here.*" She thrust her pelvis forward. "And the testicles hung here . . ."

I nodded somberly. *"Impressionant . . ."*

"I sold it for a fortune."

Not surprisingly, countless artifacts are in the sweaty palms of private collectors.

And Le Chabanais' relics?

Although the brothel closed its doors in 1946, she said, the contents were not auctioned off until May 8, 1951. She pulled from her shelves a hefty volume by Romi, the antiquarian who had attended the sale. At 9:30 a.m., the famous building was mobbed by collectors, who snapped up all the Venetian glass, antique tapestries, and gilded Louis XVI clocks. Toulouse-Lautrec's centaur paintings were purchased by an unidentified buyer, and their location is still unknown. King Edward's copper bathtub was bought by Salvador Dalí for 110,500 francs plus 22 percent tax. (Thanks to the massive postwar devaluations of the French franc, that would be only around $3,500 today.) The surrealist installed the tub in his suite at the Hotel Meurice in Paris and equipped it with a telephone.

But what of the most infamous piece, I asked—the royal sex chair?

There was a paper trail. At the 1951 auction, it was snapped up for a bargain 32,000 francs (around $1,000 today) by Alain Vian, brother of Boris Vian, a popular Parisian writer and jazz musician. The sex chair changed hands again in 1982, then was obtained by the famous Parisian auction house Drouot in 1992. They soon sold it to the great-grandson of the original nineteenth-century manufacturer, Soubrier. But Madame Canet had heard rumors that it had left Paris. "Four or five people have told me it was sold to a collector in the United States," she said sadly. "It's a pity. It should be in France!"

Madame Canet then greeted the first customers of the afternoon, a couple of shy men she proceeded to work on.

"Once, erotic archaeology was my passion," she sighed as they left, sounding a bit like a disillusioned girl from the provinces trapped in a *maison close*. "But when you run a boutique like this one, you're really a prisoner."

REMAINS OF THE LOVE TRADE

I looked up the Soubrier company's address. The family furniture emporium was in the same location it had been since the 1850s, on the Rue de Reuilly near the Place de la Bastille. So I sent the current dynastic patriarch, Louis Soubrier, a friendly e-mail, saying that I was a researcher pursuing the history of the shuttered houses of Paris. Would he perchance know who currently possessed the *fauteuil d'amour* of King Edward VII?

I didn't hold out much hope for a reply, but I couldn't let the matter drop.

In the meantime, Madame Canet had kindly drawn me a series of maps to other brothels mentioned in *Pretty Women*, where fragments of decor from the era could still be found. Easily the most evocative was 32 Rue Blondel, once known as Aux Belles Poules, The Cute Chicks. The alleyway ran off Rue St. Denis, the last of Paris's streetwalker strips, which has been continually operating since the twelfth century. (Other medieval alleys, now gone, were Rue Tire-Boudin [Cock-Puller Street], Rue Pute-y-Mire [Tart Idler Street],

32, Rue Blondel on the Left Bank, site of the bordello Aux Belles Poules, "The Cute Chicks."

and Rue Gratte-Cul [Scratchy-Cunt Street].) In Rue Blondel, mature-age ladies of the night appeared in every doorway, sporting regulation leopard-skin tights, fish-net stockings and plunging bustiers. Aux Belles Poules could be identified by the lovely red faience tiles on its facade. After the 1946 closure, it was converted into a student dormitory. Its bottom floor operated as a candy factory, then a Chinese clothing importer. Two workers in white overalls happily let me have a peek inside. On the back walls, partly obscured behind rusty pipes, were ceramic tiles of half-naked nymphs lolling back on fluffy clouds, gilt-edged mirrors, and a mosaic of a voluptuous dancer holding a fan and baring one breast. Impossible to move, they had been left by collectors; city authorities have now put a preservation order on the building.

But Rue Blondel was still a feisty place. As I took a photograph of No. 32, howls of fury began to echo up and down the alleyway. "Don't photograph the girls!" A formidable woman in a German military cap swept down from nowhere and demanded to see my camera shots. When I explained my historical purpose, she softened.

"It's beautiful in there," she said. "It should be reopened for us girls!"

Gradually I learned that the relics of the top courtesans are preserved in more refined worlds far from the rough-and-tumble streets. In the Museum of Decorative Arts, for example, part of the Louvre, the famous bed of La Valtesse de la Bigne is on display in a hushed and darkened room. Costing 50,000 francs in 1875 (roughly $375,000 today), it was modeled on the extravagant *lit de parade,* or "parade bed," of the Sun King, Louis XIV, in which he would recline to receive guests in Versailles. Cupids frolic on the gilded headboard, and fauns watch sardonically from the bed posts. In *Nana,* Zola describes the courtesan's bed as "an altar, to which all of Paris would come to adore her sovereign nudity"—but he was obliged to invent the details of the decorations. Despite his pleas, La Valtesse had refused to let him inspect the inner sanctum of her bedroom. (*"Chasse gardée, maître,"* she reportedly answered, laughing. "Private hunting ground, maestro.")

Sadly, La Valtesse's mansion at 98 Boulevarde Malesherbes is gone, as are most of the extravagant nineteenth-century abodes along the Champs-Élysées, where the *grandes cocottes* once lived cheek by jowl with high-society families. At No. 124, an Italian-born courtesan known as La Barucci, whose real name was Giulia Benini, had once told an army colonel that she would not sleep with him until he had paraded naked in front of her house—so he wrapped himself in a cloak, rode his horse at the head of his troops down the avenue, and then opened the cloak to her window out of the soldiers' view. Nearby, at No. 103, the exotic dancer Mata Hari was arrested for espionage in 1916. She insisted to the police officers that she dress properly, then stripped naked in front of them. Abjectly enough, the officers reported that they were "revolted by such impudence. . . ."

In fact, the only nineteenth-century courtesan's house to survive on the Champs-Élysées is No. 25, former home of La Païva, a steel-willed, Russian-born beauty whose real name was Esther Lachmann and who became the lover of composer Richard Wagner, among others. Today, the basement has been turned into a sepulchral restaurant called (of course) La Païva, swathed in velvet drapes, its banquettes framed by columns evoking the classical caryatids of the Acropolis. The mansion itself has managed to survive the last century as the Travellers Club. When I rang the bell, a liveried doorman summoned the

Interior of La Païva's mansion on the Champs Elysées, now an opulent private club.

director, who turned out to be a passionate devotee of courtesan lore, though frail and in her sixties, with the wonderful
name of Roselyne Winklarik. She proudly gave me a tour of
the Païva palace, which blends French and Italian Renaissance styles in gaudy splendor. At last, I was breathing the air
of the *grandes cocottes*! The onyx staircase and agate bathroom
were inspired by the *Arabian Nights*, while the marble nudes
supporting the drawing room mantelpiece were modeled from
life by the irrepressible La Païva herself.

THE ATTIC OF ROYAL SEX

The next day, when I opened my e-mails, there was a message
from Louis Soubrier, with the riveting subject heading
EDWARD VII CHAIR. "When you are in Paris," it read, "I
will show you the *fauteuil d'amour* with pleasure."

I was on the phone within minutes, getting directions to
the warehouse. In the nineteenth century, the Soubrier family
had made its fortune in historical replicas of Roman and ancien régime furniture—which is why, no doubt, it was a candidate to create this royal fantasy piece. Today, Soubrier deals in
antiques, often renting for period films.

Dashing from the Métro, I met Monsieur Soubrier as he
was leaving the building. A dignified gentleman in his sixties,
with a full moustache, tweed coat, and yellow silk cravat, he
reminded me of a retired flying ace from the Western front.

"Oh, I forgot to tell you that we close for lunch!" he said,
mildly bemused by my ignorance of Gallic tradition. "Come
with us, we'll dine together!"

Oh no, I thought, worrying that I would say something
during the meal to make Monsieur Soubrier change his mind.

("You mean you only want to look at *the chair? I thought you wanted to buy it!")* At his favorite café across the street, we settled at a table with one of his friends, a fellow furniture maker whose dachshund kept hopping about his feet. Edouard worked in contemporary designs, he said—exactly the opposite of Monsieur Soubrier. "I loathe history!" he admitted, as the appetizer arrived. "The past, it doesn't exist for me. But for Louis, the past is *everything.*"

Monsieur Soubrier regaled us with stories of his visits to America in his youth. In the 1950s, he had been to Newport, Rhode Island, and attended the birthday party of Jacqueline Bouvier. But I was fixated on furniture. Had he always known about his family's famous chair?

"My father was a very correct man, very formal," he explained. "He never spoke of the *fauteuil d'amour* to me. But when it came on the market again in 1992, one of the very old *maison* workers took me aside. I learned that my great-grandfather had made the chair in the early 1890s, on specifications provided by the Prince of Wales himself. So I began looking in our archives. And yes, there it was! I found my ancestor's original line drawings, and a watercolor of the design. It was living proof."

Soubrier purchased the chair from Drouot—for how much he would not say, apart from admitting it was "very, *very* expensive"—and has kept it in his warehouse ever since. For a short time, it traveled to New York City for an exhibition on "fantasy furniture." This was no doubt where the rumor began that it had been sold to an American. One Midtown Manhattan gallery had apparently refused to display the chair, forcing the organizers to change venue. "The Americans were shocked," he gloated.

The luncheon continued at an excruciatingly slow French

Louis Soubrier, whose ancestor manufactured the royal "sex chair" in his Right Bank warehouse.

pace—salads were nibbled, desserts considered, coffees sipped—until I began to fear that Soubrier might decide on a nap instead. But suddenly, he put down his cup. *"Allons!"* he declared.

Inside, the warehouse was crowded with antiques of every era—ship's figureheads, chandeliers, oil paintings, porcelain vases—all the colorful detritus of French history. A hand-operated cage elevator slowly took us to the third floor, and we followed corridors through endless storage rooms, with hundreds more pieces stacked on shelves. It was too much to take in, and my eyes became exhausted.

But on the top floor, in the farthest corner, some hulking object lay beneath a blue blanket. Soubrier whisked it off, then wrestled with several layers of archival foam. Finally, the sex chair itself stood before me in all its glory.

"Voilà," Louis said proudly.

It was undeniably a beautifully made piece, vaguely like

a cross between a gynecologist's chair and a snow sled. The wooden frame was carved in eighteenth-century style, with two padded levels upholstered in pale green embroidered silk. Its practical use, however, required some consideration. The key lay at ground level, where there were brass plates, which swiveled for comfort—these presumably for King Edward's feet.

"Tradition holds that the *fauteuil* was designed for three," Louis shrugged. "But the precise arrangement . . . ? It is open to debate."

Soubrier ran his hands along the fabric. "We had to re-upholster the *fauteuil* as soon as we bought it. The chair was dirty," he said. "*Very* dirty."

"Oh?" I said, not sure if I wanted to hear the details.

We know that Le Chabanais was patronized in the 1920s

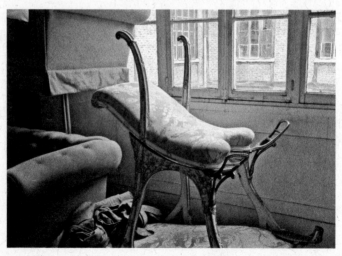

The legendary "sex chair" of King Edward VII in its current Parisian home.

by the full-bodied American comic "Fatty" Arbuckle, and during the war years it was also a favorite of the grotesque, morphine-addled Luftwaffe chief, Hermann Göring. In his memoir *Between Meals,* the rotund gourmand and *New Yorker* writer A. J. Liebling also confesses to visiting the place as a student. Presumably it wasn't just Bertie who had taken advantage of the device. And one of the owners in the 1980s had been "a very, *very* active gay man," Louis said, who had certainly put it to practical use.

Downstairs, Soubrier showed me his great-grandfather's watercolor of the *fauteuil,* which he had found in his archives and was now framed. As I said good-bye, he offered one last delicious morsel—unverifiable, but passed on as fact by the agents at the Drouot auction house. In 1951, when the first private owner, Louis Vian, had purchased the *fauteuil,* it had

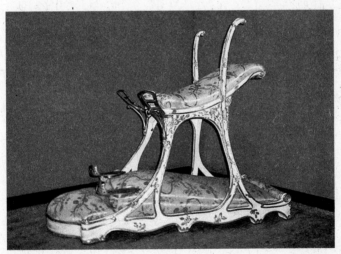

The chair on display in New York in the mid-1990s. (Courtesy Louis Soubrier)

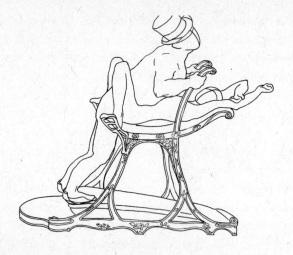

Right: An artist's recreation of the fauteuil d'amour *in action.*
(© *Lesley Thelander*)

been delivered with a battered leather attaché case. Opening it, Vian was astonished to find a preliminary drawing for the chair scrawled by the Prince of Wales himself, with notes in his handwriting. The following morning, Vian was visited at his home by two extremely well-dressed Englishmen, who offered to buy the briefcase for a fabulous sum. Vian did sell it, although he turned down an offer for the chair itself. "They were from the Secret Service," Louis said. "Covering up royal tracks."

Nineteen fifty-one, eh? About the same time they visited a certain lawyer's office in Scotland?

That afternoon, I rushed to Madame Canet to report my findings.

"The *fauteuil* is still in Paris!" she said, nearly jumping for patriotic joy. "It's still here! Still here!"

I was pleased to deliver such happy tidings. But when she quizzed me on my adventure at Soubrier's, there was a brief linguistic confusion.

"Vous êtes monté?" she asked eagerly. You mounted?

"No, no," I said, blanching. "I didn't mount it!"

A few minutes later, when I was describing the chair in detail, she clapped her hands again. *"Alors! Vous êtes monté!"* You *did* mount!

"No, really . . . I just looked . . ."

I finally realized that she meant *monter* in the sense of "to ascend"—that is, I went upstairs to the third floor, where the chair was kept, rather than tested it out.

That will have to wait for a more intrepid researcher.

Chapter Three

INFERNAL PROVENCE

The Marquis de Sade Is Dead!
Long Live Pierre Cardin!

France has always been a Coney Island for literature lovers: The land is lousy with shrines like Victor Hugo's apartment in Paris, George Sand's mansion in Nohant, or Balzac's cottage in Passy, where even the author's old coffeepot is revered like a piece of the True Cross. But a more select breed of bibliophile has long made the pilgrimage to a remote southern village called Lacoste, where the château of one Donatien-Alphonse-François, Marquis de Sade, looms in decaying grandeur. Born in 1740, Sade remains one of France's more outrageous cultural heroes—an aristocratic libertine who has gone down in history for his maniacal lifestyle and bizarre pornographic novels, including *Justine, Juliette,* and *120 Days of Sodom,* each one overflowing with sexual fantasies of such nightmarish cruelty that they gave birth to the term sadism. For generations, interest in Sade's crumbling refuge in Provence was limited to the cognoscenti. Then, one day in 2001, word leaked out that the Château Sade had an illustrious new owner, the celebrity fashion designer Pierre Cardin. Ever since, the king of leisure suits has stirred things up in sleepy Lacoste, introducing upmarket boutiques, cafés, galleries, and hotels, even an annual arts festival, until the villagers are once again revolting.

As for me, I didn't care how famous the new lord of the manor was. This devoted literary tourist just wanted to get inside that castle.

Few writers' homes are so intimately connected to their distinctive creative process. Constructed in the Middle Ages as a fortress against Saracen marauders, the ancestral château had captivated Sade ever since, as a boy, he first saw it crouching above the village like a wolf in ambush. His father gave it to him as a wedding present in 1763, when Sade was a charismatic and promising twenty-four-year-old, and it soon became his most beloved residence, where he lived for energetic interludes over the next fifteen years—his feral prime. Essentially, the château became the mise-en-scène for some of Sade's more controversial real-life escapades, including a light-hearted romp dubbed "The Little Girls Episode" by biographers. This edifying incident occurred in late 1774, when the marquis, then aged thirty-four, came to winter in Provence with his wife and a string of fresh-faced household servants he'd hired in Lyon. The newcomers—five unsuspecting virgin girls and a handsome teen male "secretary"—were intended to supplement his more experienced castle staff, such as the luscious housekeeper Gothon, whom Sade had hired because she sported "the sweetest ass ever to leave Switzerland," and a studly valet, Latour, by whom Sade liked to be sodomized while prostitutes watched and cavorted.

As far as historians can discern, over the next six weeks, Sade dedicated himself to corrupting the captive minors.

Holding them hostage in the château's dungeon, he forced them to act out scenes from pornographic novels and his own intricately stage-managed sexual rituals. (Obsessively controlling, he liked to choreograph every detail. As a character complains in one of his fictions, "Let's please put some order into these orgies!") Modern French wives are legendarily indulgent of their husbands' peccadilloes, but Sade's wife, Pélagie, took conjugal freedom to new heights by overseeing this marathon debauch, keeping the five girls compliant, then hushing up the ensuing scandal. When the police came knocking, she helped bribe the outraged parents and spirit the girls, decidedly damaged goods, away to convents.

Over time, the château also took pride of place in Sade's literary imagination. As the biographer Francine du Plessix Gray points out in her classic *At Home with the Marquis de Sade,* its position hovering above Lacoste fed his outdated fantasies of feudal inviolability, where he could act out his rabid carnal desires with no fear of reprisal. Even later, when Sade was in prison, the château remained a font of inspiration for his grisly literary output—a Walden Pond for the polymorphously perverse.

Speculation has long been rife as to what remained inside the château, particularly the dungeon. Although the edifice was looted during the Revolution and pillaged for its masonry, connoisseurs of erotic literature began arriving in the nineteenth century to soak up its aura. In 1871, the French art historian P. L. Jacob was told by villagers that the walls of the dungeon were once painted with naked figures dancing in "a type of witch's Sabbath" around supine women, a vision Jacob breathlessly compared to an absinthe hallucination. Later, the bestselling author of salacious history Dr. Augustin Cabanès was informed that revolutionaries had discovered in the dungeon "instruments of torture that served at the marquis' debauches." ("Or is it just idle gossip?" he mused.) Farmers spoke of secret tunnels all through the countryside, used by the marquis to evade police raids.

By the twentieth century, the château had become a louche must-see for the avant-garde traveler to Provence. Surrealists like André Breton, who inflamed the modern fascination with Sade's work, explored it; Man Ray sketched it; Cartier-Bresson and Brassaï photographed it; Lawrence Durrell wrote the racy parts of the *Alexandria Quartet* in one of Lacoste's cafés. In the 1960s, at the same time as censorship restrictions were finally lifted on Sade's works, artists began moving into Lacoste's cheap stone houses, creating a modest bohemian community. A local schoolteacher, André Bouër, purchased the abandoned castle and made the first basic repairs to it in decades. He held energetic parties there every summer; locals would wake up to see comely *filles de joie* from Marseilles, their lipstick smeared, teetering down the lanes in high heels.

But it is the château's new owner, Pierre Cardin, who has caused more tumult in Lacoste than anyone since the marquis himself. The billionaire haute couturier was evidently tickled by the literary connection when he bought the seventy-acre estate. He erected a shiny bronze statue of Sade next to the castle, pumped a million euros into improving the structure, and started a summer theater festival that lured crowds from Paris and the Riviera. (Cardin's website states that the event is a homage to Sade, who loved the stage and put on plays in the château himself.) But it soon became obvious that Cardin had grand plans for the village as well. He began buying up Lacoste's historic structures, then converting them into galleries and stores. It seemed as if Cardin wanted to take over the whole village, turning it into a "St. Tropez of culture." The reaction to this real estate grab among most of the original villagers was violent—much more so than if he had been hosting mad orgies in the château. Ever since, Lacoste has been torn apart by a mini–civil war with a viciousness that only French provincials can manage.

I had no difficulty selling Lacoste to Les, who was so dewy-eyed about her first trip to Provence that she didn't care which village we went to. The boys liked the sound of the menacing castle, thinking they were going to Gondor perhaps. I was relieved to learn that, despite all the renovations, the basic structure of the Château Sade was intact, including, I gathered, the former dungeon. But getting an invitation into the private lair of any celebrity can be a tricky business—and the volatile politics of this weird little village made the task of even meeting Monsieur Cardin difficult. But I wasn't heading into the hornet's nest unprepared. I had a connection that would melt any Sade fan's heart.

THE MARQUIS AND I

While researching Sade's life in Provence, I came across a flimsy booklet on the history of Lacoste. At first, I paid it little attention. It seemed the typically myopic local study that wallows in eye-glazing statistics, with rosters of grape harvests and treatises on pâté production. But as I flicked through the pages, I froze in shock. There in the village tax census for the year 1608 was my own name, Antoyne Perrottet.

My Gallic family moniker had been, until now, deeply obscure, so this was quite a coincidence. From the Middle Ages to the mid-nineteenth century, it turned out, a veritable army of Perrottets had infested this Provençal village—well, about ten extended families, roughly a quarter of the total population. Then, around 1860, Provence fell into economic decay, and the Perrottets all cleared out to Australia, America, Argentina. A quick call to the family genealogist confirmed that Lacoste was indeed our font.

Even stranger, I discovered, a certain André Perrottet had risen to prominence in Lacoste in the late 1700s—*as an employee of the Marquis de Sade himself.*

Now, I've never been one for roots tours, but the idea that my forebears had hobnobbed with the divine marquis put a whole new spin on things. It seemed that this ancestor of mine was a personal assistant of some sort, arranging Sade's wide range of needs. *Zut alors,* I was Costain (a native of Lacoste) myself, give or take two centuries. If that didn't give me license to talk to Cardin and demand entry into the château, I don't know what did.

While we were in Paris, I made an appointment at the Bibliothèque Nationale to read the correspondence between the marquis and Monsieur André Perrottet. In the imposing old building on Rue Richelieu, I followed a red carpet up the marble staircase—past the former Enfer, or Hell, the room for banned books—and into a magnificent, walnut-paneled reading room, where the windows were flung open to let in the warm summer breeze. I was surprised to find that, once I had a reader's card, the librarians were happy to hand over Sade's original handwritten letters. They hadn't even been scanned or microfilmed. I was presented with a volume so unwieldy it had to be propped on an easel to peruse. Bound together inside were hundreds of pages scribbled in the marquis' spidery

Sade correspondence in the Bibliothèque Nationale of Paris.

hand; many were on small shreds of paper, like small napkins, to save on expensive writing materials. I ran my finger over the Sade wax seal and the marquis' florid signature, which must be worth thousands at auction today. Finally, although the scrawl was often barely legible, I managed to piece together the ancestral saga.

Young André Perrottet was first singled out by the marquis in 1767, when he organized a successful memorial service for Sade's father. From then on, he was hired as an all-around fixer for the seigneur. André helped oversee renovations to the château. He stage-managed rites of feudal homage by the villagers. (Sade sat in an armchair lapping up the adulation, while officials swore fealty on bended knee—a tradition that had been abandoned in the rest of France for centuries.) Perrottet became a trusted courier, carrying sensitive letters to lawyers in Marseilles, three days away by coach. And he kept an eye on unruly castle staff. In 1776, André reported to Sade that the shapely maid, Gothon, had become lost in the countryside one rainy night, apparently because she had been drinking, but André found her the next morning in the forest, cold but unharmed.

I flipped through the pages greedily. The references to Sade's delicate legal problems ("the parents from Grenoble are taking action") were interspersed with casual domestic orders for new bedroom curtains or types of wallpaper. My ancestor's name popped up at regular intervals. When Sade was hiding out in Italy in 1775, he sent a letter to his lawyer, Gaspard Gaufridy, wishing he was back at home in Lacoste, enjoying *un dindon* (little turkey) and gay banter with his *"loyal* and *frank* friend, Perrottet. . . ."

So my ancestor was the Marquis de Sade's toady. Excellent. But he was also, I learned, something of a survivor. He managed to escape the plunder of the château during the 1789 Revolution and the ensuing Terror. And there is a reference to him in 1806, under the rule of Napoléon, when André had became mayor of Lacoste himself.

I took photographs of the correspondence, and had them

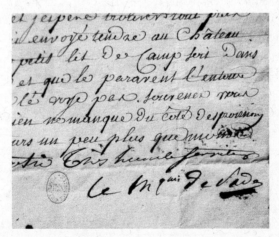

The Marquis' signature on his correspondence.

printed up into a dossier. These were my Gallic credentials—
*one of the Perrottets, Monsieur Cardin, was the Marquis'
right-hand man!*—I was ready to take on the village. All that
was left was the trifling matter of finding accommodation in
Provence in high summer.

"So how small *is* this garret?" Les grilled me, as we drove the
twenty-five miles from Avignon in a sky-blue Citroën, a model
they called the Picasso. I had snapped up the only lodging
still available within Lacoste itself. Sure, there were all sorts
of fabulous villas and gentrified farmhouses dotting the countryside, but being in the *heart* of things was key to my meeting
Cardin. I had to admit that space was going to be tight even
by East Village standards. "The boys' have got beds, right?" Les
asked. "Right?"

"We could pretend we're in a reality TV show," I suggested, "where we have to recreate the living conditions of
eighteenth-century peasants!"

A serious heat wave had settled over southern France.
Many of the forests were tinder-dry. But Lacoste still managed to look verdant and dramatic, the château looming on
its lush crag like something out of a 1930s horror movie. We
maneuvered cautiously up the winding road to the base of the
village, wondering where on earth to park the Picasso. Lacoste
is miniscule, with a network of cobbled lanes, two cafés, and
a single boulangerie of erratic hours. Of course, there are
Cardin's new galleries and boutiques, but no supermarket, no
bank, no ATM, no public transport, no bicycle hire, no escape
other than by walking.

I hoped everyone liked it: We were going to be there for
two weeks.

The Château Sade looming over Lacoste today.

Madame Colette, the shrewd, white-haired cleaning lady, handed me a fistful of iron keys, then slammed her door. After trudging up the steep cobblestones of the Rue du Four, I cranked open a huge wooden door and ascended a cold stone staircase. This was it. Our eyes adjusted to the darkness of a tiny room with bare stone walls and two narrow pallets, underneath which were two thin mattresses for the boys. The mod-cons included a rusty sink, a gas burner, and a bar refrigerator. Things were looking grim as we spun about in the darkness, but when I pushed open two shuttered doors, Les's bleak expression dissolved. It seemed our garret also came with a small balcony, which had views that would make an Impressionist drool. Lacoste, we now discovered, floats above the region called the Luberón like a hot-air balloon, with sweeping vistas across vineyards and cherry orchards. In the distance loomed Mount Ventoux, which appears snow-capped but is actually covered in chalk. I breathed a sigh of relief. This was the mythic Provence of Peter Mayle novels, beloved by British retirees and anyone with a passion for cheese, flea markets, and renovated barns.

We could thrive here. Les could sketch on the balcony for weeks. Even the toy kitchenette had a view over the rooftops. Hanging out the window, Henry spotted one of the village cats on the neighbor's roof, a snow-white apparition, nimbly negotiating the terracotta tiles like a snow leopard. From then on, the boys made it their mission to track him down and befriend him. Rather like me and Pierre Cardin.

The Marquis de Sade was by all accounts a devoted father, I mused to myself as I set out for the château. On summer evenings, he would frolic with his three young children—two sons, Louis-Marie and Armand, and a baby daughter, Madelaine—in the garden estate, displaying a fondness for play-acting, hide-and-seek, and musical chairs. The dashing aristocrat also doted on his wife, Pélagie, and lovingly addressed her as "celestial kitten," "fresh pork of my thoughts" and "star of Venus," and had quite a green thumb, planting many of the quince trees that still blossom throughout Lacoste.

A steep trail above the village led me into the castle's former moat, now dry and littered with weeds and loose chunks of masonry. The Château Sade still managed to look forbidding. French preservation laws made it illegal for Cardin to alter the exterior structure, which is essentially a ruined veil of fortress walls; the only embellishments on the blank facade are a few high windows now fitted with one-way glass. The decaying remains of the top floor give the castle a sinister appearance, like a set of rotten fangs—still the ideal refuge, you might say, for a deranged priest or bestial nobleman from one of Sade's own porn classics, like *120 Days of Sodom*. At the very least, a Dungeons and Dragons computer game designer. *Au contraire*. French magazines reported that its medieval interior is now renovated into a chic abode suitable for the global fashion icon. Of course, Lacoste is only one of Cardin's international addresses. Having made billions from an epic career that included prêt-à-porter suits, space-age dresses, and avant-garde furniture, Cardin flits between dozens of other luxury abodes. But every July, he potters about in Lacoste, working to put it on the European cultural map. Needless to say, Cardin is remarkably spry at eighty-eight years of age, his only caution being to avoid the afternoon sun. Was he inside now, I wondered, having his afternoon siesta?

His château also appears impenetrable. Apart from a sleek new metal walkway that traverses the moat to a wooden portal, which is fitted with a state-of-the-art security system, the only way inside would be to scale the ramparts with a giant ladder. The French police had done precisely that one midnight in 1774, bursting in on a terrified Madame Sade with swords and pistols, only to find that their quarry, the marquis, had fled. The villagers had tipped Sade off about the raid. The next year, officers again stormed through the château, but failed to find Sade hiding under the eaves of the roof.

The most striking addition is Cardin's shiny bronze sculpture of the marquis, perched on a precipice with commanding views of the valley. It displays Sade's bewigged head surrounded by a metal cage: Sade the perpetual prisoner. In 1777, the Marquis' own primitive security system—basically, peasant lookouts in barns around the valley—failed him, and he was seized here in the château. He spent most of the rest of his life incarcerated, thirteen years in the Bastille and eleven in Charenton Asylum. Both attempts to censor his literary outpourings proved futile. In fact, since he was allowed furniture, a library, and gourmet food in his cells, the confinement actually served to focus his literary inspiration, as if prison were an eccentric writers' colony. His lurid novels generated an underground cult following, which only grew after his death in 1814.

Within a generation, the besotted poet Baudelaire wrote that if a statue of Sade were ever erected, thousands would one day come to lay flowers at his feet. Well, it may have taken a few decades longer than expected, but there is no question that the divine marquis can bring in the fans today. Tourists arrived in a steady stream to wander the estate and take snaps of the gleaming statue. And back down in the village, all Cardin's commercial ventures seemed to be cashing in on the Sade name brand.

When I saw that his boutique gift store was even named after the marquis, my imagination ran riot. Would it be a high-end sex shop for the dominatrix and fetishist? Would it stock Sade's favorite accessories, like the hand-carved *prestiges,* or dildos, he favored for his autoerotic rites or like his beloved enema syringes, which bore tasteful engravings of men kneeling in worship before plump buttocks? At least it could offer some books from the Marquis' own library, I thought, classics like *The Fornications of Priests and Nuns,* illustrated editions of his own phantasmagoric works, or maybe a vial of Spanish fly. (This supposed aphrodisiac derived from insects was popular in the eighteenth century, even though it was mildly toxic: Sade had slipped a quantity to prostitutes in Marseilles with disastrous results and was accused of attempted murder.)

Statue of the Marquis de Sade at his château, now owned by Pierre Cardin.

No such luck. Instead, when I entered the cool stone cavern of Le Moulin de Sade, I was confronted with an array of local gourmet foods: foie gras, jams, pâtés, and honeys. When I quizzed the elderly shopkeeper about Sadist souvenirs, she gave me a bookmark with his profile and a bottle of Marquis de Sade wine.

The truth is, Sade would probably have been delighted. He was a fervent gourmand, who loved Provençal delicacies such as quail stuffed with grape leaves, cream of chard soup, and local jams. He once demanded that his wife send him a chocolate cake that was black "as the devil's ass is blackened by smoke." Fine food appears in all his writings about orgies, inspiring the participants to fits of lust. As one character notes: "Our cocks are never so stiff as when we've just completed a sumptuous feast." An early version, perhaps, of the saying that the way to a man's heart is through his stomach.

THE TORTURES OF PARADISE

When the heat finally ebbed in the late afternoon, the village began to ring with activity. Construction workers were scurrying like ants along the Rue Basse, Low Road, where Cardin had purchased a dozen buildings and was speedily gutting them. On the work permits, someone had crossed out Cardin's name by hand, and scribbled in slogans like *Sauvez Votre Village,* Save Your Village. Long before Cardin's arrival, Lacoste had been violently independent. For centuries, it was a Protestant island in a sea of Catholics, and more recently, it was run by a Communist mayor for fifty years. Now the villagers, *les Costains,* were rebelling against what they regarded as a hostile capitalist takeover. They accuse Cardin of leeching the traditional life from their village and denounce him as an arrogant aristocrat trying to turn the clock back to the prerevolutionary days of Sade.

Still, not everyone in Lacoste was ready to light torches and storm the château. A small but vocal minority view Cardin as saving the village from provincial stagnation.

As it happened, I got the latter view first when I met Finn Mac Eion, a wild-haired poet and landscape gardener who was known to be the most committed Sade specialist in Lacoste. I found him watering a row of shrubberies. Tall and gangly, wearing cut-off shorts and a khaki T-shirt as if he'd just stumbled back from the battle of Tobruk, Finn was also a one-man PR team for the new regime.

"I'm pro-Cardin and I'm pro the Marquis de Sade," he immediately declared, before denouncing the conspiracy of idle Socialists who were trying to block Cardin's noble plans for the village. Tossing aside his watering can, Finn took me on a proud tour of the twenty-five buildings that Cardin now owned. Suddenly carried away with the grand ambition of it all, he stopped to orate a celebratory poem.

"I call this one 'Resurrection,'" Finn said, striking a mock-heroic pose like a Shakespearean actor on the tiles. "It's dedicated to Monsieur Cardin."

Raising one hand, a knee up on a stone wall, Finn swept back his curly hair and pronounced in his rolling Irish brogue:

> Up from ancient ruins in Phoenix flight,
>> Domaine de Sade Pierre'd before my very eyes—
> Stone by stone this titan feat rose and rose beyond a dream
>> Where lark and passing cloud can meet—

He pointed with a flourish to the village of Bonnieux in the distance, for centuries Lacoste's bitter Catholic enemy and far more prosperous.

> Now, a beacon on this once Lacoste'd hill has
>> Far-off Bonnieux put to shame. And soon the moon it will.

"Cardin's got that poem up on his wall in the château," Finn exulted. "Right next to the Marquis de Sade's portrait."

A villager stuck his head out of the window to see what all the noise was about, but seeing it was Finn, snorted in disgust and pulled his head back in.

"Ah, they hate me here," Finn chortled. "They fucking hate me! I don't care. Friends make you weak. Enemies make you strong! I'll make 'em hate me more."

Finn invited me back to the safety of his house to discuss the Sade connection. Since moving to Lacoste a decade ago, he said, he had become obsessed with the divine marquis. He was planning to write a "creative biography" of Sade, and he had traveled to Vincennes prison and managed to prise a chunk of stone from the walls of Sade's very cell as a souvenir. I had to admire his dedication. "I want to do everything Sade did. I want to understand him. I've been everywhere he went. I've been to the prison cells he was stuck in, and the ones he escaped from—been out the same window he went out."

"You want to do everything?" I asked.

"Everything!"

Most impressive of all, Finn said that he had read every word that Sade had ever written. Even many leading academic biographers admit they have never been able to slog through the deadening litany of carnal horrors that is *120 days of Sodom,* or the twin volumes *Justine* and *Juliette,* each of which clock in at about 1,200 pages, with an inventive new outrage on almost every one. Personally, I agreed with the nineteenth-century English poet Algernon Charles Swinburne, who after hearing so much about the forbidden marquis, was dismayed to discover that his actual words, when he finally found a copy, were not particularly erotic or even shocking—just wildly absurd. Some scholars have argued that Sade's books were intended as parables rather than porn, closer in spirit to eighteenth-century philosophical fictions like *Candide* and designed to show that virtue is never rewarded and vice never punished. The final effect, Swinburne decided, was outrageous black comedy. He and his reprobate Victorian friends, like Henry Spencer Ashbee, took to reading Sade with gales of uproarious laughter. What else can one make, for example, of the scene where the ever innocent Justine discovers a mad surgeon who is dissecting one daughter while ravishing the other. "Oh, monsieur," she gasps. "Look what you have done!" No wonder the surrealists were inspired.

"But you've got to read the man's letters from prison," Finn said. "That's where you get the real Sade. They're beautifully written. They'll make you fucking weep."

Finn was out to vindicate Sade's memory. The Marquis was never given a trial, he raged, but locked up by royal decree and dictatorial edicts from Napoléon. His grand plan was to one day create a mock trial of Sade at Lacoste in order to educate visitors.

"People don't know shit about the Marquis de Sade," he said. "They come here to Lacoste and they tell me, oh, do you know he killed his wife and cut out her heart? Such crap! So much misinformation. He loved his wife! She was like Florence fucking Nightingale to him. But you get that from people. Everyone wants to see blood."

Certainly, there are subtleties to Sade's life that get lost in all the hype clinging to his name. As the biographer Plessix Gray points out, he should perhaps be termed "a nonviolent sadist." He never drew blood in his rituals, preferring to use psychological torture. He denounced the death penalty during the Revolution at considerable personal risk. And unlike other aristocrats, he was never in a duel or even went hunting. The very word "sadism" was not coined until 1886, seven decades after Sade's death, by the German psychiatrist Richard von Krafft-Ebing. (His groundbreaking *Psychopathia Sexualis* was the first "scientific" categorization of "sexual perversions," including fetishism, exhibitionism, pederasty, bestiality, nymphomania, flagellation, necrophilia, incest, homosexuality, lesbianism, and so on.) Surprisingly, Sade himself fits more into the masochist slot: He liked to be whipped, often demanding hundreds of lashes to achieve an erection. But as to his being violent, it's the old story of how we confuse writers with their writings. Sade's real life story was blurred with his exaggerated creations and their demented acts of cruelty.

"So what if Sade was a rapist?" Finn railed. "A lot of French aristocrats did much worse. And if he was such a bastard, why did the villagers help him whenever the police were raiding? Why did his servants refuse to leave him?"

Finn's wife Caron, a New Zealander, was patiently chopping a salad throughout this tirade. I asked her if she shared Finn's passion for the marquis. "I think it's good in a marriage to have different interests," she said sweetly.

WAITING FOR PIERRE

Next morning I visited L'Espace Lacoste, the tiny office for Cardin's summer festival, and applied for an official audience with the seigneur. The manager, Fabienne, stifled an incredulous laugh at my folly. "You want to visit Monsieur Cardin's château?" she said. "I'm afraid he is a very busy man." She suggested I contact the media director of the sprawling Cardin Empire in Paris, one Monsieur Hoesse—a man who, I soon discovered, never answered his phone or e-mails unless you were a head of state. Instead, Fabienne offered to sell me tickets to the first festival show, *Marco Polo*, for $260 each.

In fact, everyone I met took pleasure in telling me how impossible it would be to even talk to Cardin, let alone wangle an invitation to the château. "Monsieur Cardin is a very generous man," confided one official at the Savannah School of Design, an American art academy that had set up in the village, "but he is also a very *private* man." Expats shook their heads consolingly, recalling their own fleeting exchanges with Cardin; they talked to me in gentle tones, as if to a mental patient. I could hear them thinking: "Why should you get into the château when we've never been invited, not even for a lousy café crème. Why don't you just go on back to New York?"

Biding my time, I tried to behave like any other Francophile visitor enjoying the Provençal idyll. I would wake up early, wander down to boulangerie, buy a ridiculous quantity of croissants, then hang out with the gang on the balcony, watching the morning sun creep over the valley floor. You could see why there are no secrets in small villages. We soon found out that every word we said was being overheard by our next-door neighbor, Margaret. Margaret was a tiny, eighty-five-year-old grand dame who lived in the dark, antique-filled hobbit's house across the lane but made sudden theatrical appearances in her doorway. She had moved here from Zimbabwe decades ago and had once run the most lively bar in the village, but now she spent her time chatting with friends and adopting stray felines. Her favorite was a tough ginger pussy named William.

"Here's William," she would announce to the boys. "William the Conqueror, I call him. I was going to have him spayed, but he has such lovely hairy balls.

"William with the great big conkers!" she added, and cackled maniacally.

I spent much time in the Cardin-owned Café de Sade, a minimalist terrace that looked out over the village square.

The village of Lacoste.

After a couple of days I was officially a regular and began chatting with the affable manager, Gérard, who had worked with Cardin for twenty years in Maxim's restaurant in Paris. "Don't worry," Gérard reassured me. "Monsieur Cardin is here almost every day. You will meet him!" But I didn't.

Slowly, I began to insinuate myself into the village, with the help of my Gallic credentials—"We are the Perrottets, *mes amis,* our ancestor used to be mayor under Napoléon!" True, it was a sure-fire conversation starter. Locals knew there was once a horde of Perrottets here. There was even a tiny hamlet called Perrottet nearby, so I dragged the gang there to have our photo taken standing beside the sign. In the Lacoste cemetery, there were still a few faces of my ancestors, in 1920s black-and-white photographs enshrined at family plots, the last of the Perrottets to expire in Provence.

Les kept saying "Wow, they all look like you!" which I found mildly disconcerting.

And I got to learn a lot about Lacoste's miniature class war. It didn't take much prompting for villagers to air their grievances against their new châtelain, Cardin, which echoed the bitter feudal resentments of the eighteenth century. Jacques Trophemius, a wiry farmer in his fifties, declared Cardin a "megalomaniac" drunk on his own wealth, who was destroying the village by buying houses at triple their value. Old people can't turn the money down, and young people can no longer afford to move in. "These streets used to be filled with children playing! Where are they now?" He waved a hand theatrically. "This village is dying." I also dropped around to a farmhouse to meet Yves Ronchi, founder of the radical Association for the Harmonious Development of Lacoste. A grandfatherly vigneron who came up from his basement in galoshes and an apron as if he'd just been stomping grapes, he argued that modern France was recreating all the inequalities of the ancien regime. "This country should stand for liberty, equality, fraternity. That's why we fought the Revolution! But the rich today have a new sense of privilege. They ignore laws and trample our democratic rights." Yes, Cardin had poured €30 million into his renovations, he said, but the result was bricolage—a rushed job, makeshift, not serious. "When you look inside Cardin's houses, there is no character, no history, no soul. The details are gone. It's just empty space."

Still, there was life in the village yet. One morning, I noticed a half dozen women sitting in the plaza, all intently shelling green beans, like Madame Defarge knitting before the guillotine. "Are you coming tonight, Monsieur Perrottet?" a large woman with pink hair asked pointedly, fondling a wad of tickets from the Lacoste Association for Parties. The beans were for a monstrous aioli feast, she said—the whole district would be there.

Our arrival had coincided with the start of Lacoste's "popular festival," whose revelries resembled an outtake from *Jean de Florette*. Every day saw a different rustic event. There were donkey races through the Rue Basse, which littered the streets with excrement for days. There were three-legged races for adults, which were so violent that bones were broken. And there were nightly feasts, Breughelian affairs where hundreds of families sat along trestle tables and devoured unlimited supplies of pistou soup, washed down with a watery wine that cost less than Coca-Cola. After dark, there would be either a rock concert or theatrical piece, both shockingly bad, while the kids could watch the latest blockbuster on an outdoor screen, Jacques Tati style.

The festivities sometimes got out of hand, keeping the local gendarmes busy. One night, a brawl began between rival village members when a roulette table was set up in the plaza, and someone got stabbed in the chest with a broken bottle.

The boys became obsessed by the seedy carnival games. Sam never tired of plucking plastic ducks out of a water trough, while Henry became smitten with a real shooting gallery. Apart from winning a vast number of key rings, he got lucky one night and won a pellet gun from the prize rack. "It is prohibited for children under fourteen," the lady snapped, then immediately handed him the gun. "You could have your eye out," she added angrily.

"Don't shoot the cats!" Les yelled, running after Henry. "Or Sam . . ."

I had sometimes wondered whether my wayward progeny paid any attention to dinner conversations with Les about the

Marquis de Sade. But I gathered they did one morning when they begged for chocolate croissants for breakfast.

"They must be black!" Henry said. *"As the devil's bottom is black!"* Then tried to stifle his laughter.

"No," Sam observed. "The devil's bottom is red. He's red all over."

This theological discussion was repeated whenever black was mentioned, with the phrase becoming an embarrassing catch-cry.

I'd been stalking Cardin for a week without success when the day arrived for the festival's most anticipated event, the village bullfight. This Provençal version didn't involve any animal torture; instead, it was the human participants who suffered. In the blistering heat, a young bull chased teams of teenagers around a makeshift arena, while they tried to throw plastic hoops over its flailing horns. Whenever the enraged animal butted an unlucky player headfirst into a bale of straw, the crowd let out a roar of approval. A brass band would break into raucous music. Drunks danced about in glee, waving beer bottles and screaming insults. Of course, Henry and Sam were also up on the fence, howling for blood like pagans at the Colosseum.

At one point, I saw Les on the opposite side of the bullring, waving her arms frantically. At first I thought she was just getting into the festivities with surprising enthusiasm. Then I realized she was pointing up at the château high on the hill above us.

"Cardin!" she mouthed. "He's up there!"

I wheeled around, shielding my eyes against the flaring sun. I could just make out two figures on the castle's roof, leaning over the battlements—two men, one older with florid white hair, the other much younger. As I watched, the younger one handed something over. The lenses glinted in the sun. Binoculars.

He's watching us! I realized. *The lord of the manor is inspecting the peasants at play.* It was a relief to finally confirm Cardin's presence in Lacoste, but I also felt a vague sense of dread. How the hell was I going to get inside that castle?

"Oh, putain!" screamed one of the players, as the *vachette* raked his ribs with its horns. The crowd roared even louder as the ambulance men reluctantly put down their beers and prepared to enter the arena with the stretcher.

The binoculars remained fixed for a few more minutes, then the two figures disappeared back inside the château. Cardin was preparing his own festival, which he would personally open the next night. At last! He was emerging from seclusion.

Enough of these rustic diversions. Like my slippery ancestor André, I would have to start mingling with the aristocrats. Even if sitting through a $260 French rock opera was the price I would have to pay.

THE RULING CLASS

In this schizophrenic village, I was realizing, everything came in pairs. Cardin's swank Café de Sade, where the chef would throw together a fine *chèvre chaude* salad, had its counterpart in the shabby Café de France—refuge of the anti-Cardinites, where grizzled yokels would tear at roast chicken like gourmandizing Orcs. Now Lacoste's gritty festival would be countered by Cardin's upscale extravaganza catering to the Paris-Riviera crowd. Instead of wheelbarrow races and fistfights, the diet would be classical concerts and avant-garde art. No watery *vin ordinaire* and buckets of soup for them: Cardin's audiences would enjoy chilled champagne and imported shellfish.

The rock opera would be staged *en plein air* right outside the castle. Maybe I could even crash the after-party. So I dashed back into the ticket office and from the smirking Fabienne bought the last two standby tickets to *Marco Polo* that night. The show was too late for Sam, so Les missed out and Henry was my date. This actually made sense, a French rock opera being better entertainment for ten-year-olds.

"Come, Henry!" I declared, after we'd dressed in our finest summer threads. "The game is afoot!"

While the alleyways of Lacoste were as dark as Salem on a witch-hunting night, high above the village, Sade's estate was throbbing with life once again. Hundreds of BMWs, Mercedes, and Jaguars were parked in the fields around the château, and we fell in line with streams of society women stiletto-hobbling across the rocky terrain. Cardin's conversion of Sade's old rock quarry was like something out of science fiction. We entered past monstrous carved blocks like the pillars of an Egyptian temple to the brilliantly lit venue, a 1,600-seat amphitheater beneath the stars.

At the bar, models in sheath dresses were serving bubbly with the Maxim label.

"What, no Coke?" Henry wailed.

In the distance, I spied the man himself. He looked fabulous for his eighty-eight years, in a dark blue blazer and crisp white shirt, his mop of tousled white hair over designer glasses. A bevy of peroxide blonde women fluttered around him. Forming an outer ring were young men in silk jackets and designer stubble, like hipster bodyguards. Soon *Marco*

Polo began with samurai break-dancers on stage, while a giant screen came to life with scenes from Japanese anime. Henry and 1,600 French people were agog.

It struck me that the Marquis de Sade would surely have approved of Lacoste's artsy new life. The stage was his most enduring passion. One of the first renovations he made to the château was to install a sixty-seat private theater, and he lured out-of-work actors from Paris to join his theatrical troupe. They performed a string of surprisingly staid comedies, which Sade would write, direct, design, stage manage, and star in. The marquis also had a philanthropic streak. In 1772, he began to invite the Costains to his plays. At dusk, the villagers would pass the Goat's Gateway in their Sunday finery, the Perrottets along with the Appys, the Layandes, the Payans, and Fontpourquières. Democratic as it all sounds, Sade wasn't entirely certain of his rustic audience, and he hired a string of musclemen to act as château security, in case of a "tumult."

To his dying day, despite the notoriety of his pornographic works, Sade's dearest wish was to be recognized as a playwright. Even at Charenton mental asylum, he put on theatrical shows with the inmates as actors, which became a popular night out for chic Parisians. (Actually, Sade's youthful crimes also sound like one-man performance art pieces. On one notorious occasion, he kept a prostitute hostage while he defiled her with an array of Christian symbols. If Sade had lived in the 1980s, he might have won a grant from the National Endowment for the Arts—"Piss Christ Returns.")

Come to think of it, Sade would have approved of Cardin's profession too, for he was also obsessive about fashion. His prison letters are filled with demands for the latest styles. "Send me a little prune-colored riding coat," Sade ordered his wife in 1781, "with a suede vest and trousers, something fresh and light but specifically *not* made of linen." In the same missive, he requests a suit that is "Paris Mud in hue—a fashionable color this year—with a few silver trimmings, but definitely not silver braid. . . ."

Three hours of French rock opera took their toll. Henry was fading, so we slipped out past the looming château. While I was peering up at the windows, now lit from within, he asked: "Dad, how come you're so interested in getting inside the castle?"

"Well," I began evasively, "a very strange man used to live there."

"What did he do?"

"Um, he had this dungeon, you see, and . . ."

"Dungeon?"

Luckily, Henry spotted a ginger cat darting through the shadows, and the subject was dropped.

FIRST BLOOD

It was 9:00 a.m. the next morning when I ran into Cardin in the street. I was returning with my morning haul of croissants when I saw him heading straight toward me. He was with a couple of immaculately coiffed women about to enter a gallery; one of them was opening it with a wad of keys. Half-asleep and taken by surprise, I hovered uncertainly. Then, not knowing what else to do, I followed them inside.

"Bonjour," I chirped to the consort with the keys, when she looked at me inquiringly. "Do you mind if I look at the art?"

I wandered the gallery, doing my best to look like a sophisticated collector, while preparing myself to engage Cardin in winning banter. But when I turned around, he and his friends had vanished. I looked out in the street desperately. No sign. It was as if they'd just popped down some secret trapdoor.

"Oh my God, you didn't talk to him?" Les said, when I returned to the garret. "That could have been your only chance!" I was plunged into depression. It was true. So many Costains despised him that he must have fled for his safety.

That afternoon, I confessed my flub to Gérard. He told me not to worry—while the festival was on, Cardin liked to come to the village at that time every morning, when it was still very quiet and not too hot. "You should look for him then," he advised.

And so I did, lurking on the Rue Basse again at 9:00 a.m. the next day. I was about to give up when I glimpsed Cardin walking into one of the old mansions being converted into a hotel. OK, I thought. This was my big chance. Why was I even so nervous? I took a deep breath, pretended I was just passing by, then entered the work site.

"Bonjour!" I said cheerily.

"Qui êtes vous?" Cardin asked immediately. Two laborers stared at me.

I introduced myself, trying not to babble. "I'm a historian from New York. I'm curious about the renovations. Do you mind if I have a look?"

To my surprise, Cardin walked up to me and shook my hand. He was wearing tailored slacks and a floral shirt with the cuffs casually rolled; up close, he seemed far taller and stronger than his advanced years would suggest.

"The upstairs is finished, if you would like to see it?" Cardin said.

"Bien sûr."

We had to use an exterior staircase where a worker's truck

was parked, blocking off the lower steps entirely. But Cardin simply grabbed the fence and began to hoist himself up. It was too ambitious at first; he swung back and forth like a limbo dancer under the metal bar. I hovered beneath him with my arms outstretched, terrified that he was about to crack his skull—*oh my God, I'm going to be responsible for the death of a modern fashion icon!*—but no, with a renewed effort, he got himself up.

On the second floor, he proudly showed me the different suites, each decorated in a different style and color and filled with angular modern furniture. I made appropriately admiring noises, trying to play it cool, and complimented him on *Marco Polo*—a work of genius—while I racked my brain for how to steer the conversation. I couldn't just *ask* to see his home; that would be vulgar. An invitation had to arise organically.

Then, in the entrance hall, I glimpsed a Dalí-esque painting of a figure in a powdered wig hovering in a starlit sky. Here was my opening.

"Ah, the marquis!"

I casually mentioned how I was researching Sade's life in Lacoste.

"Yes, I've studied Sade a great deal," Cardin said. "Naturally, I am very interested in his theatrical works."

"You know, my ancestors used to live here," I said. "A certain André Perrottet, he actually worked for Sade in the 1770s . . ."

But my words were suddenly drowned out by shouts and grunts. Two workmen were lugging a monstrous scarlet lounge the shape of a potato chip up the stairs. Cardin suddenly had his hand out to me. And before I knew it, he had disappeared up the stairs, directing the workers around a tight corner.

I stood there dumbfounded. I wanted to wail, *"Show me*

the damn dungeon!" but thought better of it. Contact had been made.

THE TOUR DE SADE

"Thank God!" Les said, when I told her of my breakthrough. "Now let's go for a drive in the countryside!"

"Well, we don't want to get carried away . . ."

"But look at it out there!" she said desperately, pointing at the ravishing view and waving a guidebook to Provence I'd foolishly left lying around. Apparently there were antique markets all over the place, not to mention restaurants, wineries, waterfalls, truffle museums, and much, much more. "Can't we do something *different* today?"

Admittedly, Lacoste was becoming a tad claustrophobic. We had trudged the same four cobbled lanes about a thousand times between the same two cafés, running into the same handful of villagers. The boys were now tearing around the village like their feline friends. Trying to include them at refined artistic functions had not been a success. One night, we'd gone to a reception at Lacoste's last independent gallery when Sam's piercing shrieks interrupted the party. He ran into the crowd with blood spurting down his nose in a scarlet river, the result of ninja fighting in the lane outside. As I whisked my howling offspring from the immaculate space, I noticed a wave of relief emanating from the other guests. I could hardly blame them. But I was beginning to feel as if there was a cosmic conspiracy against my mission, with my family as the agents of sabotage.

While I floundered about like a lost butterfly in the village, Les pointed out that there were some basic logistics to consider—including the teensy problem that there were no actual groceries available in Lacoste, apart from croissants and jam. Eating out was stressful. Every dinner was spent trying to stop the boys from disturbing the other, childless diners, who sat in silence, contemplating the view through their cigarette smoke and shooting us disdainful looks. Worse, the heat wave in Provence had become unbearable. Lacoste is also one of the only villages in southern France that lacks a public pool, and none of the genteel expats we'd met had offered to share their villa *piscine*.

So as the mercury broke 100 degrees, we began a Kafkaesque routine of driving for miles to find municipal pools, only to be denied access because of our American-style swimwear. Board shorts had just been declared unhygienic by the French authorities; only Lycra briefs would be tolerated for males of any age. Every time we tried to slip past the ticket office window, we were caught and had to open our bags.

"Forbidden!" the crones would snap.

"But *why* are board shorts unhygienic?" I pleaded.

"Loose hairs," they retorted. "One needs to be *contained*."

We peered into the pool enclosure, where scrawny French boys were frolicking in tiny stretch underpants and purple swim-caps, like *Tintin en Vacances*. Henry blanched at the sight. "I'm not wearing those things!" he railed. "Let's get out of here!"

I tried to see these jaunts as part of my research. After all, Sade had managed to drag his thirty-two-person theatrical troupe all over this part of Provence in the summer of 1772. Biographers have marveled at the manic energy needed for this touring enterprise, as the Marquis trundled over mountain roads and Roman bridges with carts full of scenery and a support team of valets, cooks, and disgruntled thespians. I could sympathize. Every time I mobilized my own crew to hit the road, it was like Napoléon's army breaking camp.

After these forays, I would return to Lacoste with heightened anxiety, wondering what I had missed. I was like Martin Sheen in *Apocalypse Now*—every day I was away from the jungle I felt myself getting weaker and the enemy stronger. I had to remain in the village, stay focused, avoid distractions, if Cardin was going to be ensnared.

The low point came when Lesley announced one morning that she had been concealing a painful rash on her neck that she could no longer tolerate. I groaned inwardly. This meant we had to spend yet another day driving to another infuriatingly pretty hill town in order to find a doctor.

The French physician was so young, tall, and statuesque, he looked as if he'd stepped out of a Gallic TV soap—*Hôpital General,* perhaps.

He took one look at Les's back and solemnly pronounced, "*Le pox.*"

"*Le pox?*" Les gulped. This was getting a little too eighteenth-century.

The doctor kept going on about *le pox* this and *le pox* that. I started to think he just liked saying *le pox*. *Was this bubonic plague or syphilis?* I wondered. We had drawn up a list of French words before the visit to describe her symptoms—useful technical terms like *agonizing* and *blistering*—but that one hadn't come up.

"*Monsieur,*" I interrupted, "*qu'est-ce que c'est, le pox?*"

We all hunched over a computer to find an online medical dictionary.

"Oh, shingles!" Les said. She knew it was stress-related.

The next morning, I ran into Jasper in the Rue Basse. Jasper was a grizzled local sculptor I'd met in the gallery where Sam had disgraced himself.

"You should have been at the party last night," he grinned, a little too cheerily it seemed to me. "Cardin was *there!*"

"What?" I was stunned. "What party?"

"Oh, the American school has a little art gallery at the top of the village. Cardin always turns up at their receptions. He was in great form! I chatted to him for ages."

Jasper shook his head in consolation. "What a pity you didn't know about it. It was quite an event. Why, you could have asked him about visiting the château."

Oh, yes. Sade himself was on my trail, twisting the knife.

Now I put a ban on unnecessary excursions. Why be tourists when we could be locals? I reasoned. It was true we had finally become fixtures in Lacoste, thanks to our own eccentric rituals. Every morning, the boys would crawl out of bed and go on "Cat Watch." Les would sketch on the balcony and make trips to the well for drinking water. I would stake out a corner in the Café de Sade and idly chat with Gérard about Carla Bruni, soccer, or the Tour de France, which was passing nearby. By now, everyone in the village knew I wanted to visit the château, from the mayor, the charmingly named Madame Louche, down to the café's dishwashers. I ran into Cardin on three more occasions, but always in the company of his coiffed entourage. I dropped heavy hints about my interest in the dungeon. He never took the bait. His minders would suddenly start flapping and shuffling him along to the next appointment.

"You don't get a lot of time with Cardin," one villager said, when I explained the problem. "He leads the conversation, and he moves fast."

I tried to remain calm, but time was running out. Every time I returned to our hovel, Les's eyes would dart up at me inquiringly, then look away with a mixture of fear and pity. There was less and less to say. Even Sam was getting suspicious.

"Where's Daddy going?" he started asking whenever I slipped out.

"Oh, he's got work to do," Les would mutter dryly, pushing my copy of *Juliette* under the bed with her foot. The cover displayed the heroine with a strap-on dildo brutalizing a gagged shepherdess.

Contrary to my previous image of Provence, Lacoste was never dull. Strolling down the Rue Basse one morning, I was caught in a scene of mortal combat. Our cleaning lady, the sweet, white-haired Madame Colette, was leaning out of her front window, whacking the windshield of a car with her kitchen broom as it tried to maneuver down the lane. The driver and his wife were cowering in fear as Madame screamed insults like a longshoreman. Many locals believed that the narrow medieval streets should be taboo for all cars—except their own—but some tourists just wanted to drive everywhere. Suddenly, the wild-haired figure of Finn Mac Eion sprang from the bushes, and started yelling at Madame Colette in defense of the tourists' civil rights.

When I returned fifteen minutes later, the argument was still raging, with Colette's husband now involved. The tourists had long since driven off in terror.

It hadn't taken me long to realize that Finn was ubiquitous in Lacoste, and an invaluable resource for gossip. At least twice a day he would pop up with his watering can from a secret garden or hail me from his balcony as I walked by, to update me on the latest skirmishes between the peasants and the seigneur, Cardin. By now, I'd also heard much of Finn's colorful life story. I knew about his former drug addictions. About his AA meetings in Aix. About his youthful flirtations with the IRA, his prison terms and his escapes. ("Prison is a very interesting place, everyone should go there once!") About his vendetta against Peter Mayle, who had apparently reneged on a promise to let Finn quote him in his gardening advertising ("I'm Irish, and the Irish never forget!"). About his meetings with celebrity visitors like Tom Stoppard and John Malkovich, and his friendship with the daughter of Albert Camus. The great French existentialist had lived in Loumarain and is now buried there in a quiet, flower-filled cemetery. In Finn's study, I saw Camus' battered old bicycle hanging on the wall, a gift from the daughter.

"I'm like the Marquis de Sade, I am," Finn said. "Always in trouble. I wake up in war, I go to sleep in war. I don't know what's the matter with me. I see injustice, I have to throw myself into the middle. I can't help it. I wish I could, but I can't."

His pro-Cardin-Sade stance has made him a pariah in the village, he continued. His gardening van is broken into almost daily. His tools are stolen. The windows in his house had all been shattered by enemies. Finn even blamed the villagers for the recent drowning death of his dog, Bono Bono, in a local pond. "The poor creature was murdered," he says. "No doubt about it." Admittedly, Finn has a special talent for exasperating the locals. He printed a T-shirt with a photo of Cardin and a quote from Albert Einstein: GREAT FLIGHTS OF GENIUS WILL ALWAYS BE BATTLED BY MEDIOCRE MINDS. "Villagers come up to me in the street and ask, 'Are you saying *we've* got mediocre minds?'" he roared with laughter. "*Yes*, I tell 'em. That's *exactly* what I'm fucking saying!" He self-published a book about Lacoste, portraying the villagers as indolent provincial parasites. Now he had written a play, called *Camel-lot,* which seemed designed to provoke his neighbors to violence. In it, Pierre Cardin dies just as Lacoste is taken over by an influx of Arab immigrants. The newcomers fill the parking lot with camels, elect the village's Algerian-born homeless man as mayor, and shatter the decades of Socialist control. The play ends as an Irish flag is raised over the Château Sade. It turns out that Cardin has bequeathed the castle to his most ardent supporter.

"So you get on well with Cardin?" I asked.

"Oh, he loves me," Finn said. "He thinks I'm fucking brilliant."

When I delicately inquired if he might get me a private audience, Finn grew more protective. "Everyone is after Cardin for something," he apologized. "Some favor. Summer isn't a good time. He's surrounded by all his people. You'll never get near him. Come back in the autumn! Things are quieter. You'll have your chance then."

I slunk out of Finn's house, hoping nobody would rush up and denounce me. Staying neutral in Lacoste was a difficult business. Every time you stopped to chat in the street, someone was watching. Every time you chose one of the cafés, you were making a political statement. Like my ancestor André, I wanted to stay on good terms with the revolutionaries. It was hard not to admire the villagers' stubborn resistance to change. It reminded me of the Groucho Marx song: "Whatever it is, I'm against it!" It felt doomed, but oddly heroic. Well, *almost* heroic. One artist I met, who had grown up in the village, declared that she was just waiting for the day the haute couturier keels over and croaks.

"I've bought a nice bottle of champagne to open when I

get the news," she declared. "Cardin's in his eighties. He'll die before I do. I'm waiting for the day!"

Things have clearly gone downhill for a feudal overlord, I reflected.

At first, the Marquis de Sade could do no wrong in Lacoste. When he'd arrived on his first official visit, the Costain yokels had danced and sung for the lovely woman on his arm: "Oh, the happy news . . . Our Marquis has married a young beauty. There she is! There she is!" The beauty turned out to be one of the most noted prostitutes in Paris, but the Costains took no offense. In fact, as the years passed, even the darkest rumors about Sade's behavior could not dull the villagers' admiration; such antics were expected of any red-blooded nobleman. Sade took care to procure his playmates from faraway towns, a gesture of consideration to the locals. The villagers, in return, warned him about police raids and assisted his white-knuckle escapes. But the idyll couldn't last forever.

THE ZEN OF DUNGEONS

As for me, time was running out.

After another troubled sleep, I woke up cursing the marquis' blighted village. Our two weeks there had almost slipped away. Cardin's glam festival was ending soon, and after the last performance, Gérard confided, the seigneur would leave for his Cannes villa. Now, I asked myself, what on earth had I been doing all this time? Why hadn't we just spent our days gamboling in the lavender fields of Provence like normal folk? Instead, I'd been lingering in Lacoste like a ghost, tormenting my family day in, day out.

When I opened the shutters, I couldn't believe my eyes.

Dark blue thunderclouds crackled over the Luberón. The heat wave was over.

"Come on," I said to Les, "let's go get a slap-up breakfast."

We staggered through the downpour to the Café de Sade. Since the place was deserted, Gérard allowed us to sit in the VIP antechamber, a chic update of Louis XIV style. It was usually reserved for Cardin himself, but Gérard figured that he would also be sleeping in today. The menu was as expensive as the Ritz in Paris, but for the first time we ordered with wild-eyed abandon, demanding fresh-pressed juices, double espressos, pyramids of brioche, and every fruit compote known to man. After two weeks in the village, we were finally showing a proprietary air, relaxing in Cardin's sumptuous mahogany armchairs like aristocrats on a sugar binge.

As the rain hammered down outside, Henry and Sam became strangely calm. They pulled out their art books and began drawing with a studious concentration. It might have been the barometric pressure, but we all breathed a sigh of relief.

Suddenly, Les was elbowing me in the ribs. Cardin had wandered into the café with his usual entourage. As they all shook the rain off, their eyes settled on us, in prime position. I almost choked on my apricot jam. Our table looked like a bomb had gone off.

"Uh-oh, he's coming over," Les whispered. "I guess we'd better clean up." But there was no time.

I stood up to shake Cardin's hand and introduce him to Les, stammering something apologetic for having taken over half his establishment.

"Not at all," Cardin said approvingly as he surveyed the debris. "It is important to introduce the next generation to café life. Especially young *artistes*."

He towered over Henry, and said, *"Bonjour."*

"Hey," Henry said, waving casually.

"Do you mind if I see your work?"

Henry shrugged and handed over his creation, a series of robots shooting lasers in intricate geometric patterns. Not quite da Vinci, but not bad, either.

"I like the use of black here . . ."

Please, guys, I thought, *don't say, "black like the devil's bottom is black."*

"Wow," Les exhaled, after Cardin had shuffled off. "So that's the big man."

It may have been my imagination, but it seemed that Cardin saw me a little differently now. I wasn't just some lone nut stalking the village. I had progeny here—evoking a quiver of sympathy, perhaps. After all, Cardin had several nephews, now middle-aged, who occasionally swept through town in their sports cars.

About half an hour later, we saw Cardin in the street below. It had stopped raining for a moment, and he seemed to be waiting for something. For the first time, his entourage was nowhere to be seen. He was all alone.

"Now!" Les said. "You've got to go down there! I'll take the boys."

I jumped up, clutching my wad of historical documents. When I approached, he turned to me with eyebrows raised, and I blurted out my story—all about my ancestor who used to work for the Marquis and carry his letters and . . .

Cardin interrupted gently. "What would you like to do?"

I took a deep breath. "I want to see inside the château."

He nodded thoughtfully and said, "Yes. It would be very interesting for you. Are you free at five p.m.?"

"Five? Today? What should I do?"

"Just knock on the door."

THE DEN OF SIN

And so at five p.m. precisely, I crossed that forbidden metal walkway over the moat and pressed the buzzer. No response. I banged the iron door-knocker. A sepulchral silence. After ten more buzzes and bangs of increasing urgency, I looked around in exasperation. *Was this some sort of practical joke?*

A gaggle of French tourists looked at me with bemused smiles. I snarled back. Then I heard the nerve-shattering strains of an electric guitar coming from the quarry. Of course. The festival finale was tonight. I stomped across the rocky plateau toward the stage. Security guards dashed up to intercept me, but this time I confidently squirmed past, declaring that I had an appointment with Monsieur Cardin. He was sitting in the empty amphitheater in a Panama hat, alongside one of his stubble-chinned assistants.

"Ah, Monsieur, I hope you remember, we had an appointment at five?"

"There is a rehearsal in progress," said Cardin, looking puzzled.

"But . . . to inspect the château?"

"Why don't you sit down?" Cardin said. "It would be very interesting for you."

I looked at the stage forlornly. The show was a musical fantasia. Men in First World War uniforms were pirouetting through the trenches. Women dressed as sexy French housemaids spun around a young nun. Gendarmes leaped exuberantly into the air. It was like a cross between *Saving Private Ryan* and Cirque du Soleil.

"French theater is very nonlinear," said Cardin's colleague, Nicolas, a young director who, I hoped, had not noticed my appalled expression. "This style would never translate to Broadway, for example."

Cardin shook his head at the literal-mindedness of American audiences. "I commissioned this piece especially for the festival. Tonight is the world premiere."

"I have a ticket," I sighed, inwardly vowing to tear it up.

On went the rehearsal, but I was wilting. Sade was really getting his pound of flesh from me. Suddenly, the music stopped and Cardin stood up.

"It's over?" I said, trying not to sound thrilled.

There was one last glitch—Cardin couldn't find his château keys—but then, finally, we were crossing the moat together. This time, tourists took our photographs. The outer fortress door opened onto a grassy courtyard, where the castle's inner portal stood. Cardin led the way into a pitch-dark room. As my eyes adjusted, I made out a foyer crowded with theatrical props and boxes of empty champagne bottles. But then Nicolas opened the door to the eighteenth-century entrance hall, and we were all blinded by the afternoon sun as it flooded through tall windows onto the raw stone walls.

I almost dropped to my knees with relief.

We have a very good idea of the château's interior decor in its Sadistic heyday, thanks to an inventory of its contents made in the mid-1770s. The reception halls were crowded with marble statues Sade had bought as souvenirs in Italy, including a copy of a Roman Hermaphrodite, and hung with a fashionable selection of paintings on uplifting historical themes—Socrates in Athens, the death of Alexander the Great—plus one risqué portrait of Mademoiselle de Charolais, a comely Parisian debauchee who posed half-clad as a Franciscan monk. The upstairs bedrooms were lavish. Madame Sade's boudoir was wallpapered with scenes of her native rolling Normandy hills, and her four-poster bed was hung with gold-trimmed blue wool. Sade's chamber included the obligatory secret cabinet for his erotica. And there were many, many toilets. Sade was a hygiene freak—especially by the standards of the day—so the castle was equipped with fifteen portable commodes, six bidets, and a large copper bathtub with a state-of-the-art water heater. To Costains, the contraption must have seemed like an object from the beyond.

Today, the château feels more like a storage space than a residence. I cast my eye over a haphazard array of Renaissance chests, marble busts, lamps made from animal horns, and stacked modern canvases. A thin layer of dust covered every surface.

Cardin waved at one heavy table. "I found that at a Paris flea market," he said, in an offhand way.

I had seen books of Cardin's avant-garde interiors from the 1970s, where whole buildings were gutted and transformed into adventurous creations. Being unable to completely redesign the château had perhaps thwarted his artistic imagination.

We moved into a salon that was clearly in more regular use, with liqueur bottles scattered on a card table. Sade had designated this as his reception chamber, to take advantage of its sunny, south-facing aspect, and Cardin uses it for the same purpose today. The walls were now painted peach. (An *Architectural Digest* feature on the castle described the effect as "intimations of innocence.") In one corner, I saw a famous pencil sketch of the marquis in his early twenties—famous because it is the only known portrait of him—looking lean, aquiline, and surprisingly delicate in profile.

Cardin sank into one of the silk lounge chairs and pointed at an antique wooden sideboard. "*That* belonged to the marquis. Open it. You will find it interesting."

Inside were piles of ancient parchments. The first wad seemed to be legal documents, page after page of them. Who knows what was in there? I didn't have time to even scan. There were also random scraps of paper that looked to be in the marquis' own scrawl. I feverishly made out the word *framboises,* "strawberries." "Pâté de foie gras." "Good sausages." "Marzipan." Were they the Sade family shopping lists?

Cardin interrupted my reverie to suggest that Nicolas show me the rest of the castle. I eagerly agreed. As we wandered up and down various stone staircases and into chambers littered with dusty artworks, I kept an eye out for a door to "the subterranean level," my primary goal. Only half of the castle's original forty-two rooms survive, but it still felt huge. One room was a makeshift library with copies of Sade's novels. In the guest room, the bed was covered in plastic, and an empty coat rack stood in a corner.

"Does Monsieur Cardin actually live here?" I asked Nicolas.

"Well, he owns a château for every day of the year." He smiled. "This one he uses when the summer festival is on."

At last we passed a stone staircase spiraling down into darkness. A thick chain lay across it, with a yellow sign blaring ACCESS INTERDIT, "access forbidden." Oh no, I thought, the subterranean level is dangerous! They'll never let me down there.

"Let's go up to the rooftop," Nicolas said. I tried to look enthusiastic as we surveyed the 360-degree view of the Luberón. This terrace was once the castle's third story, with bedrooms for servants. Only one wall had been salvaged, with wooden

View from the roof of the Château Sade.

frames rotting in their windows. *Magnifique,* I muttered distractedly. *Like a dream.*

"I understand there was once a basement . . . ?" I suggested.

"Oh, yes," Nicolas smiled, still captivated by the view.

"Can we go down?" *Without having to bother Monsieur Cardin,* I thought.

Nicolas looked at me uncertainly. "Well, I *think* so."

He examined the ACCESS INTERDIT sign and hesitantly moved aside the chain. Foot-worn spiral stairs coiled into the murk. Above our heads, the cantilevered bricks did look as though they might come crashing down at any minute.

"Did you ever play a game called Donjons et Dragons?" I asked Nicolas. He looked at me blankly. "We should have brought wooden crosses."

About twenty feet down, our way was blocked by a large wooden door, which was kept shut by a heavy metal stake wedged into the floor. Before Nicolas could change his mind, I heaved it aside. The door creaked open into pitch black. A breath of stale, icy air hit our nostrils, and we both hovered uncertainly, unwilling to be the first to enter.

"There should be a light switch on one wall," Nicolas said uncertainly.

I remembered I had one of the keychain plastic torches that Sam had won at the village carnival. It had a two-watt bulb the size of a pimple, but it would have to do. I shone a feeble beam into the void.

So this was it, I exulted. The dungeon Sade.

It was like stepping into deep space. Creeping forward a few inches at a time, I had a terrible premonition of being trapped in the darkness like a character out of Poe. I could see the floor was smooth, but the walls looked roughly hewn from raw, damp rock. Above my head, arches sagged unevenly. About thirty feet into the vault, I detected the remains of two ancient chambers, now little more than outlines in the wall. In Sade's time, these had delineated two underground rooms, one a wine cellar, the other the château's prison, for which Sade had the only key. Then I saw something that made me freeze. It looked like a rectangular stone trough, with a lingam-like protrusion in the center and four gutters running to a drain. If I didn't know better, I would have thought it designed for human sacrifices.

In the icy blackness, my imagination boiled. It was here that key scenes of the charming Little Girls Incident had played out for six weeks in the winter of 1774–75. Because the event was so thoroughly hushed up, the precise details of what the five virginal girls and lone boy "secretary" endured have been the subject of scholarly debate ever since. One

French historian suggested that every night was "a witch's Sabbath," wherein the nymphets "offered their flanks to . . . gashing" (whipping) while the boy "had to play the role of flutist" (to Sade's engorged member). Even the most sober depiction, culled by du Plessix Gray from the surviving letters and legal documents, suggests a relentless menu of "whips and cat-o'-nine tails; a great deal of sodomy, both homo and hetero; plenty of daisy chains," regular dollops of "psychic terrorism," and inspirational readings of pornographic literature from Sade's library. The servants joined in with gusto. Madame de Sade aided and abetted. For the entire time, she made the château's domestic affairs run smoothly, seduced, as ever, by her husband's magnetic charm. Perhaps she simply felt freed while the children were away in Paris.

It's even possible that the innocents played along. With Sade, nothing is ever black and white. After the scenario was discovered and most of the girls were smuggled from the castle, one of them decided to stay on at the château as a scullery maid.

I finally spotted the light switch, and stumbled over to flick it on. A set of industrial lights exploded on the roof, flooding the chamber in sickly yellow. Now the grotto was decidedly less forbidding. In fact, I could see that the floor had been freshly concreted. But what was that sinister sacrificial trough . . . ?

"Oh, it was used for stomping grapes," said Nicolas. Sade wasn't much of a drinker, he added, but had a soft spot for fruit liqueurs.

I took a deep breath. I could do with a glass myself.

The Little Girls Incident was the turning point for the Marquis. He was at first bemused by the scandal he had caused in Provence. "I'm being taken for the *werewolf* in these parts," he

The "subterranean level" of the Château Sade.

wrote to Gaufridy in mocking tones. "Those poor little chicks with their *terrified* comments." But as outrage began to brew about his domestic hiring habits, Sade realized it might be wise to lie low, and he slipped off to Italy for a clandestine sightseeing tour. But from then on, he was increasingly a hunted man.

Even the love affair between Sade and his faithful villagers began to sour. The Costains tired of their master's antics. And while Sade remained passionate about his estate, he began to see the peasants as nothing but irritants. "I've come to the conclusion that all Costains are beggars fit for the wheel," he wrote in a 1776 letter (sounding not unlike a certain Irish gardener I'd met), "and one day I'll surely prove my contempt for them. . . . I assure you that if they were to be roasted one after another, I'd furnish the kindling without batting an eyelash." This outburst came after the father of one of his alleged victims had burst into the château and tried to murder him by firing a pistol inches from his chest. The shot misfired, and the culprit wandered Lacoste for days, drunk on local wine. Rather than forming a lynch mob to punish him, the villagers reacted with indifference. The marquis was forced to bribe his stalker to depart.

And so nobody warned Sade on the night of the August 26, 1777, when ten policemen staged a four a.m. raid on the château and carried him away in shackles. He would never return. Workers managed to keep up the estate for the next fifteen years, but in 1792, a revolutionary mob sacked the castle. It was led not by Costains but by radicals from the nearby town of Apt, who broke down the door, slashed the oil paintings, destroyed his precious library, and tossed the furniture from the windows. Still, once the damage was done, the pragmatic Costains became resigned to getting what they could from the site. The records name one Pierre Perrottet, who pillaged the castle for stone by demolishing the pigeon loft and later removed a trough, a dinner table, and two nice water casks.

Sade was devastated when he learned of the destruction. "No more Lacoste for me!" he wrote. "What a loss! It is beyond words. . . . I am in despair!" Broke, he was forced to sell the château.

Which makes the sprouting of today's Sade-inspired tourist industry in Lacoste seem all the more ironic. It's tempting to think that the marquis has come back to take revenge on the peasantry for betraying him so cruelly—in the form of a billionaire capitalist, slowly calcifying their village.

I did attend the final performance that night, and I wasn't even bothered by the bumblebee costumes or dancing gendarmes.

It was a full moon, and Maxim champagne was flowing like water. I was in such high spirits, I crashed the after-party at the Café de Sade. Gérard raised his eyebrows when I walked in to the private feast, until Cardin came over to shake my hand. "An excellent end to the arts festival," we agreed.

This was the way I should have behaved all along, I decided. With an air of noblesse, the world simply falls into place.

The next morning, I couldn't resist a little gloating, so I went to the Café de Sade to casually mention to a few naysayers that I'd managed to penetrate the château.

"Well, congratulations," said Jasper the sculptor, through gritted teeth. "Mission accomplished."

A few minutes later, Cardin arrived with a few friends and waved me over.

"This is the historian from New York!"

I was introduced to Cardin's guests: the governor of Thessalonika ("Greece's second city!"), a trade envoy from Russia ("We are proud to be doing business with the Cardin empire!"), the owner of a Marseille shipping company, and three comely blonde women with lacquered nails, dripping gold earrings, and pearly white smiles, who adroitly translated among Greek, French, Russian, and English. Cardin was delighted to learn that I had actually been born in Australia. "This table is international," he rejoiced. "All we need now is someone from Africa!"

Toasts were raised. Gifts offered. The Greek mayor presented Cardin with a marble replica of the Winged Victory of Samothrace, which I could already see gathering dust in the Château Sade. Then we all stood up for endless photographs. As I stood with my arm around a bevy of blonde translators, I saw Les trudging uphill toward the café. She had spent all morning packing.

"What are you going to do now?" she asked. "Run for mayor?"

Chapter Four

SEVEN-HUNDRED-YEAR ITCH

The Love Lives of Medieval Peasants

It's no secret why, in the history of sexuality, the upper classes get all the attention, while the huddled masses are pushed into the shadows. The problem is simply the dearth of source material. The voices that survive from the distant past tend to be those who had the education, time, and funds to record their intimate lives. The result is a little skewed—imagine if future historians reconstructed twenty-first-century mores with only the *Hamptons* magazine social pages to go on—and matters only get murkier the further back in history you explore. By the Middle Ages, we have an approximate idea of the romantic dramas of poets, nobles, and clerics who put quill to vellum, but the lower orders might as well be small burrowing animals as far as their mating habits are concerned. This absence has allowed a fantastical view of the medieval era to fester, riddled with weird and savage sexual practices. Peasant life, it has been assumed, revolved around the bovine tilling of the fields, eating month-old gruel for supper, and being raped by the local lord, not to mention some serious hygiene issues. If nothing else, we assume they were too riddled with plague, pestilence, and weeping sores to think much about getting it on.

But a peculiar twist of fate has shed a glimmer of light on daily life in one forgotten village in the Pyrenees mountains, named Montaillou. Historians have managed to piece together the sex lives of a whole string of colorful personalities there, dashing our dour preconceptions of the medieval era. Instead, peasant life comes off as a type of comic soap opera with as much bed-hopping as a Pedro Almodóvar film.

Montaillou's improbable path to fame began on September 8, 1308, when soldiers of the Inquisition surrounded the village and arrested all 250 adult citizens. The raid began a long series of investigations that would eventually expose the villagers' most private secrets. This isolated hamlet in the mountains of Languedoc was the last bastion of the heresy known as Catharism, which had maintained a subversive resistance against the official Catholic Church of Rome for over a century. A century earlier, the Papacy had ordered a brutal crusade to wipe out the heretics, and one great castle after another fell to the sword. But the Cathars had survived in isolated Montaillou, with many of the holy men, called Perfects, holding underground meetings and hiding out in barns and attics. The Church investigation reached its most intense phase after 1318, when an up-and-coming bishop named Jacques Fournier took the reins. A heavy-drinking, corpulent cleric who would later become pope, Fournier mixed his heretic-hunting with an almost anthropological interest in Montaillou's social customs. He summoned villagers to his courtroom in the town of Pamiers and extracted much more detailed information than usual about their personal lives. (Contrary to its grisly image, the Church-run Inquisition could not use torture in its proceedings, but was obliged to hand witnesses over to the state if they needed to be roughed up or executed. Later, the Spanish Inquisition, which was overseen by the Crown in Madrid for political ends, was far more brutal.) Court scribes transcribed the witnesses' declarations. Although it was not word for word—the peasants spoke in their native Occitan, which was then translated into Latin with some paraphrasing—the 325 folios of testimony constitute a unique transmission from the past.

Fournier's Register was unearthed in the Vatican archives in the late nineteenth century, but it was not until the 1970s that French historian Emmanuel Le Roy Ladurie sifted the trove. His book, *Montaillou: The Promised Land of Error*, became an international bestseller. And its huge popularity had little to do with Le Roy Ladurie's abstract theorizing on social history. What amazed modern readers was the cinematic vision of medieval sex. Montaillou in the early 1300s had a compelling cast of characters—horny farmers, adulterous damsels, lecherous priests, and lovesick shepherds—and was as promiscuous as any California commune. What's more, the evidence suggested that Montaillou was essentially no different from hundreds of other rural villages in medieval Europe, for Catharism was, in theory, more austere than Catholicism. The holy men preached that this world was the creation of the devil, the human body was polluted, and all forms of sex were sinful, even between married couples—a verdict that villagers roundly ignored, as premarital sex, adultery, fornication, and pederasty flourished. They paid lip service to the repressed official culture but did whatever they wanted.

Part of the "Cathar Trail" once used by heretic holy men above Montaillou.

I'd heard that the village of Montaillou still existed, some-where in the Pyrenees Mountains near the French-Spanish border. What's more, the current mayor, Jean Clergue, proudly traces his lineage back to the most licentious character in the fourteenth-century transcripts, a playboy priest named Pierre Clergue. The outpost isn't exactly a tourist attraction today. After all the hype about Le Roy Ladurie's book calmed down, it had drifted back into obscurity. I couldn't even find Montail-lou on the road map—I needed a detailed French hiking chart. Overlooking the wild frontier with Andorra, it could only be reached on a winding drive that connects a string of ruined Cathar castles.

A few history buffs have excavated parts of the medieval village, although I had no idea how many landmarks from the Fournier Register still existed. A more direct link to the past, I speculated, might be the thirty or so permanent residents. It seemed unlikely they were holding key parties in the mountains these days, but I still wanted to meet them. After all, nobody had expected their ancestors to be a wild bunch, either.

THE LOST WORLD

The heat wave penetrated the eerie medieval gloom of the Pyrenees, so like good penitent souls we purified ourselves in the first river we found, slipping like eels beneath the golden arches of a Roman aqueduct while French families basked on the rocks around us. Languedoc felt like a different dimension of France. Provence had been for wealthy Parisians and high-strung expats. This was where the humbler Gallic classes escaped to the country. Friends gathered at the same holiday units every summer as they had for decades, and we relaxed with them in makeshift garden enclosures, drinking cheap rosé and playing *boules* while the kids ran riot.

Always taunting us on the horizon was the Mediterranean Sea, sparkling with the promise of crystal waters and seafood bouillabaisse. Les and the boys would press their noses to the car window as we drove past one turnoff after another to the beach.

We were going somewhere *much* more interesting, I assured them. Into the very bowels of the Dark Ages.

"Heretics!" I enthused. "Knights and witches, gore and blood, mud and filth."

I left out the bit about wife swapping.

To whet the gang's appetite, I steered us toward the city of Carcassonne, medieval history's answer to EuroDisney. With its restored double ramparts and witch-hat turrets, the place has a fairy-tale quality—from a safe distance. Crossing the crowded drawbridge is more like entering Dulac, the "perfect" medieval town in *Shrek*. Falconers in period dress saunter about with hunting birds on their arms, minstrels serenade café crowds, and souvenir shops sell every form of reproduction sword, helmet, and halberd like a vast Halloween store. The boys got into the spirit, vying to test one murderous-looking weapon after the next. The shopkeeper looked at me in horror when she realized I was considering a hunting dagger for Henry. "These are not toys, you realize! The children will lose fingers, eyes!" Apparently they were for serious boar hunters who must be mingling in the crowds. With his new weapon safely sheathed, Henry was the happiest kid at the jousting show, another classy Medieval Times event with knights thundering about on horseback and wenches baring cleavage.

Over further objections from Les, I took Henry to the Museum of Torture. What demographic this institution pitches for is hard to guess. We nearly tripped over a gaggle of four-year-olds scampering around a mannequin of a comely blonde about to burned at the stake, her tunic torn open to the waist. A pair of vicious-looking priests attended to another half-naked damsel on a rack. Among the displays was a rusty chastity belt, with a drawing of how it might be worn. It was an unconvincing-looking item, two bands of metal and a cheap lock. Henry shrugged, more interested in the thumb-screws.

This vision of the Middle Ages as a barbarous fantasia was first concocted in the Renaissance, but it was the Victorians who really refined the sexual element, reveling in macabre tales of diseased prostitutes, incest, rape, necrophilia, and coprophilia. Myths like the *droit de seigneur*—the feudal lord's "right of the first night" over newlywed peasant virgins—were a nineteenth-century invention and became part of tourist lore repeated in castles across Europe. For Victorian sight-seers, there was soon a brisk souvenir trade in medieval tor-ture implements, which were passed off as authentic but were almost all fabricated in modern workshops. Some Pari-sian brothels even offered them for role-playing games. No. 9 Rue Navarin in Paris had its own Chambre Medievale for S&m fans; the torture chamber offered everything the ama-teur bondage and discipline fan might require, including iron shackles, a rack, a St. Andrew's cross—where the victim's four limbs can be secured—and for the committed fetishist, a hangman's scaffold.

Perhaps the most symbolic favorite was the chastity belt, *la ceinture de chasteté,* which epitomized, for repressed Victo-rians, the Middle Ages' secretly compelling misogyny. In the late nineteenth century, two of these artifacts were actually displayed in the esteemed Cluny Abbey of medieval art on the Left Bank of Paris, where they were almost as popular with tourists as the Cathedral of Notre Dame. While staying in Paris, I had made a detour to the museum to see if they were still in the collection. There was no sign among the exhib-its, so I asked at the information booth and was handed, with some irritation, a printout from the Conservation Department in three languages:

For the attention of those who ask for information on

CHASTITY BELTS

The two chastity belts in the museum (famous in the XIXth century) are not shown for two reasons:

— on the one hand, these things were only used in the West between the XVIth century and about the middle of the XVIIIth century (and then only in exceptional cases) and did not exist in the middle ages. Therefore they do not enter the period the museum covers.
— on the other hand, the two examples in the museum formerly attributed;
   • one to the XVIth century then to the XVIIth or XVIIIth centuries
   • the other to the XVIth century

ARE BOTH NINETEENTH CENTURY FAKES

The meaning was a little obscure, so I decided I should inspect them for myself. After some cajoling, the guards reluctantly ushered me up a stone turret, where a mousy, bespectacled curator in a black turtleneck sweater, Elizabeth Taburet-Delahaye, led me up to the storage facilities in the abbey's attic, now filled with enormous archival drawers requiring special weights and pulleys to open. With a fetching blush, she unwrapped the two objects in question. They were tiny, as if made for size 0 models, and meticulously crafted.

Their designs were very different. One was a large iron ring lined in decaying velvet, with a smooth ivory "eagle's beak" that was supposed to clamp over a woman's nether-regions. The other belt was a more advanced open-jaw system, with two hinged metal pieces that would go between a woman's legs and then be secured to a metal band around her waist. Two small barbed openings were provided for sanitary purposes. This one was ornately engraved, with an image of the chaste Adam and Eve holding hands.

They were undeniably creepy, even more so knowing that they were the product of male fantasy. In 1931, a broad-minded British Museum curator named E. J. Dingwall published the first real study on the subject, *The Girdle of Chastity*, which became an underground classic. It established that the earliest chastity belts were actually made not in medieval France but in Renaissance Italy. The first reference to them in any text is a 1403 Venetian tract on military hardware. Even then, they were almost certainly never used, but simply shown off as conversation pieces.

No matter. Today, chastity belts fit our image of the medieval world too perfectly not to remain a fixture of its mythology.

And in the Torture Museum gift shop, business was still brisk.

South of Carcassonne, roads curled like mule tracks into the Pyrenees mountains. The skies turned a brooding gray. The villages became lonelier, the people more reserved, their accents thicker. Culturally speaking, this border region has more in common with Catalonia than France, and the traditional tongue of Occitan, wherein, for example, *oc* is said instead of *oui*, is almost unchanged since the Middle Ages. (In other words, Les explained to Henry, these were *The knights who say Oc!*) The

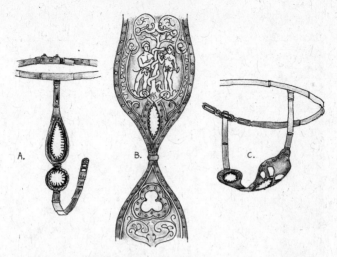

Three examples of chastity belt design, shown off in 19ᵗʰ century museums as examples of "medieval" barbarity. A: from the Doge's Palace in Venice, dating from the Renaissance. B: from the Cluny Museum of the Middle Ages in Paris, a 19ᵗʰ century fake. C: from the British Museum, once kept in the Secretum, another Victorian-era forgery. (© Lesley Thelander)

descendents of the Cathars, we soon discovered, are still resistance fighters—only these days, they battle the growing tide of tourists lured to the majestic castles. With heretical obstinacy, they refuse to change their ways to cater to outsiders. Signs are nonexistent, services have erratic hours. We walked into one restaurant, and the owner pointed angrily at his watch. "We close at two p.m.! Go away!" (It was 2:05.) The only other eatery for miles around was a decrepit gas station. Soon enough, there weren't even any decrepit gas stations, just cliffs and dark forests. As the jagged Pyrenees protruded over the horizon ahead, it was easy to imagine the Cathar holy men were still hiding out here. This was French *Deliverance* country, where you didn't want to turn down the wrong dirt lane.

Memorial to the Cathars on the road to Montaillou.

We finally spotted Montaillou near the River Ariège, its few dwellings clinging to the sides of a grass hill, which was crowned by a poetic tower of golden stone. Turning the car engine off in the empty plaza, we were enveloped by an eerie stillness. The only sound was the tinkling of a dripping pipe into a stone water trough. From somewhere in the distance came the music of cowbells. It was as if the residents had all been carried off by the plague. The main thoroughfare for the past thousand years led to an austere little church and shabby café, but both of their doors were firmly shut. There was one modern element—a trailer from which the local amateur Radio Montaillou would broadcast—but it, too, was silent. And the mayor's office? A handwritten sign on the door said it was open on Thursday mornings. The only sign of life was a lone black dog that followed us from the shadows.

"Can we go back to Lacoste?" Henry asked. He missed the swizzle sticks at the Café de Sade.

"No, to Paris!" Sam said, jumping on the bandwagon.

Then we found a small store where an elderly woman, Michelle Derine, sat half asleep behind the counter. The boys looked with mortification at the wares, hand-knitted mittens and doll's dresses for sale, convinced more than ever that they should escape.

"Things were even worse here in the 1980s!" Madame explained. "Montaillou almost didn't exist. There were only a dozen inhabitants, all older than I am now."

I asked how many lived here today. She hailed a farmer who was passing by with a rake over his shoulder.

"There are thirty in the village, no?" she said.

"Wait, there is that new family. With two children, no?"

"True. Thirty-four people then!"

"It's a renaissance!" the farmer chuckled. It was obviously an ongoing joke.

There was no hotel, needless to say. Madame suggested we talk to the church caretaker, Georges. We found him opening up the belfry, a rotund figure with pink cheeks and a white beard—Papa Noël wearing summer shorts and flip-flops. He proceeded to ring the bells by hand, swinging up and down on two ropes with the vigor of Quasimodo. He then showed us a Spartan room in his house that he rented out, with a balcony that looked over the pastures. The hills of the Ariège hadn't changed since the 1300s, with their network of shepherds' trails connecting the nearby villages. I recalled that they were used by some to reach local prostitutes and by lovers escaping on summer trysts.

Now all we had to do was drive fifty miles back along winding roads to buy supplies. My famished progeny glared at me angrily as we climbed back into the car.

That night, an icy stillness fell over Montaillou. The few inhabitants retreated to their houses and barred the doors. From the balcony, we watched the gibbous moon emerge over the black hills, where you could imagine the werewolves were prowling. I turned on Radio Montaillou to brighten things up. Tom Jones covers in French, Brazil 66, obscure rock from the seventies. In between every song came the jingle: "Radio Montaill-oo-*oo*-oo-*oo*-oo-*ou*." It barely dented the gloom. We closed the shutters and double-locked the doors, then fell into a sleep made fitful by the altitude and dreams.

LOVE IN THE TIME OF BODY LICE

The next morning, the sun miraculously bathed the earth with crystal light. These mountains were schizophrenic, I realized—bleak and melancholy when it was overcast, Shangri-La on a fine day. The boys could spend hours fishing tadpoles from the water trough. Les had her watercolors out. I was free to follow the Montaillou soap opera.

Archaeologists have uncovered the outlines of the original village square, surrounded by the foundations of about forty houses. The population back in the early 1300s was about 250, and thanks to the details of the Fournier Register, we know who lived where and can make virtual house calls on the Savenacs, the Maurys, the Belots, and the Clergues, picturing their mud-and-thatch manses, roamed by chickens and goats,

Remains of the 14ᵗʰ century village and tower.

with small pens outside for the pigs. I climbed up the overgrown hillside to the crumbling tower, which was once a fortified residence. It was here, in 1291, that the village châtelain brought his attractive seventeen-year-old bride, the woman who would become the pivotal figure in Montaillou's erotic legend—Béatrice de Planisoles.

The free-spirited Béatrice is such a striking character that historians seem to lose their objectivity when dealing with her. Le Roy Ladurie compares her to one of the passionate heroines of troubadour songs who always "follows her heart." Other historians moon over her beauty, her directness, her sexual openness. Even her name is "euphonious," sighs René Weis in his excellent *The Yellow Cross*. (At one point, he notes longingly, "Béatrice was always having sex.") It's clear that she exerted the same hypnotic effect on the men of Montaillou. For the next seven years, she was eyed with admiration by the male population, young and old, and a parade of would-be paramours tried to lure her into adultery. Even her husband's steward fell in love with her and one night hid under her bed, hoping in vain to seduce her. Then, in 1298, when Béatrice was twenty-four, her husband died and she was forced to move to a more modest village house.

It wasn't long before she received the attentions of the alpha male of Montaillou, the young village priest—and obsessive Lothario—Pierre Clergue.

According to the testimony of Béatrice and other villagers, it all began in the ancient Chapel of Notre-Dame-de-Carnesses, which still exists today. I strolled down to the bottom of the village to the squat structure of bone-white stone. There have been some alterations in the last seven hundred years, but the nave and apse are original, as is the rude stone altar. Outside, two footprints in the rocks showed where the Virgin Mary revealed herself to some shepherds. I peered behind the altar to the very spot where Pierre first propositioned Béatrice. As she knelt before him in confession, the priest suddenly leaned forward and kissed her, whispering, "There is no other woman in the world I admire as much as you"—one of his favored lines, as a half dozen of his other lovers would later attest. Béatrice ran from the chapel but may have been flattered.

It was the unlikely start to a romance that would shape the fate of Montaillou. It may not quite reach the exalted heights of Dante and *his* Béatrice, but I believe it is all the more intriguing because it is imbued by the messiness of real life.

———

Pierre is the most enigmatic figure in the Montaillou story, a man whose later life would take some unfortunate, even treacherous turns. He was at his most appealing in his mid-twenties, when he first courted Béatrice. Although he wasn't tall or particularly handsome, he was notoriously charming and had a rare smattering of education. Most important, Pierre was from the village's most wealthy and influential Cathar family. He had been anointed into the Catholic priesthood as a cover, but he showed little interest in a spiritual calling of any kind. According to the villagers themselves, Pierre pursued every woman he met with relentless energy and considerable success, although there was one woman who resisted: the feisty Raymonde Faure, who held out even though her husband was widely known to be impotent. Other village girls did not put up as much of a fight. When Pierre deflowered fourteen-year-old Grazide Rives in a sun-filled barnyard, no theology was needed. According to her testimony, the exchange went thus:

"Allow me," (Pierre) said, "to know you carnally."

And I said: "All right."

In 1298, Béatrice was slightly more hesitant. But the priest was nothing if not persistent, twisting Cathar theology in his attempts to lure her into bed. When she protested that a woman who has slept with a priest "can never see the face of God," Pierre was quick to reply: "All sex is sinful even between married people, so it is no more evil in God's eyes for a woman to commit adultery, incest, or sleep with a priest. Anyway, it doesn't matter in the end, since all sins can be forgiven on your deathbed. Why not just give in to your urges?"

Montaillou under the summer sun.

She did give in, the next summer, and thanks to the Inquisition's prying questions, we can follow their romantic arrangements. Pierre spent half the week at her small abode, for which he now paid the rent. Béatrice spent the other half at his house, sleeping in his room upstairs from his parents, to the sullen envy of Pierre's brothers, who apparently overheard their gasps of passion. Historians, at this point, feel the urge to assess the pair's lovemaking in terms of contemporary sensibilities. Le Roy Ladurie declares that Pierre "seems . . . to have been gentle, kind, comparatively cultivated, sensitive, affectionate and ardent in pleasure and love." René Weis adds: "There can be little doubt that [Pierre] cared for [Béatrice], and that she enjoyed sex with him. . . ."

Gamely, Béatrice did try to oblige her lover's irreverent

sexual tastes. He was particularly fond of making love during Lent and on Sundays, when he would even spring fresh from her arms to offer Mass at the chapel without going to confession. The pair also made love one Christmas Eve, the most forbidden pleasure of all.

Their most intimate moments were spent sitting in bed in front of the fireplace, delousing one another. In an environment that was hopping with vermin, this was a ritual of affection for all the villagers of Montaillou, the pastime of friends, spouses, and flirting couples, during which they could quietly gossip or, in the case of Béatrice and Pierre, debate religious ideas. Le Roy Ladurie is, as ever, unflinching in supplying historical detail. He deduces from casual references made during the court interviews that the villagers usually slept naked and that they never washed their private parts. The stench of body odor, he extrapolates, was overpowering, especially from farmhands back from the fields. Other data are more surprising. We learn that Pierre advocated a distinctive type of contraception—a magical necklace, with a small linen packet of herbs attached, that had to be hung between Béatrice's breasts and down to her belly button while they made love. (It was not exactly a triumph of women's liberation: He refused to leave the necklace with her, because she might use it with another man.) In fact, the bedroom was quite the place for "witchcraft," the inquisitor would discover. Village girls collected their first menstrual blood to make love potions—any man who drank it was believed to lose his heart—and women of all ages plied their lovers with arugula juice, an ancient recipe to enhance the quantity of sperm and the vigor of their lovemaking. They were the sort of folkloric concoctions that were popular all over rural Europe until the nineteenth century.

THE TWO CLERGUES

In the morning, a yellow van zoomed through the village delivering fresh bread. By noon, a couple of passing hikers turned up, and the only restaurant finally opened its doors, with a few tables on a grassy terrace. I was delighted to find that a whiff of the medieval still lingers in Montaillou. On our first visit, we were intercepted by the owner, a stooped woman with a cratered complexion and the pageboy haircut of a warrior monk.

"Where are you going to sit?" she growled.

We pondered the splintered outdoor seats for a second too long.

"Make up your mind!" she snapped, storming off.

"Sheesh," Les muttered. "What's Occitan for 'Lighten up'?"

And in Montaillou, medieval gruel is still on the menu. A couple of French tourist diners were staring at their plates in confusion, wondering how their coq au vin could drown in a glutinous brown sauce. But in this respect, even the Cathars would have been mortified. While they regarded this world as a creation of the devil himself, this didn't mean that they couldn't appreciate good cuisine. René Weis tells of two Cathar holy men, the upper crust Authiés brothers, who, even while fleeing from the Inquisition's agents, demanded fresh spices, local honeys, prepared foods like fish terrines, and especially "good wine." One of their hosts, who was hiding them in his home, felt obliged to venture out "in search of a better and more renowned wine than the one he kept in

Shrine to the Virgin Mary, who revealed herself to Montaillou's shepherds.

his own residence," at some risk to his neck. This was still the Mediterranean, after all. Nor were the Cathar Perfects immune to other worldly temptations. Guillaume Bélibaste was caught with his pants down—or rather, tunic up—with his pretty host, Raymonde Marty-Piquier. Raymonde's sister Blanche stumbled upon the pair *in flagrante* and cried out in shock, "Oh madam-the-misbegotten-bitch, you have compromised the entire cause of our holy church." ("Guillaume was in a missionary position," adds Weis helpfully, "but not the one Blanche had in mind.")

During our own visits, dairy farmers gathered at dusk every evening to enjoy an aperitif of Pernod and chilled mountain water from the centuries-old water trough. I gathered that politics has replaced sex in the Montaillou soap opera; there may be only thirty-four residents, but the village still managed to be torn by factions and scandals. They loved talking about the mayor, Jean Clergue. He was a wealthy businessman who had spent much of his life away from Montaillou, and they denounced his tailored suits, his hauteur, his penchant for luxury cars. "The incredible thing is how history is repeating itself here," one elderly firebrand railed. "The Clergues still run this village, just as they did seven hundred years ago!" Nobody ever admitted to voting for him, which led to whispers that he had rigged the elections. After all, the ballot box was just sitting in his office. . . .

"Montaillou is an unlucky village," the firebrand mourned. "Most villages in Languedoc have a small hotel, a decent restaurant. . . . Here there's nothing!"

The farmers were just as bitter about the mayor's ancestor, the medieval priest Pierre Clergue, talking about him as if he was still walking the streets and seducing their wives. He had hovered over Old Montaillou "like a spider," they said darkly, and his family, the Clergues, was no better than a mafia clan, using violence and intimidation to maintain control. I had to admit that, reading the Fournier Registry, Pierre the priest remained an enigmatic figure. His own testimony to the Inquisition, if there was any, has not survived. Our image of him, vivid although it is, has been entirely constructed from others' words. So I decided to get the verdict from the ancestral well, so to speak.

The mayor was a busy man. Whenever I called him on his cell phone, he was in the middle of a business meeting in Toulouse or driving his car to Pamiers or at a working lunch in Andorra. He always politely asked that I call back. But whenever I did, I just got the voice message. I was beginning to suspect Monsieur Clergue might be avoiding me, when I received a communiqué to meet him in the mayor's office.

On arrival, I found him barking furiously into the telephone. Tall and powerfully built, in his early fifties, he had exchanged his business suit for an oilskin jacket and jeans, and outside, instead of a BMW, there was a practical little Renault with the Radio Montaillou logo. ("It's the mayor's new look," scoffed one of the detractors later, as I hung out at the water trough. "He's no longer the Sun King. He's a gentleman farmer now!") Clergue exuded a sense of distracted urgency. His desk was covered with papers in barely contained chaos. As soon as one telephone call ended, another began. Cell phones rang in his drawer. He wanted to give me a business card but couldn't find one, searching manically through his desk before giving up.

Finally the mayor calmed down long enough to tell me how Montaillou had clawed its way back from the brink of oblivion.

He had been raised in a dying village, he said, and like every other intelligent young person, he left for Toulouse and Paris in the 1970s. "Le Roy Ladurie's book had come out, so whenever I said I was from Montaillou, people would go, *ah!* Everyone had heard of it! And yet, when I returned here, it was like a ghost town. So in 1992, I met some friends, and we decided, 'We have to do something about this village or it's going to vanish!'" Clergue and several others formed a group called Castellet to salvage the crumbling fortress on the hilltop. They secured its walls and invited archaeologists to excavate. In 1997 they started a historical festival, with actors in Cathar dress, sword-fighting, and reenactments. Le Roy Ladurie himself arrived to host academic seminars.

But now things were sliding. Archaeologists stopped coming a few years ago—there was no funding. The historical festival had been canceled this summer because the provincial authorities had withdrawn support. The momentum was being lost.

Yes, he suspected that a lot of people blamed him. They said that he was too obsessed with Radio Montaillou, which he'd begun in 2004 and which was now broadcasting all over the mountains. But he said many villagers actually disliked all the attention from the outside world and the occasional summer tourists. "In the Middle Ages, Montaillou was a village of resistance. Even today, it's not like anywhere else in France. It's independent!" He spoke about his thirty-four-person redoubt as if it were a sprawling republic.

We strolled out of the office and found the site where the Clergue family's medieval mansion had once stood. The mayor grew pensive. "I know the villagers still argue about my ancestors," he muttered. "Seven hundred years is nothing out here."

SUGAR AND BLOOD

In January 1301, Béatrice suddenly ended her eighteen-month relationship with Pierre, moving out of Montaillou to Prades, a village two miles away, and remarrying. We don't know exactly why. Perhaps she saw little future as the mistress of a priest, even one as charming as Pierre. But the encounters continued. One night in October, Pierre walked to Prades while her new husband was away, and they made love in the cellar while her maid kept guard. Their last meeting took place three years after that first stolen kiss in the chapel. Béatrice was worried that another liaison in her house would be too noisy for the neighbors, so Pierre devised a romantic plan. His assistant arrived after dark and led her through the "very black night" to the church of Saint-Pierre, where he had made up a luxuriant bed in front of the altar.

"Really!" she exclaimed (or at least, that's what she told the inquisitor many years later). *"How can we do such a thing. . . ?"*

Pierre laughed sarcastically: *"Oh, it will do the saint such grievous harm!"*

And so, I followed the same foot trail to Prades through grassy fields still trodden by cows. There wasn't another soul about. Just me, a few fat bees buzzing among the grass, and clouds of tiny gnats cascading like silver flakes in the air. Prades, if possible, was even more desolate than Montaillou. In the empty plaza was a faded sign explaining that the "celebrated heretic" Béatrice de Planisoles had once lived here. I found the caretaker to the church of Saint-Pierre, who handed me the keys.

"You won't get lost. It's not exactly the Champs-Élysées," he cackled. "And what a church! Not quite Notre Dame de Paris!"

The building had certainly seen better days. The sharp scent of cat's urine wafted from under the door. Inside, shafts of fragmented light burst down through empty windows, its stained glass shattered by vandals. Even the altar had been knocked from its foundation. Still, even though the church had been rebuilt after a seventeenth-century fire, there were the same medieval stones in the floor.

Back in 1301, Pierre escorted his married lover back to her house before dawn. It was their last liaison. Beatrice would go on to have many life adventures. Fifteen years later, in 1316, when she was again a widow, in her early forties with four daughters, she took up with another priest, the handsome Barthélemy Amilhac, two decades her junior. "I loved him to distraction," she admitted to Fournier, also explaining that in her experience, "priests desire women more than other men."

Pierre, however, would spiral into a long and rather sinister middle age.

The farmers I spoke to had mocked the mayor for tracing his lineage so proudly back to the medieval priest, Pierre. There had been a number of wings of the Clergue family in the 1300s, and the lines were confused. "Why, I could just as easily say I am a descendent of the priest," one scoffed. "But I wouldn't want to. He was a traitor!"

I had to admit that Pierre seemed an unusual choice of role model. Sure, he comes off as rather raffish in his youth, but he was also a medieval double agent, playing the Cathars off against the Catholics. The Clergue family had long made its fortune by skimming Church tithes and running protection rackets for heretics, and Pierre became increasingly Machiavellian after Béatrice broke off their affair. When the Inquisition raided Montaillou in 1308, Pierre almost certainly provided a list of whom to interrogate, fingering enemies of his family. His brother Bernard was the village bailiff—magistrate and police officer in one—so he was able to seize the property of those the Inquisition imprisoned. Pierre justified his actions by saying that he had sacrificed a handful of vulnerable individuals in order to protect the larger Cathar community. But he became increasingly ruthless. One man who threatened to expose the Clergues' heretical sympathies to Church bounty hunters had his tongue cut out. Another was hacked to death and his corpse left by the fortress as a warning to others. Pierre's physical needs also became less *charmant*. He took to stalking the bathhouses of Aix-les-Thermes and telling women he would denounce them to the Inquisition if they didn't sleep with him.

So when I ran into the mayor again outside the Radio Montaillou offices, I steered the conversation around to his ancestor's dubious reputation. Monsieur *le maire* took a more forgiving view.

"In effect, Pierre Clergue was an excellent politician," he explained. "Yes, it's true, he changed sides often. But remember, life was very hard in Montaillou in the Middle Ages—we can hardly imagine. He wanted to protect his family. That was his first priority. Who are we to judge how a man behaves under such stress?" As Don Corleone, or Anthony Soprano might put it, the family is always first.

The mayor also held no hard feelings against the crusading Bishop Fournier who shattered the village. "He was a real detective!" he said. "Very thorough."

"So where is Jean Clergue buried?" I asked. "Is it possible to visit his tomb?"

The mayor flinched.

"But I . . ." he protested. "I'm not dead yet!"

I quickly apologized. It was an easy mistake, I said, with all those Clergues. I meant *Pierre* Clergue, of course, the lecherous priest.

"Nowhere," Jean said. "His body was burned."

Eventually, the Inquisition had closed in on Pierre Clergue. His defenses began to unravel in 1320, when Béatrice was arrested and interrogated by Bishop Fournier for several days. Some of her testimony incriminated her former lover. Béatrice herself spent two years in the dungeons of Allemans, and on her release was forced to wear the yellow cross to indicate that she was a former heretic. We do not know when she died, but her health had suffered in prison and it cannot have been long after her release.

In 1323, Pierre was finally summoned by Bishop Fournier for interrogation and placed in "luxury detention" in a monastery. (The worst torment here, Weis speculates, was probably the enforced "life without women.") He was in his late forties, and he died before his court date, presumably of natural causes. If he was indeed interrogated, the transcript was lost, so the logic behind his double dealings—and his true religious convictions, if any—remain a puzzle. Although he had betrayed many Cathars within Montaillou over the years, he refused the Catholic sacraments on his deathbed. Pierre was posthumously condemned as a heretic and his remains were burned and scattered.

The end of the story is cheerless, more in keeping with our traditional impression of the Middle Ages. But thanks to Béatrice's story, as recorded by the Inquisition, there is a small burst of free-spirited rebellion within the medieval gloom.

The skies over Montaillou had turned gray again, so we decided to leave the haunted village once and for all in favor of the warmer lowlands. In a grassy meadow south of Pamiers, we all got out of the car and wandered in the blazing sun.

When Béatrice first received her summons from the Inquisition in 1320, she made a typically impetuous decision: She convinced her second priest lover to flee with her on horseback. On the run from agents of the Church, the pair actually managed to snatch one last moment of pleasure together in a shady vineyard near the hamlet of Bénagues. The historian Weis, ever intrepid, even identifies the spot where they rested as Les Vignasses, a field directly south of the modern village where grapes were grown until recently. There, like a fourteenth-century Bonnie and Clyde, the fugitives laid out a blanket beneath the vines and made love for the last time, all the time guarded by Béatrice's eagle-eyed servant.

Chapter Five

WILD AND CRAZY SWISS

Sex and Drugs and Lyric Poetry

In Europe, you can unearth a history of debauchery in the most overlooked places. Take Switzerland. That money-worshipping republic is seldom thought of as a lusty outpost of bohemian creativity. But in the early 1800s, the world's most flamboyant young artists sought out the fleshpots of Lake Geneva, where an underground party scene flourished amid the sublime alpine landscapes. A volatile mix of freethinkers, sexual adventurers, philosophers, and exiles flourished in the all-night salons, trailed by a wave of Grand Tourists who hoped to glimpse the renegade celebrities at play. Like Prohibition in New York or the cold war in Berlin in the 1980s, Switzerland's dour Calvinist facade only seemed to provoke a more extreme level of misbehavior.

The most scandalous group descended from England in the summer of 1816, in the disreputable wake of Lord George Gordon Byron. Like some deviant Adonis, the twenty-eight-year-old Romantic poet had already rampaged through London's high society, where he was dubbed "mad, bad and dangerous to know" by one former lover, Lady Caroline Lamb, for his self-destructive excesses and shocking liaisons with men and women, including his half sister Augusta. Earlier in 1816, he had been forced to abandon England in the face of an igno-minious divorce—it was rumored that his wife would expose his penchant for sodomy, which was illegal at the time and too shocking to even be mentioned in decent society—and so he traveled south along the Rhine in a reproduction of Napoléon's coach with a squadron of servants, his private doctor, a pea-cock, a monkey, and a dog. Byron had set the tone for his Eu-ropean jaunt at his very first hotel in Calais, when, according to his medical companion, "he fell upon the chambermaid like a thunderbolt." Switzerland was the obvious choice for a dashing young sybarite to enjoy the summer. For four months, Byron rented a villa by the electric blue waters, where he hosted riot-ously animated literary soirées while love-struck admirers spied on him with telescopes from the opposite shore.

Rumors of depravity at Byron's villa were fueled when the new neighbors arrived: the intense twenty-three-year-old poet Percy Bysshe Shelley, who had become notorious in London as an advocate of atheism and free love; his soulful, auburn-haired, eighteen-year-old mistress, Mary Wollstone-craft Godwin, for whom he had abandoned his wife and son; and Mary's adventurous stepsister, Claire Clairmont. (Also eighteen, she had been Byron's lover back in England, and almost certainly Shelley's, too. Spirited and self-dramatizing, she had changed her name from Jane to make it sound more like a heroine's from fiction.) The result was doubtless the most artistically productive vacation of the century.

The summer of 1816 was also noteworthy for a startling event in meteorological lore. The eruption of Mount Tambora in faraway Indonesia sent a cloud of volcanic ash across the northern hemisphere; it became "the year without a summer."

Trapped indoors by wild lightning storms, Byron proposed that each member of the group compose a horror story, with their imaginations fueled by wine and opiates. The teenage Mary came up with *Frankenstein, or The Modern Prometheus,* now a Gothic classic, while a nightmarish short story called *The Vampyre* was written by Byron's mentally disturbed physician, John Polidori. (Developed from an idea of Byron's, it was the first vampire tale in English, predating Bram Stoker's *Dracula* by more than eighty years.) The volatile combination of sex, drugs, and horror has been mythologized ever since, evoked in films like *Haunted Summer* and Ken Russell's *Gothic,* which envisions the Byron ménage as a hallucinogenic orgy breaking down the barriers of the psyche. Today, the creative audacity of the Romantic coterie seems like a precursor to all the youth culture outbursts since, from the Beats to punk.

Once the storms broke, the Diodati group also enjoyed Switzerland's more civilized pursuits, such as sailing on the lake, swimming off smooth-pebble beaches, and hiking in the Alps. Lake Geneva has its own warm microclimate, making summers (usually) almost tropical. Today, the shores are even bristling with palm trees, earning it the PR-friendly moniker the Swiss Riviera. It all sounded marvelously picturesque, and, frankly, a little dull. But I was delighted to find that our own visit would coincide with the Montreux Jazz Festival—just the thing, I hoped, to awaken the bohemian spirit of fat-cat Swiss bankers and bureaucrats.

SECOND-CLASS SWISS

On their arrival in 1816, the Shelleys were pleasantly surprised by Switzerland's democratic spirit, which lent the peasantry "a freedom and refinement of manners" and indifference to class barriers. Most British travelers, on the other hand, were in the habit of abusing their servants at whim, and they were exasperated by the Swiss commoners, who seemed to regard themselves as equals, refusing to cower, cap in hand.

These days, we discovered, the roles are neatly reversed. The Swiss are now the Brahmin caste of Europe, while visiting foreigners are scrambling for scraps at the table.

From our mint-condition train carriage, we peered out at the pristine Lego-built houses trimmed with their identical rows of red geraniums, not a whiff of disorder in sight. Every inch of spare land in Switzerland has been tidied up and accounted for. The streets have no potholes. Tidy vineyards braid the surrounding hills. Lining the shore in Montreux were five-star hotels and designer stores, housed in art nouveau palaces where the likes of Noel Coward and Audrey Hepburn came to take the mountain air. It was as if the Swiss didn't know how to spend all their money. *What should we do today,* you could hear them thinking, *buy another Rolex?*

As for us, we hiked up 343 neat stone steps to reach our rented cottage. Here we discovered that not all Swiss homes look like IKEA catalogs. Somehow I'd managed to find us the last slice of Swiss grunge, an old worker's croft in gray concrete with a bathroom tiled in seventies olive green. Henry took one look at the rusted shower and declared it "unsanitary." He and Sam then took to chanting "Unsanitary Swiss people!" for some reason, laughing dementedly as they danced in a circle. The balcony, built for two with knees touching, afforded "partial lake views"—that is, a sliver of sparkling blue water between two luxury apartment buildings, each with panoramic terraces.

But the jazz festival would soon be in full swing, I declared, so to cheer ourselves, we dressed up and plodded back down the 343 steps to mingle with the mad, mad Swiss. The waterfront promenade was now blazing with lights, its perimeter entirely lined with vendors. In fact, anywhere else in the world, it would probably just be called a Shopping Festival. There was plenty of piped music—very little of it jazz, thankfully—but live concerts were thin on the ground. Apparently, the headliners all played to seated audiences inside concert halls. Instead, we joined Lake Geneva's current youth culture—hordes of well-shod teenagers celebrating the fact that the legal drinking age in Switzerland is sixteen. Well, they were closer to Mary Shelley's age anyway. Admittedly, for the average nineteenth-century tourist, excitement could also be difficult to find around these shores. One English visitor, Lord Henry Brougham, described Switzerland as "a country to be in for two hours, or two and a half, if the weather is fine, and no longer. Ennui comes on the third, and suicide attacks you before the night."

We retreated to a bar hanging over the water and ordered a couple of glasses of wine. They arrived in what appeared to be plastic medicine cups.

I held up one of the tiny tubs in confusion. They had cost the equivalent of $12 each. The waitress impatiently explained that here in the Canton of Vaud, the standard pour was carefully measured out to one deciliter. You could buy two deciliters for $24, three for $36. And that was the *vin ordinaire*. It seemed downright un-European. Back in France, wine was cheaper than Coca-Cola and was often siphoned on tap at bars. For the rest of the night, we staggered around in shock, calculating the exchange rate from Swiss francs. Each time the boys began to ask for soda, we chanted, "No Coke for you!" It didn't take long to realize that the restaurants were also run like banks; dining out is treated like a gold bullion transaction. Every dish on the menu is calibrated by weight—200 grams of cheese fondue, 125 grams of salmon—all of exquisite quality, but all rapaciously expensive. You could imagine the chefs measuring each ingredient with calipers. Les was mortified. "There's no love of cooking here!"

We watched other travelers press their noses up against restaurant windows with forlorn expressions. Even in the supermarkets, where everyone ended up, people stared bewildered at the prices.

"We're like bums!" Les railed, as we huddled in bush shelter gnawing salami. "We're the bums of Montreux!"

The young romantics of 1816, I reminded everyone, also had to make their own fun in Switzerland. When Byron's and Shelley's parties first rendezvoused in a Geneva hotel, they were immediately entranced by the natural setting. Mary waxed lyrical in letters about the brilliance of the lake, "blue as the heavens which it reflects," and the unearthly clarity of its waters, which on dusk boating excursions revealed trout and perch zigzagging over the stones far below—an image she would work into *Frankenstein*. She spent hours in the hotel's exuberant gardens, watching lizards and listening to the female vineyard workers singing. But their idyll wasn't perfect. Byron found himself being followed about by "staring Boobies," disapproving English tourists, and the odor of opprobrium also clung to Shelley and Mary, who were living in sin while traveling with the scandalously unchaperoned Claire. So they all rented private lodgings in the isolated rural hamlet of Cologny, on the northwestern shore. Byron settled into the sumptuous Villa Diodati, with sweeping mountain views, and the Shelleys and

Claire into the more humble Maison Chapuis nestled by the leafy waterfront below.

Today, traveling by water is still the most charming way to explore Lake Geneva, with a fleet of restored fin de siècle paddle steamers drifting from one trim little village to the next. Feeling defiant, we hopped on one vessel and went straight downstairs to the walnut-paneled first-class restaurant. A maître d' escorted us with the highest aplomb to a white linen-covered table, until we ordered four bowls of soup and nothing more. After our initial financial humiliation in Montreux, a new tactic was needed. Like the feisty peasants of yore, we refused to be cowed by the aristocratic opulence but took on the challenge of enjoying the luxuries of Switzerland while squandering the barest minimum of funds. It drove

The Château de Chillon on Lake Geneva, which inspired one of Byron's most popular poems.

the Swiss nuts. The staff first tried being snooty, then cajoling, then imploring. We were unmoved. There were no regulations saying we had to order the $120 set menu or an $80 bottle of wine. Instead, we leaned back by the splendid open window and watched the majestic scenery drift by.

Back in 1816, during a break in the rain, Shelley and Byron had set off on a weeklong sailing excursion together, accompanied only by their Swiss boatman, Maurice. (Although Byron had innumerable encounters with men over his lifetime, there is no evidence that he and Shelley were ever physically intimate.) The poets were literary tourists themselves, seeking out the homes of earlier residents Edward Gibbon, Voltaire, and Jean-Jacques Rousseau, who had set his 1761 romantic novel, *Julie, or the New Heloïse,* in these hills. This heartrending saga of two star-crossed lovers was the great bestseller of the eighteenth century, going through seventy-two editions before 1800 and making Rousseau Europe's first celebrity author—a role that Byron was already taking to new and sensational heights. The climax of their trip was the Château de Chillon, a fortress whose spires jut like some Arthurian fantasy from the lake, framed by icy peaks.

With his wicked reputation and saturnine good looks, Byron made quite a stir in the small lakefront villages, and today almost everywhere he visited has some sort of memorial, if only a Rue Byron, while the pale, intellectual Shelley is largely ignored. The undistinguished house in Clarens, for example, where they stayed with the mayor has a plaque, as does the Hotel d'Angleterre in Ouchy, where Byron wrote his popular poem *The Prisoner of Chillon.* The most authentic survival is the mansion of Madame de Staël, whose star-studded literary salon in Coppet was the only one Byron would deign to attend. The writer and socialite Staël, scintillating and vivacious for her fifty years, was as famous for illustrious lovers, who included the French foreign minister Talleyrand and politician Benjamin Constant, as she was for her steamy novels. Today, the Madame's tenth-generation descendent, Count Othenin d'Haussonville, opens to the public many of the rooms, which still have the original furnishings, including her elegant bathtub. Also intact is the first-floor library, which became so crowded during theatrical events that servants would pass drinks in through the windows using fishing poles. And the upstairs salon remains as lavishly furnished as it was when the infernally handsome Byron made his first appearance dressed head to toe in black, his chestnut curls flowing, dark eyes burning, and cleft chin jutting. Upon his entry, one Englishwoman apparently fell into a dead faint. Ma-

Byron carved his name in the dungeon of the Château de Chillon (although his friend Hobhouse thought it was done by a PR-savvy guard).

dame de Staël's daughter was appalled, muttering, "This is too much—at sixty-five years of age!"

I dragged Les and the boys to see them all, with varying degrees of success. The dungeon of the Château de Chillon, on the one hand, was quite a hit: Water lapped at the iron bars next to the pillar where Byron had carved his name, now under glass and marked by a plaque. (Byron's friend John Hobhouse insisted that this famous graffito had actually been carved by an enterprising prison guard to lure Romantic poetry groupies.)

But Sam and Henry began to resist the idea of trudging for hours in the heat to behold, say, a featureless building with a dead poet's name on it. Les was also starting to roll her eyes. So I took to the only logical recourse: bribery.

I hammered out with Henry what came to be known as "the candy contract." Lindt chocolate could be had for ready francs on any street corner. What if he and Sam were allowed a piece for every stint of solid walking? Say, one square every fifteen minutes. It would be like some Brothers Grimm story, only with a happy ending.

Henry weighed the offer. "Every five minutes."

"Twelve?"

"Ten!"

"Done."

This worked for a few days. But I had left the biggest challenge until last: the actual mansion where *Frankenstein* was conceived, the Villa Diodati. For this mission, I suspected that some serious traipsing would be involved. Directions to the villa were suspiciously vague, and there was a good chance we would get lost.

I noticed Les frantically researching the luxury spa pool complexes Switzerland was famous for, planning to abscond with the boys. But these would literally cost an arm and a leg, I told her. No, this was a sacrifice we would *all* have to make.

THE LABORATORY OF LOVE

The village of Cologny, where all the excitement occurred over the summer of 1816 in Byron's Villa Diodati, is today one of the most prestigious suburbs of Geneva, home to the trophy mansions of assorted sheikhs, CEOs, and Europop stars.

"The tourist office calls Cologny the Beverly Hills of Switzerland," I read from a brochure, as we skimmed over the lake, past the famous Jet d'Eau fountain.

"Oh great," Les muttered. "I thought Switzerland was *all* Beverly Hills! You mean they get even richer?"

Unfortunately, I managed to get the ferry schedules confused, and we found ourselves traipsing in the blistering heat along a busy six-lane highway, miles from our destination. If Cologny was "the Beverly Hills of Switzerland," we were lost on the Santa Monica freeway. Our water ran out. Not even the candy contract could help.

I peered at my map. Something up ahead was labeled Geneva Plage, Geneva Beach. At least we could get drinking water there, I reasoned, if only for $10 a bottle.

"Oh man!" Henry screeched, when we saw the Plage. "It's a water park!"

The Swiss version was a little more upmarket than the average Splish Splash in New Jersey. Apart from the immaculate new slides, there was a lakeside beach with canoes and diving towers, a vast plush lawn where smokers planted their individual spiked ashtrays, self-service cafés, and an elegant bar for the adults. As if to remind us that we were light years from Wildwood, Les found a Bulgari-leather-clad iPhone dropped casually on the lawn. She returned it despondently to the front desk.

By midafternoon, the mercury had climbed to 98 degrees, but I was getting restless. The Villa Diodati was up in the hills somewhere, waiting for me to visit. When I broached the subject of continuing the hike, the boys ran off shrieking in rebellion. Les closed her eyes and lay back on her towel, contemplating a siesta.

"Why don't you take this one, hon?" she murmured. "You can tell us all about it."

Half an hour later, I was sweating up a near-vertical pedestrian lane that (I prayed) led to the billionaire estates of Cologny. Every few yards, security guards in air-conditioned glass booths eyed me as if I were a terrorist. My printout from Google Maps was not proving entirely accurate, leading me into cul-de-sacs of tall hedges and luxury McPalaces, all of which seemed to be empty. I eventually stumbled into Cologny's old village center, where the few historical buildings had been turned into real estate offices. Along with the new wealth, modern art was clearly thriving in Switzerland. The lawns were graced with avant-garde sculptures that resembled giant spanners and screwdrivers, while the town centerpiece, by a celebrated Swiss artist, was a totem pole of teddy bears. By now I was feeling sunstruck. When I lurched into the only store to buy a bottle of water, the shopkeeper recoiled as if I were the creature from the black lagoon.

Finally I found the discreet stone gatepost engraved with the number 9 and a single word, DIODATI—placed next to a very sleek and very tall security gate.

The Villa Diodati, scene of Byronic excesses, in Cologny today.

Peering through the grille, I could see the legendary dwelling, its coral-pink exterior hardly changed from nineteenth-century engravings, complete with the wraparound balcony where Byron finished the third canto of *Childe Harold's Pilgrimage*. The vineyards that once covered the grounds have been landscaped into orderly gardens, and the Shelleys' more rustic cottage, the Maison Chapuis, has vanished, but Diodati has been preserved in aspic—although still in private hands, and divided into glamorous apartments.

I pressed the buzzer and smiled into the unblinking eye of a surveillance camera, but it remained dead. Nobody was home. A meadow next door, called Byron Field, offered another partial glimpse of the villa, although the owners had planted trees to limit the public view. A sign asked visitors to respect the Swiss code of conduct: PEACEFULNESS—TIDINESS—FRIENDLINESS—SECURITY.

It added that the police and "a private security agency" were supervising behavior at the site. Presumably some visiting poetry buffs get a little rabid.

Then I saw one of the Diodati residents, a debonair senior gentleman, drive his BMW into the estate. For some reason, the gate remained wide open behind him.

Nothing prevented my strolling down the driveway, until I found myself standing almost level with Byron's terrace, drinking in its 180 degree views of the lake, which even the sprawl of Geneva's stodgy UN buildings could not mar.

Through the window, I could see the ballroom-size Grand Salon. Now it was easy to imagine the bohemian coterie gathered there by candlelight to manically debate, carouse, and bed-hop that fateful summer. Byron's reservations about resuming his affair with the buxom, gypsy-eyed Claire Claremont quickly crumbled. ("I never loved her nor pretended to love her," he later wrote, "but a man is a man—& if a girl of eighteen comes prancing to you at all hours—there is but one way.") When the elderly gardener discovered one of Claire's slippers in the bushes one morning, he returned it to her with a polite bow. Sexual tensions were rife. Shelley and Claire had been intimate in England (he called her his "Little comet"). Dr. Polidori developed an infatuation with Mary, which was not returned. Mary confessed to being both attracted and repelled by Byron, but he found her cold. The homoerotic tension between Byron and Shelley added to the lively ambience.

English expats in Geneva let their erotic fantasies run wild regarding the secretive arts colony. Tourists even hired boats to marvel at the mixed-sex undergarments on the washing lines, proof that the Villa Diodati was a free-love commune, with the young ladies as virtual sex slaves. On one occasion, Byron was accosted on his evening ride by strangers and accused of corrupting Swiss youth. The Diodati menagerie, one British newspaper frothed rabidly, was a "league of incest."

It was mid-June when the torrential storms began—an "almost perpetual rain," Mary later recalled, with walls of lightning surging to and fro across the lake. The housebound friends read lurid German horror stories aloud to one another and discussed the latest scientific theories on galvanism, the life force, and animation. Wine flowed in generous quantities, as did laudanum, a tincture of opium. One night, when Byron recited a poem about ghosts, Shelley leaped up and ran howling into the rain, having hallucinated that Mary had sprouted demonic eyes in place of nipples. It was in this feverish, incestuous environment that Mary experienced her celebrated nightmare. She dreamed the plot of *Frankenstein* (as she recounted in the preface to the 1831 edition of her book) and then told the blood-soaked fable the next night to an enthralled audience around the fireside. Byron and Shelley encouraged her to write it as a novel.

As I was envisioning this classic tale of poetic inspiration, I heard a click behind me. The villa's security gate had been automatically activated, and was whirring shut. I had to scramble to escape being entombed.

The Swiss mania for privacy was getting on my nerves. I hiked back down to the lakefront and crossed the busy highway. Then I threw myself into the crystalline water and began swimming. About two hundred yards out, I turned around. There was the Villa Diodati, completely exposed to my plebeian eyes.

"I can see you!" I yelled up at the proud owners. "I can see your villa!"

And then a water-skier nearly ran me down.

Byron Lane next to the Villa Diodati in Cologny, with Lake Geneva view.

CASUALTIES OF THE PEN

In the age before effective contraception, free love involved a harsh learning curve for women. The Swiss arts colony began to fracture in August, when Claire revealed that she was pregnant, and Shelley asked the wealthy Byron to take responsibility. "Is the brat mine?" Byron asked petulantly in one letter, before accepting that it must be. The Shelleys left Switzerland at the end of the summer so Claire could give birth in England, with Byron promising to support the child (which he did, with bad grace). He remained at the Villa Diodati until the autumn, making extended excursions in the Alps, then finally left for Italy, where he plunged further into the irreverent abyss.

Today, the "Frankenstein summer" seems a dreamlike interlude of contentment in lives blighted by tragedy. Six years later, in 1822, Shelley drowned in a boating accident in Italy, at age twenty-nine. Dr. Polidori had committed suicide the year before, at age twenty-five. Claire's daughter with Byron would die at age five, and only one of Mary's four children with Percy survived. (Another pregnancy, her fifth before age twenty-five, miscarried. Incidentally, Shelley's deserted first wife, Harriet, also killed herself, carrying his child, in late 1816.) Byron died in Greece in 1824 at the ripe old age of thirty-six.

Mary Shelley returned to Lake Geneva as a famous middle-aged author in 1840, and found Cologny eerily intact but populated by ghosts. "There were the terraces, the vineyards, the upward path threading them, the little port where our boat lay moored," she wrote. "I could mark and recognize a thousand slight peculiarities, familiar objects then, forgotten since, replete with recollections and associations. Was I the same person that lived there, the companions of the dead? For all were gone . . ."

The final word was had by the irrepressible Claire Clairmont, who lived to age eighty. In her dotage, she began to write a memoir about her experiment with free love in Switzerland. The first pages were discovered in 2009 by the biographer Daisy Hay in the New York Public Library—so on my return to Manhattan sometime later, I visited the Pforzheimer Collection of Shelley and His Circle, a dark, hushed room with felt-inlaid desks and marble busts of the poets, where I requested Claire's musings.

The librarian first brought me some other fragments from the Lake Geneva interlude, including an original letter from Shelley that arrived at the Villa Diodati that fateful summer. (Scribbling from the Hotel Ville de Londres in Chamonix on July 22, he describes for Byron a muleback jaunt into the Alps, and enthuses about hearing an avalanche among the "palaces of Nature." In a cheeky mood, Shelley had signed the hotel register in ancient Greek, putting his profession as "Democrat, Philanthropist and Atheist." The words were so volatile at the time, writes biographer Richard Holmes, they were interpreted by enemies back in London as "Revolutionary" and "Pervert.")

At last I was presented with the folio of Claire Clairmont's papers. The stack of letters and notes had not been indexed, but luckily what I was looking for was near the top: a selection of yellowed pages in Claire's small, neat handwriting, tattooed with her subsequent corrections, deletions, and annotations, some of which were barely legible.

> These papers are a record of the effects and workings of the free love system such as the writer of these papers beheld with her own eyes—this is no hearsay record. . . .

The words were written around 1879 when she was a septuagenarian living in Florence and were intended as the introduction to a book-length work—she died after writing only a half dozen pages. The radical ideals of free love were out of fashion with Victorians, to say the least, but the feelings are deeply personal. Bitterness seeps from every line. Claire viciously denounces Shelley and Byron and their self-serving idea of sexual freedom, which left a trail of wreckage among the women who fell into their orbit:

> Under the influence of the doctrine and belief in free love I saw the first two poets of England . . . the most refined and honorable specimens of the age, become monsters of lying, meanness, cruelty and treachery. . . . Under the influence of free love Lord B(yron) became a human tyger slaking his thirst for inflicting pain upon defenseless women who under the influence of free love . . . had loved him.

She reserves her most intense attacks for Shelley, whose advocacy of sexual liberation turned women's lives into "a perfect hell." Piecing together references in letters, biographer Richard Holmes deduces that Claire and Percy became lovers again in 1818, when they were traveling in Italy away from Mary, and that Claire miscarried in Naples. The 1822 death of her young daughter by Byron, Alegra, is still shocking today. While she was under his supposed care, he had sent her to an Italian nunnery at the age of four and refused to allow Claire to visit her, even as she sickened and wasted away.

As a single woman with a damaged reputation, Claire would have needed a good deal of money to compete with such company—or a few years' supply of the pill.

DOWN AND OUT IN THE BERNESE OBERLAND

Our skirmishes with the moneymeisters of Switzerland grew more intense when we followed the Romantics into the Alps, where the machinery for separating travelers from their cash has been honed by centuries of experience. Once again, it was Byron who had forged the way for millions of sightseers. In 1816, after the Shelleys had left, he took an extended horseback tour of the Bernese Oberland with his Cambridge chum, John Hobhouse, marveling at waterfalls and glaciers ("like a frozen hurricane," Byron wrote of one). The poet did manage to forget some of his angst in the celestial mountain scenery. Crossing one high pass, he cheered up so much that he "made a snowball and threw it at Hobhouse," reports the historian Emily Dangerfield. ("It is not known whether Hobhouse returned it.") They ended up in the village of

Lauterbrunnen, where the snow-capped mountains loom in perfect chocolate-box formation. Today, well-heeled travelers arrive here from all over the world—and so, slavishly, did we.

In our Hotel Oberland, the menu stipulated that diners would be charged $1 per glass for tap water. A whole *carafe* of tap water (crass indulgence!) was $3. An extra pat of butter, 50 cents. More bread? $3. Use of the bathroom was a relatively modest 50 cents. The owners took their own dinner in a back room, scowling at any guests who interrupted. We imagined them counting their coins, the gnomes of Lauterbrunnen.

We did have one small victory—petty, yes, but strangely satisfying. The city council of Lauterbrunnen gives out a "Guest Card" to those who are already paying for one of their hotels, which entitles the bearer to such extravagant discounts as one dollar off entry to the municipal swimming pool. ("Reduction is for adults only!") After a long day hiking in the Alps, we stumbled down to the pool entrance and claimed our dollar off, which the attendant, a battle-hardened woman in shorts, granted with an indignant snort. Her concrete pool was a genuine blue-collar refuge (it seems that even in Switzerland there are truck drivers and hotel cleaners) where leathery women with dragon tattoos were chain-smoking in the sun.

After a swim, I went back to the kiosk to buy a glass of sweet strawberry wine, apparently the local specialty. But instead of my credit card, I pulled by mistake the Guest Card from my wallet, which almost gave the attendant a coronary.

"You cannot use the guest discount for wine!"

I shrugged. "I didn't mean to—it was an accident."

"No! You tried for a discount! You tried!"

I dropped my voice conspiratorially. "Actually, I've heard that in Lauterbrunnen you sometimes give *free* wine to tourists."

She blanched. "No free wine in Lauterbrunnen."

"Yes," I repeated. "*Free* wine!"

From then on, whenever I went up to the kiosk, I took out my guest card.

"Free ice creams for tourists in Lauterbrunnen?"

"Free hotdogs for tourists in Lauterbrunnen?"

After three days of this, she finally cracked a smile.

On the train out of Switzerland, I opened the Geneva newspaper and saw a promising report: "Bar Owner Attacked with Knife After Presenting the Check." Apparently the customer deemed the bill so excessive he drew a knife on the publican. I wondered if this swank establishment was introducing an entirely new charge on tourists. The mind boggled at the possibilities. Was there now a cost for using the plates? Napkins? Why not the table and chair? Whatever it was, the customer had been pushed too far.

Luckily, this being Switzerland, nobody was hurt.

Chapter Six

"LITTLE DEATH" IN VENICE

The Covert Casanova Tour

I had arranged to collect in Venice a package the weight of an anvil—all twelve volumes of Casanova's memoirs, which provide a native son's insider tips for visiting his home town.

Consider his thoughts on accommodation. In the winter of 1753, Giacomo Casanova, then an insatiable twenty-eight-year-old, needed a short-term rental in central Venice where he could entertain a ravishing young nun he identifies as M.M. (Her real name, historians have discerned, was almost certainly Marina Morosini.) Like many other aristocratic girls in Venice, M.M. had been sent to a convent by her family so they could avoid paying a marriage dowry, and she chafed at her fate. With golden hair that hung down to her knees, winsome blue eyes, alabaster skin "so white that it verged on pallor" and (of course) "two superb rows of teeth," this enterprising Bride of Christ had made the first advance, according to Casanova, by dropping him a love note after a church service on the island of Murano. Several furtive meetings followed, where the pair agreed it would be safer to tryst in the heart of Venice. A common inn was out of the question. Casanova wanted private rooms. Specifically, he required a *casino*—one of the city's secretive apartments designed for the pursuit of "love, good food, and the joys of the senses." He scoured the winding alleyways inspecting the options, before deciding on the most sumptuous and expensive of all, near the theater of San Moisé by St. Mark's Square. It had five rooms, including an octagonal boudoir with mirrors on the ceiling, white marble fireplaces, and porcelain tiles from the Orient that depicted an athletic array of erotic positions. The extravagant price included a chef, who would deliver meals ("game, sturgeon, truffles, oysters, and perfect wine") from the kitchen via a revolving dumbwaiter, so the occupants and their guests could keep their identities hidden.

Casanova's choice, it transpired, was a great success. On the appointed evening, M.M. slipped from her island convent—a feat that evidently was not over-difficult—and was escorted in a gondola to San Marco by her first lover, a mature French ambassador named Joachim de Bernis, who graciously encouraged the adventure. For safety, M.M. had disguised herself as a boy, wearing black satin breeches and a pink waistcoat embroidered with gold thread; her long blonde hair was plaited down her back. The androgyny only increased Casanova's desire when the group met in the Campo dei Santi Giovanni e Paolo behind a famous equestrian statue. Thanking the ambassador for his broad-mindedness, Casanova and M.M. retired to the five-star casino, where a candlelit feast duly materialized. The twenty-two-year-old novice, Casanova fondly recounts in the second volume of his memoir, *The Story of My Life,* "was astonished to find herself receptive to so much pleasure, for I showed her many things she had considered fictions . . . and I taught her that the slightest constraint spoils the greatest pleasures."

The pair met regularly for months, swapping oysters in their mouths, then making love while M.M.'s older consort, the French ambassador, spied on them through a peephole. Eventually, the ambassador was invited for a ménages à trois, then later à quatre when another young nun, C.C. (Caterina Capretta), joined in.

Naturally, I became fixated on lodging us in a former *casino*. Unfortunately, like Casanova, I couldn't actually afford it. But as Giacomo must also have decided, Venice has never been a city for half measures.

The island republic has always held a place of honor in Europe's erotic imagination. For eleven giddy centuries, from 697 to 1797, it flourished as the boudoir of Europe. Its strategic location on trade routes to the East filled the city with luxuries and allowed Venetians a level of sensual indulgence that was the envy of the Continent. By the 1700s, as Venice's maritime empire crumbled, its reputation for decadent pleasures only grew, as merchant dynasties squandered their fortunes with abandon. The eighteenth century became a long, golden twilight, when the whole baroque city qualified as a red-light district, and travelers flocked here to cruise the canals with powdered courtesans and taut gondoliers. They rented crumbling palazzos, flirted at masked balls, gamboled in the bawdy houses, and recovered from their exertions in the *stue,* or Turkish baths. The city's pornography was revered, and the latest raunchy sonnets of Giorgio Baffo were passed in handwritten form around coffeehouses such as the Florian. In 1778, one particular Venetian love song, "La Biondina in Gondoleta," "The Blonde in a Gondola," became a hit throughout Europe. (This eighteenth-century model of "The Girl From Ipanema" ran: "Oh my God, what beautiful things I said and did, I won't be so happy again in all my life . . .") In short, Venice was locked in a perpetual Carnival, where figures in tricorn hats, cloaks, and long-beaked masks—quickly becoming a Venetian cliché, but originally taken from mischievous characters in Commedia dell'Arte theatrical shows—swept along the misty alleys in search of anonymous encounters. Poets attributed the rampant sensuality to the city's all-surrounding fluidity, whose canals suggested a well-lubricated paradise. Later, the French poet Apollinaire would go so far as to dub Venice the pudenda of Europe.

No figure sums up the era's hedonistic frenzy more than Giacomo Girolamo Casanova, the ultimate, well, "Casanova," who cut a swathe through an apparently willing female population. (Not to mention a trail of unplanned pregnancies; the nun C.C, Caterina Capretta, for one, nearly died from a hemorrhage following either a miscarriage or home abortion.) In recent years, Casanova has been so mythologized in literature and film that some even assume he is a fictional character. It's hard to think academically of a man who has been played for comedy by Tony Curtis, Donald Sutherland, and Heath Ledger, and has even been portrayed in a Bob Hope movie. In fact, Casanova the man lived from 1725 to 1798, and most of his affairs—his passions for milkmaids and princesses, his liaison with a female singer who was masquerading as a castrato, the incestuous seduction of his illegitimate daughter—have been documented by modern historians and his best-disguised lovers clearly identified.

Compared to the average fops and dandies of the era, Casanova was a striking physical presence—over six feet tall, trim and handsome, with a swarthy complexion and, as one scholar puts it, "greedy lips." The ultimate self-made man, he was the son of two poor actors who gave himself the noble-sounding title "Chevalier de Seingalt," and went on to use his wit, charm, and joie de vivre to make himself a sought-after companion in the highest courts of Europe. What many don't realize today is that, along with his amorous achievements, Casanova's intellectual versatility puts the likes of Hugh Hefner to shame. Apart from being a theater director, a violin virtuoso, and a secret agent, he translated the *Iliad* and created the French lottery system. He debated with Voltaire, Goethe, Catherine the Great, and Ben Franklin, and he almost certainly worked with Mozart on the libretto of *Don Giovanni.* Just for good measure, he knocked out a history of Poland, several mathematical treatises, and a protofeminist pamphlet. But it was his rollicking sex memoir, written when he was in his sixties, that ensured his immortality.

The innocuously named *Story of My Life* is a hilarious encyclopedia of eighteenth-century sin. It would also, I hoped, serve as my guidebook to Venice's secrets. Although an inveterate traveler, Casanova was obsessed with his home city, and the memoir teems with unusual asides and insights. Being a serious fan of Giacomo, I hoped that if I followed his path, I might be connected, if only momentarily, to the city's past magic—a notoriously difficult feat. It has become a ritual for travelers to mourn Venice, whose fall from grace since Casanova's day is more extreme than that of any other place in Europe.

The Venetian historian Claudio dell'Orso argues in *Erotic Venice* that the closure of the city's brothels in 1958 (following Paris's lead) symbolized the decline of its traditional life. By the 1970s, local artisans were departing to live on the mainland, leaving Venice a hollowed-out shell. "Desire does not live in Venice any more," he lamented in 1996. "In fact even Venice, that Venice, no longer exists." Today, a mere sixty thousand permanent residents (about a quarter of the eighteenth-century population) confront the arrival of 20 million annual visitors. Even Italians regard Venice as a lost cause, where honeymooners are ripped off by gondoliers and end up arguing over maps. Its sensual reputation hangs by the barest of commercial threads. In 2006, enterprising locals opened an Erotic Museum but it failed dismally and closed after six months.

And yet, the fact remains that no other city in Europe is so physically intact. A few guard railings have been installed on the canals, and the gondolas are no longer crowned with curtained leather booths, where lovers could withdraw for privacy as they floated through the city. But otherwise, Venice looks much the same as it did when Casanova saw M.M. shed her nun's habit. The absence of automobiles gives Venice the potential for imaginative historic wandering—outside of tourist hours, that is. If you venture out very early or very late, the only noise in many corners can still be the gentle lapping of water, and Giacomo himself might spring from a doorway at any moment.

NUNS AND LOVERS

Approaching Venice is a time-honored spectacle, skimming over the ocean with nothing but a few mooring poles and seabirds to announce your arrival. Passengers still emerge excitedly from the railway station directly onto the Grand Canal, thick with watercraft like a painting at the Met come to life. The charm frays a little when the blown-glass vendors swoop in or you try to find a bathroom and there are forty people waiting for a single stall. But a shady café overlooks the hubbub, so in our case, we regrouped over cappuccino and bottled orange juice. In the heat of optimism, I decided that our irascible Bangladeshi waiter only proved that Venice is still the gateway to the East.

"*Bellissimo, no?*" I raved, waving my arms out over the water traffic. "*Sogniamo colle occhi aperti!*"

"What the heck?" Henry said, looking at me as if I'd finally lost it. He'd just gotten used to ordering soda in French.

"We're dreaming with our eyes open!"

Fearing the worst, Les had patiently held off asking where we might be staying in Venice. I pulled out a scrap of paper that had the address of a certain Signor Luca. Before I could conjure visions of randy nuns, I had some business to transact.

"You guys stay put for a few minutes."

It had been quite a stretch to find a luxury *casino* worthy of Casanova on our budget. For weeks, the only places I found were dark shoeboxes in remote ghettos for astronomical sums. Finally, I'd come across *una offerta dell'ultimo minuto,* "a last minute special," that looked suspiciously attractive. All I had to do was bring $2,000 in cash to this fellow Signor Luca, and the keys to a pleasure dome worthy of Kublai Khan would be handed over. So what if I'd be paying off this trip until I was ninety-five? There's something about Venice that makes you throw logic to the winds.

"You're serious?" Les asked, as I slipped into the crowds. "They've probably been running this scam since 1750!"

An illicit atmosphere certainly endures in Venice. All those towering facades promise that mysterious worlds are still contained behind closed doors. Even on the busiest canals, Venetians will appear for just a moment high on their balcony or in their lavish bedrooms before velvet curtains are drawn tight. Signor Luca's office, I had to admit, looked like a drug-dealer's front in Uzbekistan. There were three souvenir T-shirts hanging in the window and a pair of flip-flops. The signor himself was a corpulent, goateed fellow in dark glasses, sipping macchiato from a teacup. He took my cash, slowly counted out the crisp bills, then dangled three keys on a ring before me.

I had to ask why the apartment was so discounted.

"August is low season in Venice," he wheezed. "*Very* low season." He gestured weakly at the window. "The heat. The humidity. The people. But you will enjoy it."

I shuffled out, hoping Signor Luca wasn't about to pack up his "office" and disappear the moment I turned the corner.

Those mysterious Venetians, we soon found, were not quite as timid as rumor held. After wrestling our luggage onto a ferry, a creaking steamer out of Joseph Conrad, one of the quirky old "characters" decided to chew me out. "Foreigners shouldn't be allowed to bring luggage on public ferries!" he orated to the other passengers, sweat pouring down his face. "They should be forced to take a water taxi!" (This would have amounted to $200 for a five-minute ride.) "What do they expect coming here like this. . .?" The other Venetians, mostly women with shopping bags returning from the markets, rolled their eyes at him. "So much talking!" one matron scoffed. "He's in love with the sound of his own voice!" Others chimed in on an animated discussion of the iniquities of public transport the world over. Soon we, too, were commiserating and gesticulating as if we were on a New York bus. Quite a change from Switzerland, where you have to almost pull a revolver to make someone talk to you.

Henry and Sam, meanwhile, were mesmerized by the reflections on the canals. A whole city where the streets were made of water? This was worth seeing.

Venetian street addresses haven't been updated since the eighteenth century. Signor Luca had made me a helpful drawing of what our new home looked like, but it still involved impromptu explorations of the canals behind the Piazza San Marco.

"Is this it?" Henry asked, dubiously. I held up the drawing. "I *think* so . . ."

"It looks like a prison."

A defensive iron grate opened onto a tiny courtyard, where sacks of garbage were piled up like sandbags at a bomb shelter. The dark vestibule smelled powerfully of bilge water. It seemed as if a canal was flowing just beneath our feet. We crept up cracked marble stairs in darkness, with the prospect of a Coleridgean pleasure dome more remote with every step. But once I'd wrestled open the door, I was flooded with relief. The place was not bad, not bad at all. In fact, it was vast. The master bedroom had twenty-foot ceilings and a four-poster bed. Corridors went off at strange angles to reveal endless extra bedrooms, all with antique furniture decorated with hunting scenes. The hallway was a gallery of original sketches by the owner's friend, Hugo Pratt, creator of a graphic novel series called *Corto Maltese,* about a sailor-adventurer in the early 1900s. The lush ink illustrations revealed Venice's dark taverns where buxom gypsy girls worked the bar and toothless sailors sharpened their knives, plotting kidnap and mutiny.

It was like something out of a Visconti movie, where a fallen aristocratic family drifts along in frayed splendor. Casanova might have demanded a few more *chaises longues,* but Tom Ripley would surely have approved.

Les was never happier. Henry and Sam had their own room for the first time in months, and the kitchen overlooked a Renaissance courtyard.

"I'm like a bird," she said. "If you want to get me in the mood, I need everyone to be fed and the laundry to be done."

It was a promising start for channeling Venice's most famous son.

THE RAKE'S PROGRESS

Casanova loved that Venice was saturated with erotic historical reference, and today every corner still evokes an anecdote. We crossed the Ponte delle Tette, the Bridge of Breasts, where Venetian *puttane* were once permitted to lounge with their dresses open in order to drum up business. (Laws against female nudity were relaxed in the 1400s when a series of scandals made it clear that homosexuality was rife.) We located the original door of an eighteenth-century brothel called Scalon, still bristling with iron spikes designed to deter roustabouts from breaking it down with their shoulders. Eating pizza in front of the Church of San Barnaba, I could recount how, in 1443, Enrico Dolfin, a young noble, was caught under the church organ with a prostitute named Margarita, and so prosecuted for committing a "crime against God." A short stroll away was the Church of Santa Maria Formosa, dedicated to the "shapely" Virgin Mary, whose full figure so aroused a Venetian bishop when she appeared to him in a vision that he plunged into a spiral of guilt. And on a more contemporary note, we called at the villa of the voracious American heiress Peggy Guggenheim, whose canalside terrace is graced with Marino Marini's statue "The Angel of the City," a naked man on horseback with an erection. In the 1950s, she would apparently unscrew the phallus and present it to whichever male visitor she intended to bed that night. Later in life, when asked by a journalist how many husbands she'd had, she replied, "Mine, or other people's?"

But as for Casanova's physical presence, there is only one official memorial in all of Venice—a hard-to-spot plaque on the fissure-like Calle della Commedia, Comedy Street, in the San Samuele district, where he was born and spent his childhood. It's as if the Venetians themselves are ashamed of his wastrel ways; nobody is even quite sure in which house he was born. Although he developed a superhuman constitution, Giacomo was a surprisingly frail, simpering child, whose permanent nosebleed made it seem unlikely that he would survive. His father died when he was eight years old, and Casanova nurtured an obsession with his mother, a beautiful, self-absorbed actress who was surrounded by male admirers and who regularly left her children to tour the theaters of Europe. (His was an early case of *mammismo*, the mother-worship that Italian psychiatrists have recently denounced as the curse of the country's males.) Around the corner stands the modest

The only memorial to Casanova in Venice, on the corner with Calle della Commedia, the street of his birth.

Church of San Samuele, where the teenage Casanova trained, improbably enough, for the priesthood. He even had the top of his head shaved in the clerical tonsure—a seriously unsexy look for us today, but according to his own account, when he gave his first sermon, the money collection tray included feverish love letters from female parishioners.

By his late teens, Casanova had tossed in the cowl and fallen in with a clique of seven loutish friends, who ran around Venice at night playing pranks on gondoliers. I prowled the old red-light district around the Rialto markets to find Alle Spade, the last surviving *bácaro,* or bar, that Casanova frequented. Hidden from the noonday sun, its dark wooden interior was strangely devoid of customers. I nibbled cicchetti, dried cod snacks on crackers, while the jowly owner informed me in oft-rehearsed tones that "Casanova was the greatest *chiavatore* (fucker) who ever lived." No plaque would dare to recount the most notorious episode to occur in Alle Spade, which began when Casanova's gang spotted three men drinking with a pretty girl and decided to play a hoax. The leader, a young patrician, convinced the drinkers that he was an agent of the ruling Council of Ten and that they were under arrest. The quaking trio, who even included the girl's husband, were then spirited to a remote island and stranded for the night. The girl, however, was spirited upstairs to the comfortable, firelit salon of Alle Spade, plied with good wine and food, and informed that if she offered her favors, she would win leniency from the council for her captive husband. First, the leader had his way with her. "She was surprised when I presented myself second," Casanova notes. "By the time she saw the third . . . she had no more doubt that her happy fate promised her all the members of our band." The eight friends then escorted the girl home.

"We had to laugh after she thanked us as frankly and sincerely as possible," Casanova notes of this quaint jest.

From Alle Spade, I tracked down the Palazzo Bragadin, a mansion opposite the site of Marco Polo's house, which was the scene of a lucky break in Casanova's life. At age twenty-one, he recounts in his memoir, he was making a bare living as a violinist when he noticed an elderly gentleman drop a letter after a high society ball. The grateful old man offered Casanova a ride home in his private gondola, only to be seized en route by an apoplectic fit. Casanova remained overnight, nursing him back to health and keeping away the doctors who advocated leeches and bloodletting. The victim turned out to be a powerful senator, Don Matteo Bragadin, who on his recovery treated Casanova like his adopted son. He gave him a room in his palazzo, a gondola, and an allowance of ten sequins a month, which instantly vaulted Casanova from the rank of impoverished rascal to young man-about-town. (In *Erotic Venice,* the author Dell'Orso convincingly argues that this meeting was hardly as innocent as Casanova claims, for a "dropped letter" was a standard ruse for wealthy Venetian men to pick up younger men. Casanova was showered with gifts not because Bragadin was a kind-hearted soul, but because he was Bragadin's boy toy). Outside the palazzo, two Franciscan friars in brown robes were sitting on the steps with their bag lunch and Evian water. I was later impressed to learn that the building had just been purchased by none other than Pierre Cardin, who was born and raised in Venice before moving to Paris. Real estate agents must have him pegged.

With Don Bragadin's assistance, Casanova came into his own, winning fortunes in the gambling houses, spending them on extravagant fashions, and seducing the upper-class women

*Entrance to the Palazzo Bragadin (on the right), Casanova's home
for many years, thanks to an indulgent Senator.*

of Venice. But to the end of his life, he regarded his romance
with the frolicsome nun M.M. as the most magical of his
many romances. The site of her convent, Santa Maria degli
Angeli, lies at the tranquil tip of Murano Island, which was
even in the eighteenth century given over to glassware production. (The factories were relocated here in the Middle Ages
so as not to burn down the city.) A sign informed me that the
convent had been demolished in 1823, although the church
where Casanova and M.M. first met still stands. The historian
Judith Summers learned that Marina Morosini, despite her
passionate nature, never left the nunnery and ended her days
as the abbess. C.C., however, managed to win her freedom, if
only to marry a rich lawyer.

On Guidecca Island, another old convent called Convertite is more intact. It became notorious in 1561 when the rector was convicted of treating the four hundred nuns as his private harem. Appropriately enough, today it is a women's prison, where the old canalside entrance still conjures the silent comings and goings by gondola.

Stay long enough and you realize that Venice still proceeds at an eighteenth-century pace. Life in our *casino* revolved around the tides and wind. Usually, a romantic breeze would waft through the curtains, but every now and then, when the mercury rose, an unhealthy stew of humidity and bilge-water would settle over the city, permeating every corner, bringing armies of mosquitoes, and no doubt inspiring Signor Luca's discount. In Thomas Mann's day, wealthy Venetians would escape the heat and diseases at the beaches of the Lido. Thankfully, the pungent odors would seep away after a few hours.

Depending on the sounds emanating from the alley below, you never knew quite which century it was. At dawn, I'd be woken by the street cleaners, the whisk of their straw brushes interspersed with greetings at the top of their lungs, sounding as if they were inside our bedroom. By nightfall, once the tour groups went back to their cruise ships, the city became eerily silent. If anyone loitered too late in the street, Venetians would bellow oaths at them from their windows. Once, when a group of boozers refused to move on, someone upstairs emptied a whole pail of garbage on their heads. I made a mental note to try it on the clubbers back in New York.

Italian summer traditions began to rub off even on me. Our strolls into Casanova territory proceeded at a more leisurely pace, punctuated by pit stops for iced wine or cordial in the piazzas. The heat grew so intense that Henry and Sam would fill their baseball caps with water from the ancient cisterns and douse themselves, to the horror of passing Venetians, who dress in their Sunday best even to go to the grocer's. The boys' main pastime, however, was extracting as much as they could from us in the form of souvenir treasures. Stores are piled high with glass knickknacks in tutti-frutti colors, so the "candy contract" was replaced with the "Venetian crap contract." Soon they were demanding fantasy chess sets and hand-crafted parchment notebooks. One day, we stumbled across Ca'Macana, the oldest mask store in Venice, which had designed the masks for the Hellfire Club vehicle *Eyes Wide Shut,* where Henry became besotted with a priceless cyborg mask, encrusted with hundreds of jewel-like electronic parts. With so many wealthy visitors to Venice, the sky is the limit. Another store offered a model apothecary's desk, complete with miniscule glass bottles and leather-bound books, for a mere $4,000. We shuffled the poor boy away, muttering to himself in shock.

My favorite time was early morning, when I'd rise at dawn and creep out into the hushed city to enjoy the calm before the storm. By the waterfront, church bells drifted across the mirror-flat Lagoon. Only a few others were out—clusters of ferry captains, waiters setting up restaurant chairs, and vendors en route with their carts. I'd take a seat at one of the early-opening workers' cafés and lose myself in Casanova's memoirs—escapist literature for a family holiday, if ever there was.

THE OFFICE OF VENETIAN SECRETS

Casanova's charmed life went awry one hot July morning in 1755, when, just after his thirtieth birthday, soldiers burst into his rooms at the Palazzo Bragadin. He had been singled out by the spies of the Venetian Inquisition as a con man, a card sharp, a magician, and a Freemason. He had also read aloud in a wineshop a blasphemous poem that "speaks both directly and indirectly of copulation." But the real motive for his arrest, historians have speculated, was that he simply offended the wrong people. Casanova had won money from powerful men, had seduced their wives, and was recently courting a young lady sought by the Grand Inquisitor himself. The officers ransacking his quarters found plenty of suspicious evidence that could be used for trumped-up charges—banned books on astrology, kabbalah, and "how to converse with demons." After Casanova had dressed (in protest, he chose to wear his finest clothes, "as if to attend a wedding"), he was spirited by gondola to the Doge's Palace, the intimidating nerve center of the old republic. There was no trial. Venetian state policy was to tell prisoners neither the charges against them nor the length of their sentence. Instead, he was ushered across the Bridge of Sighs into I Piombi, the Leads—so called because the cells were directly under the lead roof—where he was condemned, for all he knew, to rot forever.

The most astonishing part of the story is that Casanova actually managed to escape from the Leads, the only inmate to ever do so, making him the toast of European courts. In recent years, historians have even delved into the republic's archives to identify his cells and escape route in the off-limits attics of the Doge's Palace.

The building is still one of Venice's most famous, its gleaming Moorish facade overlooking the lagoon. When I entered, ticket vendors were lined up beside each other like some languid tribunal. The Doge's Palace was huge, they explained, and only certain rooms were open to the public. Access to the rooftop cells was strictly limited because of the delicate nature of the physical space.

"You should have booked *Il Itinerario Segreto.*"

Of course! I clapped. The old Secret Itinerary . . .

Italians love their secret tours, which appeal to their sense of drama. There are several in Florence, where small groups are allowed into closed-off nooks of the Palazzo Vecchio and Uffizi by special permission. The downside is that it is often an enigma how to actually sign up for them. Here in the Doge's Palace, I found the bureaucrat in charge of "special visits" sitting alone in the far corner of the room, a mass of frizzy black hair, painting her nails with blood-red polish. She was not encouraging.

The Secret Tour was *very* irregular. She sighed. Spaces fill up months in advance. Often it was *cancellato,* cancelled. The only tour that was planned anywhere in the near future was . . . here she ran her finger down a handwritten ledger . . . *pieno.* Full.

Could I get on a waiting list?

"*Impossibile.*"

Anyone higher up I could talk to?

"*Nessuno.*"

Pondering a bribe, I asked if any special fee could make things . . . easier?

"*Niente.*"

Finally, just to get rid of me, she wrote down the department within the Ministry of Culture that, on some cosmically remote level, masterminds the operation of Venice's great historical sites. Perhaps I could go and plead my case in person.

It took me two hours to locate the office of the Foundation of the Civic Museums of Venice, which was unmarked in a nameless back alley. In August, it also appeared to be deserted. Up on the fourth floor, I finally found the sole remaining worker, a woman at her desk who was bathed in blinding light, reflected off the linoleum floor. The *dottoressa* wavered at my request—it was all rather unusual—but for a committed foreign scholar, a specialist in the life of Casanova, well, perhaps it could be done. . . .

When I rushed home to tell Les the good news, I found everyone in a state of exhaustion. They had gone out trying to buy groceries, become lost, and couldn't find the way back. Les had gotten into an argument with a produce vendor, who was offended by her touching his tomatoes.

"You can buy any kind of jewel-encrusted mask in Venice twenty-four hours a day," she railed, "but you can't get toothpaste, toilet paper, or soap."

It was true that living in the heart of the city had its practical difficulties. But after a couple of glasses of wine, looking out over the stately courtyard, we'd be dreaming about moving here with the boys for a year, me writing in the Macano Library, her sketching at the Accademia. We'd just have to bring our own groceries.

THE THEATER OF PAIN

Next morning at the Doge's Palace, the woman with blood-red fingernails cracked her ledger for the Secret Tour. I was amazed to find that my name was now scribbled on the list, as if by kabbalistic magic. A handful of other invitees arrived one by one, all dignified and nattily dressed Italians, including a philosophy professor from Milan with his aged and fragile mother. I wondered whether she'd be able to stand the excitement.

The Palazzo Ducale, or Doge's Palace, nerve-center of the Venetian Republic. Casanova was imprisoned in the attic cells.

At first, when our guide, Luciana, arrived, she seemed hardly Casanova's type in her thick-rimmed reading glasses and all-enveloping white lab coat. She briskly handed out clothing stickers with SECRET ITINERARY stamped on them, then clomped up the Golden Staircase. But the costume was just a ruse. At the top of the stairs, she suddenly spun around, opened her coat, and dipped a hand down her plunging neckline to produce a key on a silver chain. This she inserted with a graceful, practiced motion into a keyhole, which opened a hidden panel in the bare wall. Luciana was decidedly more alluring now.

"Signori and signore," she whispered huskily. "Welcome to the sanctum of the Venetian Republic. No bags are permitted inside. No photographs. No video."

We nodded obediently. Luciana without her coat was transformed into Sophia Loren from one of her later films—say, *The Priest's Wife*—as she beckoned us to enter. The rest of the milling visitors in the Doge's Palace could only stare in slack-jawed envy as we stepped into the forbidden netherworld. As we passed, Luciana touched us each lightly on the hair, counting our numbers, then stepped inside to lock the door behind us, slipping the key with a smile back into her magnificent décolletage.

This was how a Secret Tour *should* start, I was thinking.

We ascended a dark stairway into corridors made from raw wooden planks, which began to shudder and sway. Soon it felt as though we were clambering about inside a galleon at sea. The route to Casanova's cell ran via the original offices of the Republic's top bureaucrats. In contrast to the baroque luxury of the rest of the palace, which was designed to impress foreign dignitaries with Venice's wealth, they worked in no-frills cubicles with special hinges on the doors to create an airtight fit, in order to prevent eavesdropping. Next came the State Inquisitor's Room and the Torture Room, where prisoners had their arms tied behind their backs, then were dropped from ropes.

It was through these gray corridors of power that the despondent Casanova was ushered after his arrest that steamy July morning in 1755. He knew that the attic cells of the Leads were reserved for long-term prisoners, and in his detailed account of the day in his memoir, he recalls that he was paralyzed with despair. His body felt "as if crushed by a wine press." (The sentence was actually five years, but Casanova was not informed.)

Now as our little tour group approached Casanova's rooftop cell, we became as hushed as if we were entering a chapel. A low doorway led into a tight wooden box, about eight feet by eight, with a five foot high ceiling, all made of dark planks encrusted with metal studs. Near the door was a horseshoe-shaped device. Casanova recalls asking its purpose of his jailer, who gleefully told him it was a garroting machine, handy for quick executions. Then he was left alone, his only company rats, "the size of rabbits."

"*Alora,*" Luciana breathed sadly as we crouched inside. "This was Casanova's *first* cell. You can imagine what it was like for a man like him to be trapped here! He couldn't even stand upright! He was attacked by fleas constantly. In the heat, he could do nothing but sit half naked, sweating. For a man who had devoted his life to sensual pleasure, this was like a living death. So he decided to escape, even though nobody had ever succeeded in doing so from the Doge's Palace before."

By eleven a.m. on our visit, the summer temperature in the Leads was already as "pestilential" as Casanova describes it. The perspiration was pouring off us, and we could hardly breathe. The philosopher's elderly mother was looking shakier by the minute. I noticed that Luciana didn't go into the more graphic details of Casanova's suffering, which included an extreme case of hemorrhoids. ("A cruel affliction from which I never recovered.") Instead, she enthusiastically related his Great Venetian Breakout.

Plan A, concocted in this very cell, was an embarrassing flop. Casanova got hold of an iron bolt left by some workmen and began to dig through the floorboards at night. He hid the damage beneath a carpet and armchair provided by his patron Don Bragadin, who had also sent some books and food to help Casanova survive. But agonizingly, after several months of painful labor, the guards decided to grant their most likable prisoner a favor and transfer him to a nicer cell. The

Entrance to Casanova's first cell in the Doge's Palace, which he shared with rats "the size of rabbits."

tunnel was discovered. "It was just as well," Luciana said. "Directly below is the Grand Inquisitor's chamber. He was about to break through the ceiling, which would have destroyed a Tintoretto fresco!"

The Italians shook their heads in horror.

We filed into Casanova's second cell, which had slightly better ventilation and light, to hear about Plan B, whose details have been verified by historians from the prison archives. Now more closely watched, Casanova smuggled the iron spike, which he had hidden in the spine of a book, to a fellow prisoner, a disgraced priest and first-class neurotic named Martin Balbi, and put him to work making a hole in the ceiling. At midnight on October 31, 1756, the odd couple made their break. After wriggling from their cells, they climbed onto the palace roof, two hundred feet above St. Mark's Square. The priest suddenly realized the danger—not to mention the fact that Casanova had no actual plan—and tried to back out. Casanova refused to let him. They nearly slipped to their deaths but managed to get back inside the palace through another window, using ropes made from torn sheets. At the bottom of the Golden Staircase, they discovered to their horror that the main prison gate was locked from the outside. This was when Casanova's savoir faire came to the rescue. He was carrying in a bag around his neck the flamboyant wedding clothes he had worn the morning he was arrested—a lace-trimmed coat, ruffled shirt, and tricorn hat with long feather—and now he put them back on. Glimpsing this chic figure through the grille, a guard assumed that he was a rich visitor accidentally caught inside after visiting hours. As he opened the door, Casanova and Balbi elbowed past and scampered for the first gondola.

"The escape made Casanova famous, but he would not return to our beloved city for nearly twenty years," Luciana sighed, as if mourning on behalf of Venetian womanhood. "When he did come back, it was to a hero's welcome. Even the inquisitors wanted to hear him tell the story of how he got away!"

I was trying to visualize the scene when I had a stroke of luck: the philosopher's mother announced she was about to faint from the heat. The Italians went into fits of shouting, then proceeded to carry her downstairs, with Luciana leading the way, barking on her cell phone for medical assistance. I found myself standing alone in Casanova's dismal little cell. After all the high security and mystery surrounding the Secret Tour, the solitude was intoxicating. At last I had a tiny glimpse of Casanova's presence. I took a few photos—*frutto proibito*, forbidden fruit!—then went back to the first, even more dismal cell, and photographed that, too. Nobody was going to chase me out. In fact, I probably could have stripped down naked and really channeled Casanova.

But then it occurred to me that I might actually be locked in. The next Secret Tour might not be for weeks. So I slunk sheepishly down the stairs to face Luciana, now decidedly annoyed.

When I emerged into the Piazza San Marco, it took a while for my eyes to adjust to the sunshine. Unlike Casanova in his flight from Venice, I plopped myself down in a café chair, ordered a prosecco, and pulled out his memoir.

As Luciana had said, the escape from the Doge's Palace made Casanova an exile from his beloved home city. Despite all his brilliant adventures as he zigzagged from Paris to Madrid to London to St. Petersburg, his fondest dream was to return to Venice. When the Inquisition finally did pardon him in 1774, he was nearly fifty years old, broke, his looks fading. (One of the more disconcerting elements of *The Story of My Life* is Casanova's unsparing assessment of the ravages of time. It was at age thirty-eight, he reported, that he "began to die"; middle age was merely a step away from "sad and weak, deformed, hideous old age.") Slipping back to Venice, he moved in with a young seamstress and almost resigned himself to domestic retirement. But he became ever more prickly and cantankerous. In 1782, now aged fifty-seven, Casanova published a libelous pamphlet about a powerful patrician who had offended him, and he was forced to flee Venice once again.

Running up debts as he skulked around the scenes of his former glory, he was finally forced to accept a job in exchange for bed and board—as, of all things, a librarian. A nobleman named Count Waldstein offered him the position at Castle Duchcov in Bohemia, part of the modern Czech Republic.

To the elderly Casanova, it was a humiliating final act. He was tormented by the castle staff, who mocked him for his self-important airs and refusal to learn German. When the count was away, the cook would serve Casanova curdled milk, scalding soups, and, worst of all, pasta that wasn't al dente.

Casanova's nostalgia for Venice now grew unbearable. The crumbling city mirrored his own lost youth, and the knowledge that he would never return finally pushed him into a black depression. When he turned sixty, a doctor suggested that he write his memoirs in order to stave off suicide. Today, the world should be grateful. According to his letters, Casanova began writing for twelve hours a day, laughing out loud the whole time and piling up 3,500 manuscript pages. He died thirteen years later in the castle, without ever seeing Venice again. "I lived as a philosopher," were his last improbable words, "and I die as a Christian." His gravesite on the grounds has since been lost.

The posthumous journey of his memoir is one of history's miraculous publishing success stories. On his deathbed in 1797, Casanova bequeathed the monstrous manuscript to his nephew-in-law in Dresden, who eventually sold it for a pittance to a local printer. It was written in French because this was more commonly read than Italian, let alone Casanova's own Venetian dialect. A heavily censored edition was finally published in 1822, a quarter century after the author's death, and became a runaway hit; for the next 140 years, pirate translations and bowdlerized versions of this censored edition flooded the bookshelves. The original French manuscript, meanwhile, was kept locked up in the Dresden printer's safe, where it only narrowly escaped destruction by Allied bombing in the Second World War. It was not until 1961, thanks to the efforts of eighteenth-century literature experts, that the first uncensored edition saw the light of day—just in time for the sexual revolution and renewed bestseller status. In 2010, Casanova's original manuscript was purchased from the family of the nineteenth-century publisher by the French government for a record $9.3 million. Its return to France was hailed as a triumph. The fact that Casanova was quintessentially Venetian, whose French was an idiosyncratic version filled with Italianisms, has clearly been forgiven. (The purchase was arranged by a private French donor; it's unknown whether the Italians bid.)

I can easily imagine Casanova bristling over his fame solely as a great lover. In his memoirs, he repeatedly insists on his own exalted status as an intellectual and becomes childishly resentful whenever he feels dismissed as a "merely" handsome voluptuary. His carnal adventures—122 affairs—take up only a third of the memoir, while there are endless digressions on philosophy, history, and the arts. But nobody would deny that this third includes the most energetically written sections. "I have devoted my life to the pursuit of pleasure," he declares on page one without the slightest regret.

Our current view of Casanova as history's ultimate playboy may be unfair, but it's hard to feel sorry for the guy.

Chapter Seven

VATICAN VICE

The Pope's Pornographic Bathroom

Long before the sensational inventions of Dan Brown, the Vatican has had trouble explaining away long chapters of its history. The discomfort becomes most acute with the Renaissance, when popes were princes first, not men of God, and cardinals were their flamboyant, worldly courtiers. Like all Italian aristocrats, the top Roman clerics lived in Babylonian opulence, hosted feasts with beautiful courtesans, sired bevies of children, and were more likely to die of syphilis, poisoning, or cross-fire on the battlefield than natural causes. As the intellectual leaders of their age, they were also avid patrons of the arts; they relished the rediscovery of the Greco-Roman world and a more sensual, pagan direction in painting and sculpture. But in later centuries, as the Papacy became more conservative and puritanical, an awkward silence fell over the hedonistic past.

The Church denial grew more intense after 1870, when Pius IX was forced to abandon control of Rome and retreat behind the fortified walls of the Vatican Palace. What really lay within that 110-acre enclave on the left bank of the Tiber became the subject of rumor and speculation, especially among the anticlerical elements of Italian nationalists, who advocated expelling the pope from Rome entirely. It was said that the Vatican Library contained the world's largest collection of pornography. (A not illogical notion, since the Church list of banned books, the Index, had been going strong for centuries, and a copy of each volume was kept.) Underground tunnels were thought to be decorated with hardcore obscenities. (The story was perhaps inspired by the Passetto di Borgo, a real eight-hundred-yard-long passageway that links the Vatican Palace with the Castel Sant'Angelo, and was used by Pope Clement VII to escape during the 1527 sack of Rome.) A special chamber was believed to contain hundreds of male genitalia lopped from marble statues and replaced by fig leafs.

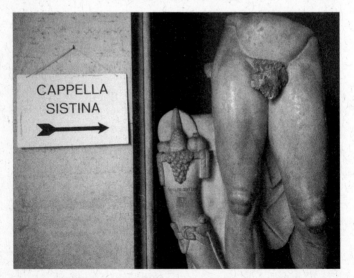

Sign to the Sistine Chapel in the Vatican Museums; fig leaves figure prominently in Papal mythology.

(Well, the Vatican did gather the world's greatest concentration of classical art, which became subject to odd censorship attempts over the years.)

But the most improbable story of all happens to be quite true: In the heart of the pope's private residence, a bathroom was covered with erotic paintings by Raphael.

Almost from the day it was created in 1516, the so-called Stufetta del Bibbiena (the "little heated room," or bathroom, of Cardinal Bibbiena) has been the Vatican's most mysterious site. Hidden in the top floor of the Papal Apartments, its wicked array of frescoes was commissioned by Cardinal Bernardo Dovizi da Bibbiena, the charming and worldly secretary to Pope Leo X. Even among the sophisticated clerics of Rome, Bibbiena stood out as the proverbial Renaissance man, an energetic party host and the author of a risqué theatrical comedy, *La Calandria,* whose scenes of adultery and cross-dressing delighted Roman high society. He had also been one of Raphael's closest friends since the pair had been teenagers in Rome. When Bibbiena wanted something provocative for the decor of his Stufetta, he knew whom to ask. Raphael was an obsessive womanizer who often dabbled in erotica. (He was even engaged to Bibbiena's own niece for several years but was too enamored of philandering to commit to marriage.)

The inspiration for the Stufetta came, quite literally, from underground. Like other Roman artists, Raphael had been lowered with ropes and torches into the recently discovered catacombs of Emperor Nero's Golden Palace on the Quirinal Hill. The colorful interior designs inspired an immediate vogue for erotica in the "grotesque" style. (The word's original meaning was "common to ancient grottos"; later, it came to mean anything monstrous or misshapen). Bibbiena chose as the theme the triumphs of Venus and Cupid, which would have also appealed to his master, the pope. Leo X was from the Medici family of Florence, raised to love art and literature, and had a cultivated interest in all things classical. He also pampered himself splendidly—he is said to have declared on his election by the Sacred College, "God has given us the Papacy, now let us enjoy it!"—and took to parading through Rome with a white elephant in his entourage.

In 1516, Raphael executed the drawings for two dozen raunchy scenes, which were painted on fifteen-inch stucco panels across the walls and ceiling of the vaulted bathroom. Some images the maestro painted himself; others were completed under his supervision by his workshop staff. Cardinal Bibbiena had also hoped to include a nude statue of Venus in the room, but it wouldn't fit into the wall niches. Another cardinal, his friend the poet Pietro Bembo, took it for his own pagan-themed lodgings, boasting in a letter that he would "desire her [Venus] more every day than you ever could."

News of the entangled lovers, priapic satyrs, and curvaceous goddesses spread around Rome, and friends of both Raphael and Bibbiena came to admire the work. But after the untimely deaths of both patron and artist in 1520, visits by outsiders grew less common. Thirty years later, even Giorgio Vasari, the famous biographer of Renaissance artists, was unable to gain access at all, lamenting that "the frescoes are still in existence, but are not open to the public." Still, Raphael's students circulated a number of engraved copies of the panels, providing tantalizing clues. The most notorious image involves the half-goat god Pan with a monstrous erection about to leap from some bushes upon a luscious naked nymph, who is casually combing her hair, her legs slightly apart.

One of the only outsiders to gain a viewing at the time was a German scholar named Johannes Fichard in 1536. (It's not known how.) To Fichard, the bathroom confirmed his own belief in the Papacy's shameless immorality: "Here, seated in a tub, His Holiness washes with hot water which is supplied by a bronze female nude. There are also other nudes, and I have no doubt that these are touched with great devotion." In the following centuries, Vatican residents also scorned the Stufetta. In the 1700s, the room was converted into a kitchen, when one of the panels was completely destroyed to make room for a cupboard. Then it became a storeroom. It was only in 1835 that the chamber was mentioned in an obscure German academic's monograph on Raphael, and interest in it revived. But chances of outsiders viewing the artworks remained slim.

The possibility grew even less likely when the Vatican Palace became the Pope's gilded prison in 1870. For nearly two millennia, the Pontiff had ruled the entire city of Rome, but in the 1860s, troops supporting the unification of Italy seized the Papal States, and finally stormed the Eternal City. Pope Pius IX fell back with his supporters to the Vatican complex, which, perhaps not surprisingly, began to exude a siege mentality. No pope even set foot outside the palace for nearly sixty years, until Mussolini recognized it as its own tiny state in 1929. Renovations were made to fit the pope and his bureaucrats in the thousand-room complex. Cardinal Bibbiena's bedroom became part of the Papal Apartments and was converted into the reception room for official meetings with foreign dignitaries. Evidently, the door to the grubby little Stufetta next door was kept firmly closed.

I wasn't sure of the room's current condition or even if it had been bricked up. In the 1970s, I'd read, the esteemed British art historian Peter Webb, author of the classic text *The Erotic Arts,* found that many Vatican officials denied the Stufetta's existence; others simply ignored his repeated requests to see it. Today, with the current welter of Catholic scandals, the Holy See has little to gain from opening an erotic bathroom.

It remains the most secret corner of the Secret City.

When I first e-mailed friends canvassing for ideas on how to get into the Stufetta, I received some less than reverent responses.

"You mean the Pope has a special room for whacking off?" wrote an investigative journalist from Boston. "I love it. . . ."

"If you see a 50 Euro note on the floor," advised Andrea, an Italian photographer, "don't bend over!"

As I expected, the papal bureaucracy is just as formidable today as it was 150 years ago. It does have a nice website, but the inner workings remain totally obscure. You need a confirmed appointment just to set foot inside Vatican City, but how you obtain one is unexplained. Attempts to Google names of officials simply come up blank.

"What the hell did you expect?" said a friend in New York who had actually worked with the Vatican. "A pornographic bathroom? They'll never let you near it!"

MISSION IMPOSSIBLE

In Rome, we checked into the venerable and gritty Albergo Sole al Biscione, an inn that dates from the Renaissance, when it took in pilgrims from all over Europe. Even then it was a historic site, with the ground floor horse stables built into the very ruins of the ancient Theater of Pompey. Dragging our bags through the Campo dei Fiore, I told Les about the American journalist Lyman Abbott, who visited Rome for *Harper's* magazine in 1872 and who argued that home guesthouses run by down-on-their-luck noble families were far more atmospheric than overpriced grand hotels: "With their covered terraces, their obscure corridors, their tumbling staircases, their unswept halls, they are repulsive to the housekeeper, but attractive to the antiquary," Abbott wrote.

Today, the Albergo is still family-run, as we discovered upon meeting the old *padrino* and his wife, who took a liking to Henry, with his book on Roman gladiators. Instead of the usual monastic cell, they gave us a bright room on the roof, with a view of ornate church cupolas. There was a symmetry to staying by the Campo dei Fiore, I rejoiced, as we lounged at one of the square's cafés. In the center of the marketplace stands a statue of an ominous, hooded figure—Giordano Bruno, a philosopher who was burned at the stake here in 1600 by the Inquisition for his heretical musings. It had been erected in 1889, with Bruno deliberately glowering in the direction of St. Peter's, and immediately became a rallying point for anti-Vatican protesters, who took to the streets chanting "Death to the priests!" and "Death to the butchers of the Inquisition!" The riots grew so violent that the pope considered fleeing to Spain. Even today, on the anniversary of Bruno's immolation, February 17, well-wishers leave flowers at the statue's feet.

"Really?" Les said distractedly, as she scanned the menu. "Let's have the mozzarella di bufala tasting plate."

I was beginning to suspect that nobody shared my Vatican obsession. I was driven on by my mad Irish Catholic upbringing, which scarred me for life, but Les was raised in the rain forests of Australia like a godless sprite, and our wayward progeny were just as likely, in the East Village, to end up baptized into some voodoo cult. The idea of visiting the sacred Christian sites, even St. Peter's Basilica, provoked reactions from baffled indifference to open hostility. It was too hot for sightseeing anyway; they demanded pagan pleasures. I had to compromise. We didn't even join the lines at the Colosseum; instead, we walked straight past the buskers in their legion-naire's costumes, heroically posing for photos under the blistering sun, to another attraction next door on the Caelian Hill. Here, every summer, the city sets up a luxury swimming pool complex where, for a modest fee, you can swim, eat panini, and drink pinot grigio while gazing up at Rome's most illustri-ous ancient monument. This was no tawdry French municipal affair. The Italians didn't bother with lifeguards, let alone rules or regulations, but style was all-important. So we sprawled in the sun like Renaissance artists on sabbatical. The other guests were rich Italian kids, magnificently bronzed, chilling out between trips to Rimini.

The pope's bathroom could wait another few days, I hoped.

When I finally ventured into St. Peter's Square, it was packed with fresh-faced pilgrims. A bevy of Third World saints were about to be canonized, and their portraits hung on huge ban-ners above the basilica doors like Stalinist icons. Around the corner at the Vatican's main entrance, teams of Swiss Guards in their jaunty blue berets stood beneath a stone archway, turning away sightseers who accidentally approached. Wher-ever you looked, there were religious supply stores pushing life-size statues of Jesus, Eucharist holders, priest's robes, souvenir mangers. It was enough to give a lapsed Catholic nightmares.

The main entrance to the Vatican City, the Porta di Santa Anna.

At the pope's very own press office, a Mussolini-era building on the Via della Consiliazione, I pressed the buzzer.

A voice crackled over the intercom: *"Pronto?"*

Sister Giovanna, who met me inside, was a lovely old nun who appeared in full regalia of gray habit, white wimple, and horn-rimmed spectacles. Naturally, I didn't blurt out that I wanted to inspect the dreaded Stufetta del Bibbiena. Instead, I said that I was researching a sober academic subject—"the influence of pagan imagery on Renaissance art." Sister Giovanna just smiled beatifically and explained that I had come to completely the wrong place. Her office only issued press releases from the pope. But she did give me some actual names and e-mails where I might start, and she let me visit the Vatican Press Center, which was lined with vintage computers and phone booths like NASA control in the 1960s. Amazingly, the computers still worked—a small miracle in Italy, where it can still take ninety minutes to send an e-mail from an Internet café.

When I went to my own website to check something, I got a pop-up screen: THIS SITE IS BLOCKED DUE TO INAPPROPRIATE CONTENT. Egad, I thought. If the Vatican officials Googled me, I'd be doomed.

STORMING THE HOLY SEE

I did notice one crack in the pope's bureaucratic defenses that might be exploited. Scholars can worm their way into the Vatican City via the Secret Archive.

Why exactly the pontiff keeps calling his document trove the Archivium Secretum was something of a mystery to me. Didn't he realize that the word secret acts on certain people like a red flag to a bull? Dan Brown in *Angels and Demons* imagines it as a subterranean Bond villain's lair, with titanium elevators, bulletproof glass, and high-tech surveillance cameras. All I knew was that it must be full of incriminating documents, ripe for examination—including, perhaps, material relating to the Stufetta. What's more, it was my most obvious way to penetrate the Forbidden City. If I could get inside the Secret Archive, I might be able to use it as a base for exploring the Vatican's hidden recesses. Needless to say, that was quite a big if.

Since the late nineteenth century, only a small number of approved scholars have been allowed into the archive, which is unique in the world for the continuity of its records, many spanning back to the 1200s without a break; the oldest date from the 800s. The rules of access have been slightly relaxed since 1998, but the Vatican gatekeepers still remain wary of outside researchers, whom they regard as scandalmongers. A reader's pass is only granted after a grueling interview in Italian, with officials famously looking for reasons to refuse. Browsing is forbidden. Applicants have to request specific documents—a tricky business, since nobody is entirely sure what's actually *inside* the archive. (It has fifty-two miles of shelves, largely uncataloged.) Writer friends in New York who had tried to gain a card with perfectly legitimate topics were invariably rejected without a second chance. My own first e-mail request for an interview provoked the curt reply that "access . . . can only be granted to Cardinals, Bishops, Ambassadors and selected groups from Universities, but not to private persons." I tried again. After all, I've put in a few hours as an adjunct at New York University. That did the trick.

In order to invent a plausible topic, I tracked down the only book on the holdings, by Francis X. Blouin Jr., who had been allowed to make a very limited inventory in 1998. Even to Blouin, Vatican archivists had not been overly helpful, with several juicy-sounding caches of documents withheld ("Not open for research and its holdings are not generally known") or simply lost ("No records located"). The most glaring restriction is that nothing after 1939 may be requested at all, covering sensitive material on the Vatican's dealings with the Nazis over the Holocaust and recent pedophilia scandals.

On the morning of my interview, I nervously shaved, dusted off my suit, polished up my shoes—the dress code is listed on the website—and stumbled downstairs. The hotel *padrone* looked me up and down and muttered: "What happened, you've turned into a banker now?"

"I'm off to see the pope," I said.

"*Va bene,*" he shrugged. "Give him a kiss from me." .

The Vatican guards first directed me into a tiny wood-paneled office, where office workers could be seen beyond an antique glass barrier, like bank tellers in a 1930s movie. This was basically Vatican Immigration and Customs, which I would eventually dub Checkpoint Charlie. I handed over my passport and letter of appointment in exchange for a pass which I clipped to my jacket.

"Through there?" I asked, pointing to a closed door at the other end of the room. The official gave me an Italian gesture of exasperation. *What do you think?*

Inside Vatican City! Only a few yards from the main gate, but I already felt I was in a different plane of reality. Grinning idiotically, I set off toward the archives, feeling that even the most prosaic scene was exotic. Maybe I could find the world's only ATM with instructions in Latin! The Vatican supermarket! The Vatican gas station! Clerics in flowing black robes

The Porta di Santa Anna from inside the Vatican City.

and crimson skullcaps swept by, muttering in hushed tones, while other priests wearing backpacks were jabbering into cell phones. Two nuns drove by in a VW Beetle. Limousines disgorged monsignors from who knows where.

I stared up at the Papal Apartments, hovering above it all with huge picture windows. Raphael's bathroom was somewhere inside.

But my first step on the ladder was an institutional hallway. Two empty chairs sat outside a frosted glass door, which looked disturbingly like a school principal's office. I could hear someone being interviewed inside, so I sat down and began to fret. Memories of my twisted Catholic education flooded back. In elementary school, nuns would give us coloring books of the souls of the damned burning in hell. Later, priests would thrash Latin verbs into us with a leather strap. I was always violating some hidden Church code, inducing an eternal blend of guilt and panic. Matters got worse when I tried out as an altar boy at age nine. I only lasted one day. I got the choreography wrong during the Mass, crossing in front of the altar with a chalice full of wafers. The Irish priest angrily chewed me out and kicked me off the altar boy team forever.

To distract myself, I perused a display case of Vatican souvenir pens engraved with celebrity signatures taken from Secret Archive documents, including Galileo Galilei's. You had to admire their chutzpah, spinning a profit from Inquisition victims. Like the German government selling Anne Frank coffee mugs.

At last, the door to the Admissions Office creaked open, and the applicant slunk out, looking ashen-faced. I stepped inside to face a beady-eyed official with a bald pate and diabolical goatee. He cast a cold eye over my documents, then began taking sharpened pencils out of his desk—moving very calmly, one pencil at a time—before casually asking the subject I wanted to research.

"The Council for the Index of Prohibited Books," I said confidently. The Congregatio pro Indice Librorum Prohibitorum had from 1571 decided which volumes should be put on the Vatican Index to be burned or banned. One of the key tools of censorship since the Renaissance, it was something I could discuss with a straight face.

The official began putting the pencils back in his desk, one at a time.

"The Congregation of the Index is *not* in the Secret Archive," he said, rising. "It is part of the Office of the Inquisition, and thus is in the Archive of the Sant'Uffizio."

"But Francis X. Blouin Jr. . . ." I stammered. "He says the documents are here!"

The official paused and sat down. "Oh, Blouin! His work is full of errors. We have had so many problems with Blouin."

But the name had taken him off guard. Maybe I was serious.

"Oh, I don't *only* want to consult the Index records," I laughed, scanning my notes. "There's the Council on Indulgences, too . . . the Council on Sacred Relics . . . the Registri Vaticani, I'd definitely like to see. . . ."

The official harrumphed and reluctantly started tapping my details into a computer. I held my breath. Better not to babble, in case I gave away my rank ignorance. I was finally starting to relax when he sucker-punched me.

"So what should I actually *put* as your research topic?"

Now it was me who was off-guard. How could I link all the disparate subjects I'd mentioned? "Why . . . the inner workings of the Renaissance papacy."

"What, *all* of them?" he raised his eyebrows.

The entrance to the Secret Archive, where Papal documents dating back for over a millennium are kept.

"Well, um . . . the day-to-day functioning of the Papal bu-reaucracy."

He looked dubious but reluctantly handed me a pass bearing the papal coat of arms—a laminated tessera with my photograph, for Professor PERROTTET Anthony to enter the Archivio Segreto Vaticano. As I stepped inside the elevator, I was overcome with euphoria. I pulled a face in the mirror and let out a maniacal giggle. Then I realized I was probably on video. Calm, Antonio! Don't blow it now.

The Secret Archive is now a seamless blend of the medieval and the digital. The catalog room looks like Merlin's study, its walls covered floor to ceiling with index volumes bound in cream vellum, which had been compiled by hand by the

librarians since the 1600s. For book lovers, it's an aesthetic experience just leafing through their enormous yellowing pages
covered in runic script. Next door, the reading room's vaulted
ceiling is covered with faded frescoes; the walls, with prized
diplomatic documents sporting the wax seals and medals of
King Charles V and Napoléon. On the long wooden desks, by
contrast, are banks of gleaming white Macintosh computers
and piles of CDs. Today archivists are scanning the Vatican's
rarest and most fragile holdings.

I was momentarily at a loss as to what I should actually
do now that I was in here, so tempting it was just to sit back
and admire the scenery. I could call up the trial of the Knights
Templar in Chinon in 1308 or the Papal Bulls from 1521 that
excommunicated Martin Luther. But no, I had to remain focused on the Papacy's dirty linen.

The archive does have a rather creaky digital catalog, even
though it covers only a fraction of the holdings. I typed in
"Stufetta." "Bibbiena." "Raphael." Nothing came up on any
count. *OK,* I thought. *Maybe the bathroom is mentioned under
Leo X?*

This was a more fruitful tack. The librarians were all men,
in finely tailored suits, standing in rows behind a long wooden
desk. They helped me sort out arcane call numbers to summon works relating to the Papacy in 1516, when Raphael and
his crew were at work. And eventually, I manage to locate
some dusty volumes that not only mentioned the legendary
Stufetta, but provided clues to its current condition.

Evidently, in the last century and a half, at least two
gentlemen-scholars with impeccable Catholic credentials
did talk their way inside. In his massive 1887 Church history,
the Austrian historian Dr. Ludwig Pastor dispelled rumors in
academic circles that the bathroom had been destroyed, al-

though he found Raphael's frescoes "in the most deplorable condition." Nevertheless, Pastor was disturbed by what he saw. "The erotic paintings . . . prove that Bibbiena was more worldly-minded than beseemed his position," he complained, adding that the licentious adventures of Venus and Cupid made "a most unseemly subject for a Cardinal's palace." In 1931, the French art expert Michel Emmanuel Rodocanachi reported that several of the Stufetta's panels had actually been whitewashed over. His book on Leo X includes several smudgy photographs of the artworks showing vandals' scratches over some of the genitalia. ("Permission for a viewing is difficult to obtain for the curious," Rodocanachi warned, with admirable understatement.)

Another book baldly reported that, as Raphael's reputation soared in the twentieth century, restorations were conducted in 1942 and 1972. Clearly, the Stufetta still existed in reasonable condition. All I had to do was figure out who had the key.

A SPY IN THE VATICAN

After a couple of days, I became a regular at the Secret Archive. I could just walk through the Vatican City gates, flash my tessera, or reader's card, and the Swiss Guards would even give me a nod. The librarians gradually loosened up and chatted with me outside the coffee machine downstairs, providing tips on how to navigate the system.

The fabled Stufetta, I discovered, was now under the authority of the terrifying-sounding Assistant for General Affairs in the State Secretariat. "I'm not sure you'll get a reply from *them*," they shrugged. "They're in the top two or three echelons of the Papacy." Still, I decided to e-mail their office every

The Casina of Pius IV, now the Pontifical Academy of Sciences, within the Vatican Gardens.

few days, requesting permission to pursue my sober study on "the influence of pagan imagery on Renaissance art," as well as e-mailing any other official in the Vatican Museums who I was told might have some pull.

I had some surprising good luck in other departments. One morning, after inhaling too much parchment dust in the Secret Archives, I was able to arrange a tour of the Vatican Gardens, which I had often glimpsed with longing through barred windows on the stairwells. Another day, I was given access to the restricted collection of Greco-Roman art, where my fondest hope was to find the fabled cache of marble penises removed from their classical owners. The story began in the 1870s, when it was said that Pope Pius IX, maddened by the loss of his territories, wandered the chambers of the Vatican Palace, personally lopping off the genitals of pagan statues.

It has been passed on through the generations with varying details—a version appears in the oeuvre of Dan Brown—and often includes ribald jokes about frustrated nuns who take advantage of the room, where the genitalia are said to be stacked like gleaming white sausages. The most recent version I'd heard, cited by a painter who worked at the American Academy in Rome, included the juicy, unverified detail that a "female German academic" in the 1990s had been working to catalog the genitalia and restore them to the statues until her "mysterious" death. Now, as I wandered the Greco-Roman halls, I asked my aged guide about it as delicately as I could. He took it as a perfectly reasonable question.

"Well, from the 1700s, there was definitely a campaign to *cover* classical statues with fig leaves made of plaster or metal," he said. "But the process would not have required the actual *removal* of penises." We examined several male statues where the genitalia did look to be merely hidden. Later, exploring the public sections of the Vatican Museums, I noticed that many other statues, like the famous Apollo Belvedere, were casually exposed and fully equipped. I kept up this investigation, taking various anatomical photographs, until the guards started to give me funny looks.

Although there were no original parchments relating to the Stufetta in the Secret Archive, I was able to explore the lubricious atmosphere of the Renaissance Papacy.

If I had to pick my favorite Vatican scandal, it would be the Joust of the Whores, generally considered a low ebb for the Holy Church. This spirited fiesta was held in the Vatican Palace in 1501 by Rodrigo Borgia, a Catalan prince who became Pope Alexander VI and who wins the laurels as the most godless, vicious, and debauched of the era's pontiffs. We know about the event thanks to the pope's master of ceremonies, Johann Burchard, who kept a scrupulous diary of the palace's goings on called the *Liber Notarum*. On the night of Sunday, October 30, 1501, Burchard records that "fifty honest prostitutes" were invited to a banquet in the rooms of the pope's illegitimate son Cesare. (The Borgia Apartments are today a popular section of the Vatican Museums. They are covered with extravagant murals and house the collections of modern religious art.) The guests included assorted clergymen, the seventy-year-old pontiff, Alexander—once handsome but now gouty and obese—and his attractive and lascivious daughter, Lucrezia.

After a drunken feast, the fifty prostitutes were ordered to remove their clothes while roasted chestnuts, a traditional Italian food for autumn, were scattered all over the floor. Instructed to eat their fill, the naked girls went scrambling on all fours after the treats while the male guests applauded. The clergymen then stripped and turned the event into an open orgy. As Burchard delicately puts it, "Prizes were announced for those who could perform the act the most often with the courtesans." Evidently servants kept score of the cardinals' sexual tally for the evening, with rewards presented by the pope to the most virile—"tunics of silk, shoes, fashionable hats, and other things."

"That this banquet took place cannot be doubted," concludes the historian Dr. F. D. Glaser, since it is also referred to by a Venetian ambassador Polo Capello.

I found the index to the Borgia Archive—it was a foot thick and a yard tall, so heavy that it almost made my knees buckle—and I requested the correspondence from late 1501. When the volume arrived, it had 812 pages of handwritten text just for the second half of the year. I leafed through the pages eagerly, enjoying the scribes' florid quill work. Doodles that looked like fingers pointed to important sections. Finally I found October 30, *Anno MCCCCCI.* On either side of the date, there was a series of somber discussions on diplomatic meetings. Business as usual for a Renaissance pope.

Well, what did I expect? An invoice for chestnuts?

To see what the Vatican now made of its reprehensible Renaissance past, I put through a call that afternoon to Dr. Giovanni Maria Vian, editor of the official Vatican newspaper, *L'Osservatore Romano,* and an expert on Church history. Before Vian's appointment in 2008, *L'Osservatore* was regarded as a propaganda organ on a par with *Pravda* in the Soviet-era Kremlin. But today, Vian is being encouraged to take a more progressive approach to modern issues, such as women's rights, and has put forth a more nuanced interpretation of Church history. He suggested I drop by his office on Via del Pellegrino, Way of the Pilgrim, in an undistinguished corner of Vatican City, for an espresso. It was all very pleasant. The breeze wafted through the open windows of his office, as Vian, bespectacled and relaxed, explained that the misbehavior of the Renaissance clergy was now seen in historical context.

"It may sound strange now, but the most important role for the popes was waging war and inspiring the troops," he said. "Take Alexander VI, famous for his orgies. From the moral point of view, perhaps, he was one of the worst popes in history. But he was an *excellent* pope from the administrative point of view. He was a brilliant diplomatic strategist. He confirmed the Papacy's influence and guaranteed its survival. Before that, European powers would dictate terms to the Papacy. He secured its independence."

In general, Vian preferred a long-term view of the Vatican's ups and downs.

"Corruption is part of the natural dynamic of history. There's an old Latin saying: The Church must always be reformed. That is the paradox of the Renaissance Papacy. Yes, it was decadent, but it allowed the Church to be reinvented and move ahead."

As I was leaving, I casually asked if he knew how I might be able to visit the Stufetta. Dr. Vian was not optimistic. "You see, Cardinal Bibbiena's old apartments are now part of the State Office. That's where the pope meets visiting presidents!"

Maybe I should light a candle in St. Peter's, I thought.

RAPHAEL'S BATHROOM OF LOVE

When I checked my e-mails a couple of afternoons later, to my amazement there was a reply from the Vatican Secretariat:

> Thank you for your email in which you requested a visit to La Stufetta del Bibbiena.
>
> I am pleased to confirm that you would be able to make such a visit on Monday at 16:30.
>
> At the entrance to the Vatican please explain the nature of your visit and you will be given the necessary directions.
>
> I hope you enjoy the visit. With kind regards,
>
> Secretariat of the Substitute

I read the e-mail over several times to make sure it wasn't a hoax. I had no idea how this had actually happened. Perhaps they were just sick to death of my e-mails clogging up their system. Admittedly, it was a little odd that it was unsigned.

No matter! I was overjoyed.

The next afternoon, I got another e-mail.

> We regret to inform you that the State Secretariat has informed us that in this period it is not possible to visit the Stufetta del Bibbiena. . . .

It was from a completely different office. Did this overrule the previous e-mail? I wasn't sure. Maybe one wing of the Kafkaesque Vatican bureaucracy had no idea what the other was doing. Clearly the only course was to turn up as scheduled and pretend I hadn't received the second e-mail.

When Monday rolled around, I spruced myself up for the big visit, then foolishly checked my e-mails again. This time, I was appalled to find a message directly from the Secretariat itself, sent that day at noon, with the horrifying subject line UR-GENT: CANCELLATION OF VISIT TO LA STUFETTA DEL BIBBIENA.

I let out a groan as I scanned the bald letter:

> Dear Mr. Perrottet,
>
> I regret to inform you that, due to unforseen circumstances, the visit to La Stufetta has to be cancelled.
>
> I am sorry for any inconvenience caused.
>
> Secretariat of the Substitute.

I couldn't believe my eyes. There was no name, no contact number, no offer of rescheduling. It was barbaric! Without pausing to think, I shot off a reply begging for a new appointment and providing my Italian cell phone number. I even added that I would turn up at 4:30 p.m. as planned to try to arrange a more suitable time. In the meantime, I sat in the Campo dei Fiori, trying to remain philosophical. I'd managed to see more of the Vatican than I ever hoped. Perhaps seeing the Stufetta *was* too ambitious.

I was just about to change out of my suit when the cell phone rattled in my pocket. I saw the caller ID was 111-111-111. Only two places I knew had such a telltale security block. One was the *New York Times*. The other was the Vatican.

A young man with a refined English accent answered—a Monsignor Miles.

"Sorry for all the confusion," he said. "I'm happy to say that the unforeseen circumstances have been resolved, and you can in fact come as previously arranged. . . ."

"Really?" I asked, incredulous. For a second it occurred to me that Les was playing a practical joke. But no, she wouldn't be that heartless.

"Just remember, no cameras or video are allowed, I'm afraid. . . ."

"Sure, thanks, yes, *grazie*," I muttered, still in shock.

This time, when I mentioned the Secretariat, the official at Checkpoint Charlie decided to give me a hard time. I needed a much higher level of pass to visit the Papal Apartments, the sanctum sanctorum of the Vatican. He also found the stated purpose of my visit entirely far-fetched, having never even heard of any Stufetta del Bibbiena. The copies of my e-mails from the Secretariat proved very little, in his opinion.

"Do you have a *name*?"

"Actually, yes—Monsignor Miles! I spoke to him only two hours ago."

The official looked through the Vatican directory, then back up at me in surprise. There really was a Monsignor Miles in the Substituto. The lunchtime mix-up had been a blessing in disguise; without a contact, I would have been standing there all day.

Calls were placed, discussions conducted in low, serious tones. The Italians in line behind me craned their necks and grew restive.

Finally, I was given a visitor's pass—this time, a much more regal version, exquisitely printed like an invitation to an embassy banquet. I was directed toward a quiet courtyard, the Cortile del Triangolo, where a Swiss Guard in full plumage of orange, blue, and red escorted me to a special elevator. It was a huge wooden cube with walls about a foot thick. An art deco light fixture gave off a weak light.

I pressed the button for the top floor, and the box rumbled slowly upward, as if it was being raised on pulleys by teams of slaves.

When the doors opened, my jaw dropped. A soaring Renaissance gallery spread before me, filled with celestial light and lavish color. On one side were the fifteen-foot-high picture windows I'd seen from below, each one open with stunning views across the rooftops of Rome. There wasn't a cloud in the sky, and the cypress trees were glowing in the sunshine as if Saint Michael had come down and given the city a polish for the occasion. The other side of the gallery was decorated with enormous painted maps—vast hemispheres with gilded edges and majestic Latin names. I tried to walk as slowly as possible to take in the poetic details. Caravels swept through the seven seas, the stars glittered in the heavens, and the occasional sea serpent popped up from the waves. The interiors of North America and Africa were mostly blank. Australia was entirely missing. Instead, Terra Incognita, the Unknown Land, loomed from the frozen south.

I felt like a minor head of state. Two more Swiss Guards, now carrying halberds, escorted me to an office with a wooden counter, like a hotel reception desk. An elderly at-

tendant hurriedly put on his blazer, then opened the ceremo-
nial waiting room.

I was too excited to sit. I went over my spiel on "the influence of pagan imagery on Renaissance art," fully expecting to
be cross-examined.

The door swept open and in walked a cleric in a black cas-
sock, looking a little harried.

"Monsignor Miles?" I guessed.

"No, no, they collared an American to look after you. . . ."

My guide from the Secretariat introduced himself in a
broad Midwestern accent—Monsignor Wells, originally from
Tulsa, Oklahoma.

"Real sorry about the mix-up on times today," he said. "We
had an Italian minister coming to meet the pope here this afternoon, so there was a scheduling conflict. But the minister
was delayed, so hopefully we can get you in and out in a few
minutes."

We stepped first into Cardinal Bibbiena's original bedroom. It had been renovated into a sanitized meeting chamber
with cream walls and no decor other than a pair of throne-line
chairs and vases of fresh flowers. In the far corner was a narrow wooden door. Standing before it with the key, the monsignor seemed perplexed.

"We open the Stufetta up very rarely," he said. "Almost
never."

For a terrifying second, I thought he'd change his mind.
Then he opened the door.

I climbed a couple of shallow steps into a bright, vaulted
chamber, about eight feet by eight, and fifteen feet high, spun
around and craned my neck to look up. The proportions were
just as odd as legend held. And Raphael had concocted a
whirlwind of fantasy: the bathroom was spinning with delec-

table erotic scenes. The walls and ceiling were covered with fifteen-inch fresco panels with small, naked deities prancing their way through a five-hundred-year-old graphic novel. Some panels were definitely the worse for wear, with gaps that had been repaired with cement; a couple were missing completely. But you could still make out the gods and goddesses at play, and my eyes darted from one image to the next trying to take it all in at once. The Vatican had helpfully provided an armchair for comfortable contemplation of the artworks. So I lounged and slowly took it all in, while the monsignor stood in a corner, waiting patiently.

In 1516, this room was on the cutting edge of interior design. The very idea of a separate bathroom was chic, inspired by a recently discovered volume by the ancient Roman engineer Vitruvius. (This was a *bath*room, not a toilet. Hygienic facilities were still rudimentary in the Renaissance. It's possible that Bibbiena had obtained a wooden cabinet as a toilet, but these were still considered experimental devices.) The cardinal's brass bath, from which he could admire Raphael's handiwork, had been removed, but down at knee level was the original silver water faucet, crafted in the mask of a grinning satyr. Three of the walls had niches decorated with real cockleshells, where statuettes once stood. Light was flooding in through a small glass window, slightly ajar.

Some modern scholars have suggested that Raphael's images weren't meant to be erotic in our modern sense, but Neoplatonic allegories (". . . for surely the Cardinal did not intend his bathroom to be a celebration of carnal love," reasons one). The argument is a little hard to credit, looking at the depictions of Venus. One panel shows a pleasing view of her posterior as she daintily steps into her foam-fringed shell. In another, she lounges between Adonis's knees as he caresses her breast. She swims in sensual abandon or sits on a luxurious bed, admiring herself in a mirror. We know from an engraving that one frame, sadly missing, had Venus suggestively raising her leg to extract a thorn from her foot. Another had Vulcan attempting to rape Minerva.

While some of the frescoes are lovingly executed, others appear clumsy. One, of Cupid sitting on a raft tied to giant snails, is truly surreal. These are usually attributed by scholars to Raphael's assistants.

Monsignor Wells was still waiting in silence. I voiced a couple of hesitant remarks, trying to sound learned, but he just shrugged: "I don't know a thing about it." Inwardly, I let out a sigh of relief. My spiel wasn't necessary. Instead, we chatted about the prairies. I had once been to Oklahoma for a story on the Old West.

I tried not to scan too obviously for the most notorious image in the Stufetta, of the god Pan with a monstrous erection. And yes, there it was, at waist-level by the window. It was a little embarrassing, but I had to ask the Monsignor to step aside so I could get a better look. I put on my most serious face as I inspected the horny half-goat deity, spying on the full-breasted nymph Syrinx as she washed her hair in the river.

Pan wasn't all there. Someone had specifically etched away his erect phallus and testicles, leaving a solid white shape—an accurate portrayal, even still.

"I don't suppose you know when . . . ?" I began.

"Don't know a thing about it."

Pan's manhood had evidently been intact in 1931 when the French art expert Emmanuel Rodocanachi wrote about the Stufetta; in fact, it was one of the few things you could see in the poor quality black-and-whites taken for his book on Leo X's papacy. The damage may actually have been done

*Artist's copy of a Renaissance engraving by one of Raphael's
students, Marcantonio Raimondi, from the Stufetta. The draping
over the nymph's thighs was discreetly added. Today, one key area
of the satyr's anatomy has been damaged. (© Lesley Thelander)*

by a disgusted Vatican official. More likely it occurred during
one of the modern restorations, 1942 or 1972—presumably
the former.

Lovers of Vatican conspiracy theories would find rich material surrounding the Stufetta. Both Raphael and Cardinal Bibbiena died shortly after its completion, within a few months of
one another, in 1520, under unusual circumstances. Raphael
was only thirty-seven, and according to the only contemporary

account we have, by the art-world insider Giorgio Vasari, he expired from too much sex. The artist's sensual appetites had always been "immoderate," Vasari wrote, and on this fatal occasion he indulged "with even more immoderation than usual." After an all-night orgy, Raphael came down with a fever, then made the mistake of letting doctors treat him. After two weeks, he was dead. Cardinal Bibbiena died about six months later, at the age of fifty, amid persistent rumors that he was poisoned. Sadly, history is silent on his sexual proclivities.

Their deaths did not end the tradition of subversive art at the Vatican. Two of Raphael's most brilliant pupils, Giulio Romano and Marcantonio Raimondi, reproduced some engraved copies of the images. They also kept painting more traditional religious imagery in other parts of the palace. But in 1523, Romano became so enraged about late payments for his murals in the Hall of Constantine that he drew obscene images on the walls instead—the notorious *I Modi*, or *The Postures*. They depicted sixteen vigorous sexual positions, with known Roman courtesans as the female characters. These were then engraved by Raimondi, and copies were distributed in a select edition around Rome, causing a sensation. Their underground popularity grew in 1525, when the scurrilous author Pietro Aretino also wrote sonnets to accompany them. Scandalously, he had many of the more provocative sections of the poetry narrated by the women.

This became too much for the new pope, Clement VII. He had Raimondi thrown in prison and would have done the same to Romano had he not fled Rome for Mantua. Papal officers hunted down and destroyed the copper engraving plates and almost every copy of *I Modi*. (It appears that any of their images related to the Stufetta were also caught in the swoop.) As Vasari notes, examples were found "in those places one would have least expected"—presumably among the Vatican cardinals themselves.

Aretino's dirty sonnets have been passed down through the generations. But tragically, not a single intact copy of Raimondi's engravings has survived. Only nine fragments, mostly of faces removed from their sexual context, were saved in the nineteenth century, ending up—of course—in the Secretum of the British Museum. (They are now in the Department of Prints and Drawings; an engraving inspired by the Stufetta is in Paris's Bibliothèque Nationale). But all was not lost. In 1928, the son of the famous Italian tenor Toscanini discovered a copy of a pirate edition of *I Modi,* made in Venice in 1527 by an anonymous printer, including slightly blurred woodcuts of the original artworks. Although the detail is not as fine as in the Raimondi engravings, the woodcuts do convey the strength of the originals. He brought the book with him to the United States, where it ended up in the hands of an anonymous American collector. Finally, in the 1980s, a copy was published by academic presses in Italy and United States as *I Modi: the Sixteen Positions.*

Today, thousands of tourists plod daily through the Hall of Constantine in the Vatican Museums, admiring the spiritually uplifting portrayal of the emperor's conversion to Christianity. Scholars have yet to perform infrared scans to see whether Romano's paintings still lurk beneath.

The monsignor was beginning to look edgy. Maybe the Pope was about to arrive, and he didn't want to be caught exiting the bathroom with me.

"Do you want to see the Loggetta?" he asked, to move me along.

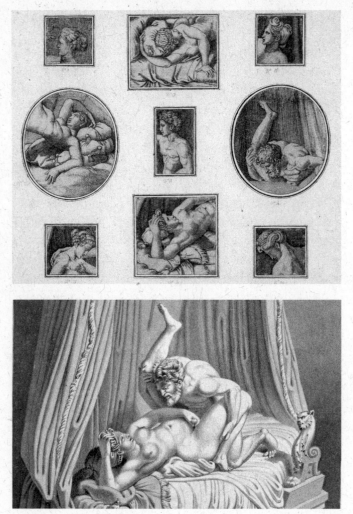

Above: Fragments of Marcantonio Raimondi's original engravings of I Modi *survived in the Secretum of the British Museum.*
Below: A copy of an original made in the 18ᵗʰ century by Frédéric Maximilien de Waldeck, an artist who claimed to have found a version in a convent in Mexico, now lost. Parts of the image do match. (Both © Trustees of the British Museum)

I looked at him blankly.

"You know, Raphael's Loggetta—it's pretty famous."

I nodded distractedly, but I was thinking of the Stufetta.

Later, as I returned to the elevator, I was so euphoric I barely noticed the bank of dark clouds gathering over Rome. By the time I was outside, the sky was black and thunder beginning to roll. I walked quickly down Mussolini's Via della Conciliazione, past the Press Office where my Vatican journey had begun, as raindrops the size of golf balls came hurtling down and a gale began to overturn café tables, sweeping umbrellas into the air. It was like something out of *The Exorcist*. I dashed into a café, took a window seat, and ordered a celebratory prosecco while I waited the storm out.

Swiss Guards outside the Inquisition Archives in Vatican City.

As the waiter approached me, he lurched and the glass fell, shattering into a thousand pieces.

"What happened?" the maitre d' demanded.

"I don't know," the waiter said, shaken.

Just to be on the safe side, I crossed myself and asked divine forgiveness for my impious investigations. Once a failed altar boy, always a failed altar boy.

RETURN OF THE PAGANS

The Once and Future Paradise of Capri

The broiling weeks in Rome had taken their toll on all of us. Enough Catholic madness and urban angst! Even the Romans had evacuated the city. I began to feel a guilty twinge that we still hadn't dipped a toe in the Mediterranean. It was time to do as travelers have done for the last three centuries and head to the southern Italian coast.

A sojourn to the island of Sirens was just what the doctor ordered.

From the sea, Capri looks like a place where the Gods would holiday, a fortress of titanic cliffs and rocky spires that rise like fangs from the blue Bay of Naples. The island may be less than four miles long and two wide but, for me, it loomed large in every sense. Its tradition of debauchery, established two thousand years ago and celebrated in art, literature, and song has reemerged again and again to inspire the reprobates of history.

The pattern was set in antiquity, when Capri became the ultimate escape for rich Romans from everyday cares. They traveled to the island to swim in its magical grottos, philosophize on the beaches, and seduce the comely locals, who were descended from Greek colonists. Many centuries later, the first excavations across the bay at Pompeii and Herculaneum in the 1750s reawoke Europeans to the erotic freedoms of the ancients. The two Roman towns buried by the eruption of Vesuvius in A.D. 79 were brimming with exuberantly carnal artworks that thrilled the most jaded connoisseurs. By the late eighteenth century, the nearby city of Naples was a goal for every educated traveler, and a visit to Capri a high point of every Grand Tour. In fact, looking back over the last 250 years, it seems that every sexual libertarian in the West made his or her way to its shores, where paganism soundly trumped austere Christian morality and inhibitions wilted under the warm southern sun. The islanders' casual attitude to sex was legendary: It was whispered that the most shocking proposals were greeted with a shrug. Living among the ruins of lost empires, perhaps they took an ironic view of human ambition and lived for the moment. Of course, foreigners had long remarked on southern Italian hospitality. As early as 1632, French traveler Jean-Jacques Bouchard referred to their favors as *la courtoisie*, "the courtesy"—as in, "The ladies are very beautiful and so are the boys and they both gladly perform the courtesy." It was as if the soil itself were irrigated with sin. The brilliant light, the crystalline water, the languid heat, all cried out, carpe diem.

The first traveling scholars were fascinated by stories of Emperor Tiberius, the patron sinner of Capri, who retired to the island in A.D. 27 at the age of sixty-nine and had a dozen villas constructed around its perimeter. His eleven-year stay there was immortalized by the gossipy Roman author Suetonius, who wrote that Tiberius indulged in perverted bacchanals with *spintriae*, "experts in unnatural acts." According to

The Hotel Caesar Augustus commemorates Roman rule in Capri.

the memorable account in *Lives of the Caesars,* one Tiberian favorite was to have boys dress up as fish and "tease him with their licks and nibbles" as he swam in his favorite grotto. In recent years, historians have discounted this depiction as a hatchet-job by Suetonius, a resentful patrician who was writing eighty years after Tiberius's death and had been dismissed from his position by Emperor Hadrian. In this revisionist view, Tiberius was actually a recluse who preferred stargazing from his observatory to ravaging adolescents. Since historians have documented far more extreme imperial behavior, the stories about Tiberius may have had an element of truth, but the reality will never really be known. True or not, the "Orgy of Capri" guaranteed its tourist industry, luring streams of Latin prose lovers to clamber up to Tiberius's hilltop palace, the Villa of Jupiter, Suetonius in hand.

Capri's golden age really began in the nineteenth century, as it garnered an international colony of freethinkers and artists, including what may be Europe's first openly gay community. The ghostly hand of Tiberius was at play again when Capri's most striking natural wonder, La Grotta Azzurra, or Blue Grotto, was discovered in 1826. A young German writer named August Kopisch had heard rumors of a haunted sea cave in the island's northwest, and he convinced some local boatmen to take him there. Swimming alone through the narrow entrance, Kopisch was astonished to find the water below him glowing "like the light of a blue flame"; the brilliant sunlight reflected through an underwater opening in the cave made him feel he was floating in "an unfathomable blue sky." Further inspection revealed a rocky platform at the back of the grotto, with a man-made opening. Islanders told him that this had once been the entrance to a secret tunnel extending directly upward to another of Tiberius's palaces, the Villa Damecuta, although the passage had since collapsed. Surely, Kopisch reasoned, this had to be where the crusty old emperor had swum with his bevy of little "fish"? (In 1964, marine archeologists did in fact dredge up three ancient statues from the grotto floor, one of the sea god, Neptune, and two of his son Triton, proving the cave had been a Nymphaeum, a Roman shrine to the water gods, and almost certainly used by Tiberius in some of his private moments. A 2009 survey of the five-hundred-foot-deep cave found seven statue bases, raising the possibility that the other four may be found. No trace of a tunnel has been found, however.)

Kopisch's bestselling account, *The Discovery of the Blue*

Grotto on the Isle of Capri, turned the trickle of rebellious visitors into a flood. Expats and artists converged from around Europe to escape the shackles of Victorian society, turning the island into the seaside alter ego of belle époque Paris. For those with ready cash, Capri was a close approximation of paradise. One could rent elegant villas, dine under the vine-covered pergolas, and argue about art and love over the light Caprese wine. Famous authors, such as Conrad, James, Turgenev, and Nietzsche, rubbed shoulders with exiled revolutionaries. Queen Victoria of Sweden came here to conduct a secret affair with the doctor Axel Munthe, who built a magnificent terraced mansion in Upper Capri inspired by his own classical visions. The libertine eccentrics included the irascible former Confederate colonel named John Cay H. Mackowen, who lived in a grand crimson mansion full of antiquities and an array of local mistresses, and the German painter Karl Diefenbach, who wandered the cobbled streets of Capri Town wearing a long white toga and sandals and gave "tormented" soapbox sermons in favor of free love and nudity in the piazza.

After the Oscar Wilde trial in 1895, the British began to predominate on Capri. Homosexuals had long been attracted to the permissive island, but many more fled London permanently when Wilde was sentenced to two years of hard labor under new laws banning "acts of gross indecency" between males. (The law had originally included relations between women, but Queen Victoria had deleted the provision, saying that the concept was patently absurd.) After his release from prison, Wilde himself arrived with his young lover, "Bosie," and laid a symbolic wreath at Tiberius's Villa of Jupiter. The writer Norman Douglas became the dean of the gay community and was known to frolic around the island's gardens with vine leaves in his hair. Decadent French poets and German art photographers came to pay homage to the pagan spirit. Capri is still fondly remembered as a progressive enclave, where nobody asked and nobody told. Even in the 1960s, filmmakers like Jean-Luc Godard chose Capri as a setting for chic and sexy thrillers, its fantastic mansions a fitting backdrop to dramas of sexual liberation.

What travel destination can withstand so much attention? The ease of modern transport has swamped Capri with admirers more interested in Dolce and Gabbana than Homeric lore. And yet the mythic pull of Capri can't be ignored. I had to find out if the pagan spirit had reinvented itself for the modern age or sunk like a stone into the Med.

THE FOUNTAINHEAD OF SIN

However, before any of us were going to swim with the fishes, we had to make a pit stop. I reminded Les and the boys that no Grand Tourist could travel to this part of Italy without visiting a certain archaeological site in the shadow of Mount Vesuvius.

Scholars have spilled oceans of ink on what Pompeii tells us about the ancient Romans' sex lives, but the most intriguing debate is over how many brothels the town had. The issue has been dubbed, endearingly, the Pompeian Brothel Problem. In the Victorian age, historians decided every house containing an erotic painting must surely be a lupanar (a den of "she-wolves," Roman slang for prostitutes) and concluded that there were thirty-five of them, which makes one for every seventy-five free male inhabitants. More recently, scholars have realized that cultivated Romans enjoyed having erotic pictures that we might consider too graphic on display in their homes, and they were particularly fond of giant penises, which were considered comic. (The ideal male body shape, seen on most statues, was actually a "dainty" penis.) As a result, some argued that only *one* building in Pompeii was actually a formal brothel. Clearly, argues the historian Mary Beard in her detailed treatment of the issue, the number was somewhere in between. But judging from studies of graffiti, paid sex could be arranged in a variety of ancient locales, including inns, latrines, backrooms in the theater, and gladiatorial arenas. (The Italian archaeologist Antonio Varone has carefully compiled hundreds of these graffiti in his exhaustive anthology *Erotica Pompeiana: Love Inscriptions on the Walls of Pompeii.* This weighty tome includes a vocabulary I certainly never saw in my high school Latin books, including endless references to *mentula,* the male organ, and *cunnuliggeter,* "a person accomplished at the art of oral sex." Most of the scrawls are rather basic, along the lines of *Hic ego multas puellas futui,* "Here I fucked many girls," or *Felix bene futuis,* "Lucky guy, you fuck well." Among the more complex attempts is the plaintive *Hic ego cum domina resoluto clune peregi tales sed versus scribere turpe fuit:* "Here I have penetrated my lady's open buttocks, but it was vulgar of me to write these verses.")

Pompeii's one undeniable brothel on Via dell'Abbondanza has been the most famous site in Pompeii ever since it was excavated in 1862. And like everyone else, I took the whole family inside the mud-walled labyrinth with its stone cubicles above which are famous painted images showing a variety of sexual positions, possibly the specialties of the house. Henry looked up at the postures with mild curiosity, noting that one male appeared to have two penises, then ran back outside squeaking *Wiener! Wiener!* Sam was terrified by a black dog that came loping through.

I hope they're not scarred for life.

To get the full picture of Roman sex, I sought out the Sub-urban Baths, which were only excavated in 1986. This luxury edifice once had an array of steam rooms and a sun terrace with sea views, but it is notorious today for a chamber with eight well-preserved scenes of copulation that appear to be satirical depictions of taboo sexual positions.

When we arrived, I was appalled to find that the baths were closed for repairs. Standing forlornly, I noticed two old guards sitting in the shade. The workers at Pompeii have legendary status: Many are descended from eighteenth-century excavators and have in recent decades been tapped by the Camorra, or Neapolitan mafia, to pillage antiquities. These two characters were definite Fellini extras, one lacking front teeth, the other with a deformed hand. I asked if there was anything they could do to show me the baths.

"Impossible," they said, with grins that said the opposite.

I folded up a €20 note, crisp and fresh from the ATM, and presented it with my card. The older of the pair took it without looking at it. For a second, I thought he would refuse to acknowledge my offer. But then he lurched to his feet.

"*Andiamo,*" he said, over his shoulder.

He removed the gate's rope like a nightclub bouncer and invited me to advance down some stairs. The damp chambers disappeared in various directions, but my guide knew exactly what I was looking for. Of the images near the ceiling, one appears to show two women in bed, among the only lesbian scenes ever found in ancient art; it is difficult to be sure, but one appears to be using a strap-on dildo. In another, a man is giving oral sex to a woman—again rare, because cunnilingus was frowned upon by Roman men as "unclean." (Not everything was accepted in the ancient world, and sex was often complicated by issues of social status. For example, relations between men were not frowned upon per se, but it was shameful for an upper-class man to be penetrated by a social inferior. The aristocrat had to do the penetrating—a situation the historian John R. Clarke helpfully calls the He-Who-Must-Insert Rule.) There are two group sex scenes, one a trio, another a foursome, the latter with a woman giving oral sex to another woman.

Below each fresco was a number in Roman numerals, and a shelf, whose purpose has exercised scholars. It's possible that the slave girls who worked in the baths doubled as prostitutes, with the numbered paintings as a visual menu ("I'll take the rear-entry position"). But Mary Beard argues more convincingly that this was simply a male changing room for the baths, and that the numbered shelves held baskets for the clients' belongings. The lewd paintings were used as a saucy memory aid. ("My clothes are in the rear-entry box.")

Beard adds one curious twist to the scenario. All eight scenes had actually been painted over with plain wallpaper patterns before Vesuvius's eruption.

"Maybe even some Pompeiians had . . . had enough of pictures of sex."

Not me. Passing through Naples, I insisted we try to inspect the mother lode of ancient erotica. For centuries, all the hardcore finds from Pompeii and Herculaneum were transported to the National Museum of Archaeology and sealed away in the Gabinetto Segreto, or Secret Cabinet. Created in 1816, it became the most sought-after cache of filth in Europe, considered so disgraceful that in 1849 it was even bricked up for several years so that "its memory could, as far as possible, be dispelled." Women have only been allowed inside the small gallery since the year 2000, and minors under the age of eighteen are still banned. All this makes the Secret Cabinet so popular today that you need a timed ticket to enter.

I was expecting a mob scene, but the grand old museum was strangely silent. A handwritten sign at the ticket booth read that a staff strike would close the museum at 1:00 p.m. Ah, Italy! There was only one hour left. We rushed past the empty entrance, along echoing corridors. Whole galleries were left unattended. We could have walked out with a handful of Roman bracelets. The Gabinetto Segreto was hard to miss, identified as it was by a big sign that reads GABINETTO SE-GRETO. A smaller sign warned that it is X-rated and bambini are not admitted. But even Italians can't keep up the pretense that the cabinet is still shocking. The ticket post was abandoned, so we all wandered inside.

"Why is this stuff locked up?" Henry asked. He couldn't really see what all the fuss was about, as we examined the scenes of nymphs by the Nile and wind chimes made from iron phalluses. As Sam frisked about, bothering the more serious connoisseurs, I tried in vain to explain the history of censorship and how the phallic imagery of the Romans, which was thought to ward off the evil eye, was thought to be rude.

We paused before one of the stranger Roman images, a painting of the god Priapus weighing his enormous penis in a scale. Henry looked at it for a second, knitted his brow, then let out a raucous laugh.

It was as comical now as it probably had been in antiquity.

THE ISLAND OF DREAMS

When we finally made it to the docks of Capri, I ran off to find a taxi while, unbeknownst to me, Les sat on her suitcase to tell the boys a horror story. When I returned, they were kneeling at her feet, listening with rapt attention and shooting me accusing glances. I already knew the plot. She was telling them about the *last* time we had come to Capri, when she was pregnant with Henry, and I'd put her through hell.

We had been traveling through Italy, researching material for my first book. Like most people these days, we decided to visit Capri on a simple day trip from Naples. Les had stopped getting morning sickness, and the weather that day was sublime. Italians rave about the *giornatta perfetta,* perfect day, when the sky is cloudless, the sea is calm, and the olives succulent, and this one qualified—almost. The evening was so warm and seductive, I'd argued, why not have dinner on the island and leave on the very last hydrofoil at eleven p.m.? Les had been more cautious, but I persuaded her. Sure enough, when we arrived at the docks, we found that the last hydrofoil had been canceled. This would hardly have been tragic, except that this was a Saturday night, and the entire island had been taken over for a festival of Italian TV soap operas. There was, quite literally, not a single room free. We visited one grand hotel after another, being repeatedly turned away by innkeepers indifferent to our Jesus-and-Mary routine. We even came back to the Marina Grande with the intention of sleeping on a ferry, but the ships were kept at freezing temperatures to discourage the rats. By now, Les was starting to look wan. After hiking all over the island, she'd already pushed herself to the limit.

We cowered in a smoke-filled bar until four a.m., surrounded by Capri's teenage in-crowd as they cavorted and lap-danced as if there were no tomorrow. Finally, when it closed, we staggered past the palatial Hotel Las Palmas, where

Orson Welles and Marlon Brando had stayed. Les insisted I inquire yet again. This time the gods smiled! One guest had failed to arrive (on that last hydrofoil), so a room was available. It was, of course, the penthouse suite, a mere $450. We took it, crawled into bed, slept for three hours, then had to catch the first hydrofoil back to Naples next morning.

Henry and Sam looked at me with troubled expressions. "Daddy always pushes things too far," Les said sweetly. I had a feeling they knew that already.

"Do we have a place to stay now?" Henry asked.

I reassured them we did. This time I would redeem myself. Capri is where all sins are forgiven, after all.

Admittedly, our expedition from Naples hadn't been in the lap of luxury. Every inch of the local Circumvesuviano (Around Vesuvius) train was tattooed with graffiti like a 1970s subway carriage out of *Serpico*. The heat pulsed through open windows, along with the scent of sulfur from volcanic vents. To reach the ferry in Sorrento, we dragged our luggage down one thousand stone steps to the port until the wheels of Les's bag broke. Then, for unknown reasons, the ferry captain wouldn't let passengers outside for fresh air. Inevitably, Sam turned green, then threw up his lunch onto Les's lap. In Capri, the docks of Marina Grande were in chaos. This was the last week of the Italian summer holidays, and the island was as frenzied as Martha's Vineyard over Labor Day.

I was grateful that I'd found us a quaint artists' studio, on the quieter southern side of the island. It had to have great views, I enthused, as we zigzagged up the hairpin bends of the cliffs in one of Capri's white convertible Mercedes taxis. We would look out over the famous Fariglioni, the three stone spires of the island that jut out of the sea like the Clashing Rocks in *Jason and the Argonauts.*

As I hoisted our luggage up the steps to our new abode, I sensed that all was not well. The lawn was bleached, the plants withered in their vases. The room was far smaller, and much darker, than the cheery photographs on the Internet site suggested. We quickly realized the "artist's studio" was in fact the former servant's quarters in the basement of a grand villa. Right on top of our heads, a gracious terrace with white columns and a bougainvillea-swathed pagoda commanded the seas, while our compact "balcony" took in the details of telephone poles. I cringed at the possibility of Italian rap stars flicking cigarette ash on our heads during their all-night parties. The sun was blasting into our windowless cell, and I could already spot mosquitoes hovering in cobwebbed corners.

The agent, Anna, a big-boned Ukrainian blonde, was keen to hand over our keys and abscond. She bellowed her every word at the top of her lungs, perhaps thinking it would make her thick Italian easier to understand. Shouting and waving her arms constantly, she pointed out the studio's eccentricities, like the cupboard doors that would not open, table legs held together with wire, and the primitive gas cooker with only one working burner. But even she couldn't ignore Les' brewing, Vesuvius-like anger.

"*No te piace?*" she finally yelled at Les. *You don't like it?*

"*Purgatorio!*" Les said, remembering her Dante.

Anna made a grunt of indifference. "*Egh!*"

Les was ready to demand our money back and look for somewhere else.

Anna barked, "*È alta stagione!*" *It's high season.*

Unpleasant memories were being evoked. Les looked ready to head for the Hotel Las Palmas and demand her old suite back. I suggested that if we bought some electric fans, *maybe* it was livable. . . .

Then Anna thundered, *"One last thing . . . !"*

She turned on the taps in the shower stall, and they gurgled dry.

"Workers came today. Now no hot water!"

Les was speechless.

"But no problem!" Anna said. *"You come upstairs!"*

Baffled, I followed her up to the villa above. I expected to interrupt a gaggle of tanned millionaires guffawing over their cocktails, but no, it was actually derelict, like a *Sunset Boulevard* mansion in decay. Its white columns were overgrown with vines, which continued clawing their way across the faience tile patio. But the most cinematic aspect was the view. I literally stopped in my tracks, stunned. The forty-foot-wide terrace commanded the entire horizon, from the Marina Piccola, or Small Harbor, far down below, to the jagged fingers of the Fariglioni, both sides framed perfectly by the soaring cliffs. These vertiginous drops were the "galloping rocks" of Capri, described by the Italian Futurist poet Marinetti in the 1920s, which provided the residents "exclusive balconies for elegant suicides." There wasn't a better view in all the island.

Anna shouldered open a doorway of the villa, revealing an alcove full of antique iron bed frames and mattresses with horsehair tufts protruding. By contrast, at the far end was a huge bathroom, completely renovated with the latest designer fittings, and a vast marble tub.

"Ecco!" Anna yelled as the water surged forth from the tap. *"You use this!"*

"So nobody is even staying up here in the villa?"

Anna shrugged. *"Needs more work!"*

"Which means this terrace . . . ?"

Our terrace view, to the Fariglioni.

"Use it, I don't care."

Downstairs, Les had our luggage ready to drag back to the street.

"Actually, hon," I whispered, as I tried to get rid of Anna before she changed her mind, "I think this place will be fine, better than fine. . . ."

That night, I tracked down the last two electric fans for sale on Capri from an old hardware vendor hidden among the Gucci and Bulgari stores. I also managed to collect some pasta and local wine from a vineyard called Tiberio in honor of the lecherous old emperor. While I tried to figure out the Italian assembly instructions for the fans, Les got the gas burner working for dinner, and Henry and Sam made a flurry of watercolors to decorate the walls. We carried the meal up to the old villa terrace, and by candlelight watched the moon rising over the Mediterranean, the lights of a hundred yachts sparkling across the water. After the tensions of the day, we were all a little delirious. The boys had found a vintage boom box with a Tina Turner cassette tape in it and began leaping about to the music like dervishes. Les and I eventually joined in.

It was a fair approximation of a bacchanal. Maybe Capri could deliver the pagan goods after all.

THE GREAT GOD PAN WEARS ARMANI

Living beneath the haunted villa was both fabulous and creepy. Every morning, I'd wake up at five a.m. and ascend to the timeless, overgrown balcony, enjoying a William Holden moment as I watched the sun erupt from the molten ocean. Only once did I push open a side door to poke around. The furniture was Mussolini-era and buried in a carpet of dust. There were mountains of old periodicals and a black armoire with all its recesses locked tight. I crept up some stairs to a boarded-up bedroom before losing my nerve. There were just too many unexplained noises up there. Soon the boys refused to stay on the terrace at all after dark. Even Les kept her spells in the marble bath short, returning with a different theory every day about who had once lived in the villa. It was a schizophrenic existence. By day, we cavorted on the terrace as if we were the Prince of Monaco, Grace Kelly, and family. By dusk, we became the gremlins in the cellar.

In ancient times, wealthy Romans came to Capri to indulge in *otium,* or "educated leisure," which involved strolls along the sands and musing on philosophy. I tried to kick back for a little Italian dolce far niente, "the joy of doing nothing," hanging out by the beach, drinking white wine, and nibbling olives. Just *existing in the moment.*

It didn't really work. I couldn't help thinking that the resilient pagan traditions on Capri weren't quite dead and buried but somehow reincarnated.

One afternoon, I noticed a poster in town—*I Paroli degli Dei,* the Words of the Gods, with a drawing of a Greek satyr playing a reed flute. Capri's annual festival was dedicated to the god Dionysius, with artsy events being held in spectacular historical sites. This I had to see. The following evening, I marched everyone through the lemon groves to the Villa Lysis, an art nouveau version of a Greek temple, built on the edge of a thousand-foot-high cliff. The sunset glittered from gilded mosaics on the columns, above which a jaunty motto was emblazoned in Latin, SACRED TO LOVE AND PAIN.

A century ago, this had been the home of another of Capri's disreputable expats, a gay French opium addict and occasional poet named Baron Jacques d'Adelswärd-Fersen, who traced his lineage back to Marie-Antoinette's lover, Axel von Fersen. In 1905, his marriage prospects and diplomatic career destroyed by a scandal in Paris (little is known, except that it involved a group of schoolboys), Baron Fersen moved to this secluded grove with his dapper Italian lover, Nino Cesarino, and threw caution to the winds. He chose this spot because it was just below Tiberius's villa, and he built a Moorish-style den in the basement, so that aesthetes in velvet jackets and hair hanging over one eye could lounge around over hookahs and discuss poetry with guests like André Gide. One day Fersen was found dead there, having ingested a lethal amount of cocaine and champagne.

This evening, while the cultured Capreses sat on the steps listening to a lecture ("Dionysius and Cinema"), we explored the art exhibition, black-and-white photographs by two of Fersen's companions on Capri, all of naked Italian boys in classical poses. A German, Baron Wilhelm von Gloeden, who lived in Taormina in Sicily, and his cousin, Wilhelm von Plüschow, based in Naples, had pioneered erotic "art photography" in the 1890s. They chose as their models young village men, no matter how plain, provided they were well-endowed, and had them pose with classical props like laurel wreaths and statue fragments, stifling any suspicion from the boys' families by paying handsome royalties. The kitschy images evoked an ancient sexual fantasia and were hugely popular in underground gay circles in Europe, collected by princes and heads of state. When in Capri, the two photographers stayed with Fersen, while his mate Nino modeled.

The festival's organizer, Ausilia Esposito, a raven-haired woman in a togalike dress and heavy gold jewelry, told me that an even more evocative homage to the Gods would be held at sunrise the next morning. I just had to find the Grotto of Matermania, a cliffside pagan shrine that could only be reached after a half-hour hike in the dark.

"Don't be late," she warned. "The music starts at six a.m. sharp!"

"You might want to go to that one by yourself," Les said.

At five thirty a.m., when I groggily arrived in Capri Town, the tuxedoed waiters were just closing down the swank cafés, and the last rich club kids were spilling out of the Bye Bye Baby disco. Trying to find the right route, I met an elderly couple dressed as if they were going to the opera; sure enough, they were bound for the dawn concert. Soon we were using our flashlights to proceed along a cobbled path through the moonlit groves.

The couple, Franco and Mariella Pisa, divided their time between Naples and Capri, much as their parents and grandparents had done. "We always try to support the arts," Signora Pisa said as she hobbled along on high heels. "No matter how strange."

After descending a stone staircase down the pitch-black cliff face, we arrived in the candlelit Grotto of Matermania. The cavern was half open to the night sky, the remains of the shrine still embedded in the wall. In antiquity, it was adorned with colored stones, artificial pools, and seashells. As shadows danced on the cave walls, other formally dressed Italians emerged from the night, one sequined diva holding a tiny white puppy. They all genteelly found rocks to sit on, until the numbers swelled to about sixty. As the starlit sky began to turn crimson, a tinkle of bells sounded and a lone musician segued into a discordant piece on a cello, inspired by research on ancient music.

I began to see that the cave gaped over a jagged coastline. Hundreds of birds in the surrounding trees began to respond

The sunrise from the Grotto di Matermania, site of pagan rites for over 2000 years.

to the dawn and the music. To the side, a team of women had laid out yoga mats and were now in Salutation to the Sun.

The audience was then offered the Dionysian repast—fresh grapes, bread, and milk. "Where's the espresso machine?" muttered Signor Pisa, sotto voce.

But the continuity with the ancient world was even more direct than I'd guessed. The organizer, Signora Esposita, excitedly told me that this very same grotto was used by Capri's artists for pagan recreations a century ago, fueled not by milk but wine and drugs. In 1911, the intrepid Baron Fersen decided to simulate a human sacrifice to the sun god Mithra here. Fersen dressed himself as the Emperor Tiberius and Nino as the sacrificial offering, while friends in Roman tunics held incense burners and sang hymns. Nino was stripped naked and bound, then Fersen pretended to plunge a dagger into his chest, which apparently did give him a slight cut. Unfortunately, the scene was witnessed by a young shepherdess, who ran in horror to the local priest. Fersen was forced to leave the island for a period—one of the few cases on record of the Capreses being outraged by anything.

The next morning, I went upstairs to contemplate the view, and lo and behold, the hundreds of yachts had vanished. There was only a single boat, a vintage three-masted schooner, in the harbor. It was as if the summer vacationers had disappeared overnight. One step outside proved it was true. "The season is over," smiled a George Clooney-esque taxi driver as we cruised along in his white convertible. "I'm happy, everyone is happy." The waiters were no longer pushy, the beaches weren't crowded, the bus drivers didn't sit on their horns.

We could also go wherever we wanted, unimpeded—even the Blue Grotto, today the biggest symbol of Capri's crass overdevelopment. I had heard rumors that if you went there just before dusk, you could swim inside the cave unobstructed by the boatmen who normally ferry tourists in and out. So I climbed with Henry down the cliff side and, ignoring a warning sign in five languages, we threw ourselves into the waves, much as August Kopisch had done in 1826. A chain is now embedded in the entrance of the grotto allowing you to pull yourself safely inside, without being brained by the rise and fall of the ocean swell. There beneath our feet, the water glowed that famous sapphire blue, which the Italian author Raffaela LaCapria describes as "more blue than any other blue, blue below and blue above and blue along each curve of its vault."

On our last weekend in Europe, I realized I no longer had any relics to chase or mad rituals to attend. Instead, I found myself chatting to locals on the beach in the Marina Piccola. I discovered it was possible to rent antique wooden motorboats by the day. Les packed an Italian feast, and we spent the day exploring the island's crevices, diving off the side of the boat and swimming around the base of the Fariglioni. By afternoon, we were just purring around Capri's soaring coastline in dreamy silence.

La giornatta perfetta for the family at last. But even then, I'm ashamed to confess, I had an ulterior motive.

I was quietly motoring us toward my personal favorite erotic landmark on Capri, the Villa Malaparte, a site that will forever be associated with the image of the twenty-two-year-old Brigitte Bardot sunbathing naked on its upper deck. This modernist fortress, built on a rocky headland in 1937, resembles a Mayan temple more than a private residence. It made a stunning backdrop for Jean-Luc Godard's 1968 film, *Le Mépris*

(*Contempt*), which has lodged in my imagination since I was a feverish adolescent. Today, the Casa Malaparte is hidden from prying eyes—that is, to all but ships at sea.

I could picture it all now. While Les and the kids drowsed contentedly on the deck, I happily imagined Brigitte rising from her towel on the rooftop, fluttering down its steps, and diving Venus-like into the turquoise sea.

And then I turned the rudder around for home.

NOTES

The best general introduction to the historical intermingling of sex and travel is Ian Littlewood's *Sultry Climates: Travel and Sex* (New York: Da Capo, 2001). The classic overviews of censorship in museums since the Victorian age are Peter Fryer, *Private Case, Public Scandal* (London: Secker & Warburg, 1966), and Walter Kendrick's *The Secret Museum: Pornography in Modern Culture* (Berkeley: University of California Press, 1996). For a brilliant survey of the history of erotica, I would also recommend *The Erotic Arts,* by Peter Webb (New York: Farrar, Straus & Giroux, 1983).

THE DEVIL'S TRAVEL BUREAU

For the *Secretum*'s formation and location within the museum, see *British Museum Trustees Minutes* 10.918, Jan. 13, 1866.

The Museum Secretum Acquisitions Register is available in the British Museum archives.

General Background

Caygill, Marjorie, *Building the British Museum* (London: British Museum Press, 1999).

Caygill, Marjorie, *A. W. Franks: Nineteenth-Century Collecting and the British Museum* (London: British Museum Press, 1997).

Gaimster, David, "Sex and Sensibility at the British Museum," *History Today,* Aug. 2000.

Gibson, Ian, *The Erotomaniac: The Secret Life of Henry Spencer Ashbee* (London: Faber; New York: Da Capo, 2001).

Thomas, Donald S., *Swinburne: The Poet in His World* (London: Weidenfeld & Nicolson, 1979).

Wilson, David M., *The British Museum: A History* (London: British Museum Press, 2002).

The Henry James quote is in: Buchan, John, *Memory Hold-the-Door* (London: Hodder & Stoughton, 1940), 151–52.

Nineteenth-Century Visitors to the Secretum

Although few left records, we do know that a core group of free-living literary gents who railed against Victorian prudery frequented the British Museum cache. The aptly named Sir William Hardman, magistrate and "genial connoisseur of smut," was alerted by staff whenever an interesting new erotic object was obtained ("for my Pantagruelian fancies are well known to one of two of the Museum people," he wrote in a letter). The bibliophile Henry Spencer Ashbee, presumed author of the Victorian porn classic *My Secret Life,* was a regular, and he wrote to Museum trustees to complain about the Secretum's lighting, lamenting that the inspection of such "interesting specimens" could only be conducted "only under the greatest disadvantages." The clique of randy connoisseurs included the poet Algernon Swinburne, aficionado of the history of birching; the explorer Sir Richard Burton, translator of the *Kama Sutra;* and Richard Monckton Milnes, expert on the Marquis de Sade, whose erotica-filled country mansion was known among friends as Aphrodisiopolis, and who would become a British Museum curator himself in 1881. All, not coincidentally, were inveterate travelers.

CHAPTER ONE: HELLFIRE HOLIDAYS

General on Eighteenth-Century Sex Clubs

Dashwood, Sir Francis, *The Dashwoods of West Wycombe* (New York: Aurum Press, 1987).

Linnane, Fergus, *London, the Wicked City: A Thousand Years of Vice in the Capital* (London: Robson Books, 2006).

Lord, Evelyn, *The Hellfire Clubs: Sex, Satanism and Secret Societies* (New Haven, CT/London: Yale University Press, 2008).

Rubenhold, Hallie, *The Covent Garden Ladies: Pimp General Jack and the Extraordinary Story of Harris' List* (London: Tempies, 2005).

Peakman, Julie (ed.), *Lascivious Bodies: A Sexual History of the Eighteenth Century* (London: Atlantic, 2004).

The Beggar's Benison and Wig Club

Book of the Old Edinburgh Club for the Year 1910, vol. 3.

Fairnie, Henry, *The Fife Coast from Queensferry to Fifeness* (London, 1860).

Jones, Louis C., *The Clubs of the Georgian Rakes* (New York: Columbia University Press, 1942).

Records of the Most Ancient and Puissant Order of the Beggar's Benison and Merryland, Anstruther (printed for private distribution only, Anstruther, 1892; repr. Edinburgh: Paul Harris, 1982).

Stevenson, David, *The Beggar's Benison: Sex Clubs of Enlightenment Scotland and their Rituals* (East Linton, UK: Tuckwell Press, 2001).

King George IV

Ambrose, Tom, *The King and the Vice Queen: George IV's Last Scandalous Affair* (London: Sutton, 2005).

Prebble, John, *The King's Jaunt: George IV in Scotland, August 1822* (New York/London: HarperCollins, 1988).

English Flagellation Habits

Gibson, Ian, *The English Vice: Beating, Sex and Shame in Victorian England and After* (London: Duckworth, 1978).

Cooper, Reverend W. M., *Flagellation and the Flagellants: A History of the Rod in All Countries from the Earliest Period to the Present Time* (London, c.1885).

London Clubs

Brooks's Club, founded in 1764, is the oldest of the surviving clubs in London, and one of the first to have permanent rooms; the current building dates from 1778. On my visit, somewhat to my surprise, a very amicable attendant named Alistair showed me around the upstairs parlor. They had an original wooden gaming table from the club's earliest days, with a semicircle cut into it to accommodate the girth of Charles James Fox, an eager but obese card player. The walls were decorated with oil portraits of the first Dilettanti Society members in fancy dress. Today, the twelve members of the society still meet at Brooks's Club every three months; the initiation rites, devised by Sir Francis Dashwood, are still secret, although it is known that they involve fancy dress.

Pubic Hairs as Lovers' Gifts

When the young Lady Caroline Lamb sent a pubic lock to Lord Byron in 1812, she went one step further and dipped it in blood—perhaps as a sign that she was not pregnant.

CHAPTER TWO: PARIS TO THE GUTTER

Anonymous, *The Pretty Women of Paris* (Paris, 1883; repr. Ware, UK: Wordsworth Editions, 1996).

Anonymous, *The Shuttered Houses of Paris: Being a Companion Volume to "The Pretty Women of Paris"* (Paris, 1906; repr. New York: Grove Press, 1996).

Baldick, Robert (ed. & tr.), *Pages from the Goncourt Journal* (London: Oxford University Press, 1980).

Bernheimer, Charles, *Figures of Ill Repute: Representing Prostitution in Nineteenth-Century France* (Cambridge, MA: Harvard University Press, 1989).

Boudard, Alphonse, and Romi, *L'Age d'Or des Maisons Closes* (Paris: Albin Michel, 1990).

Canet, Nicole, *Maisons Closes: 1860–1946.* (Editions Nicole Canet, Paris, 2009).

De la Bigne, Yolaine, *Valtesse de la Bigne, ou Le Pouvoir de la Volupté* (Paris: Librairie académique Perrin, 1999).

Harsin, Jill, *Policing Prostitution in Nineteenth-Century Paris* (Princeton, NJ: Princeton University Press, 1987).

Hussey, Andrew, *Paris: the Secret History* (London: Bloomsbury, 2006).

Lemonier, Marc, and Alexandre Dupouy, *Histoire(s) du Paris Libertin* (Paris: La Musardine, 2003).

Romi, *Maisons Closes dans L'Histoire, L'Art, La Littérature et Les Moeurs,* 2 vol. (Paris: Robert Miquet, 1952).

Seigel, Jerrold, *Bohemian Paris: Culture, Politics, and the Boundaries of Bourgeois Life, 1830–1930* (New York: Viking Penguin, 1986).

Weintraub, Stanley, *Edward the Caresser: The Playboy Prince Who Became Edward VII* (New York: Free Press, 2001).

Zola, Émile, *Nana,* intro. Luc Sante (New York: Barnes & Noble, 2006).

CHAPTER THREE: INFERNAL PROVENCE

The classic biography of the Marquis de Sade is Francine du Plessix Gray, *At Home with the Marquis de Sade: A Life* (New York: Simon & Schuster, 1998).

On Lacoste

Fauville, Henri, *La Coste: Sade en Provence* (Aix-en-Provence, France: La Calade, 1984).

On Early Visitors to the Castle

Cabanès, Dr. Augustin, *Le Cabinet Secret de l'Histoire*, vol. 3 (Paris, 1901).

Courtet, Jules, *Dictionnaire Géographique, Historique, Archaeologique, Biographique* (Paris, 1857).

Jacobs, P. L., *Mélanges Bibliographiques* (Paris, 1871).

The Perrottet Connection

Bourdin, Paul, *Correspondence Inédite du Marquis de Sade: de ses proches et de ses familieres publié avec une introduction des annals et des notes* (Paris: Librairie de France, 1929).

Laborde, Alice, *Correspondences du Marquis de Sade et de ses Proches Enrichies de Documents, Notes et Commentaires*, vol. 7, 1773–1776, *La Vie Quotidienne au Château de La Coste* (Geneva: Slatkine, 1994).

Lely, Gilbert, *Vie du Marquis de Sade, écrite sur des données nouvelles et accompagnée de nombreux documents, le plus souvent inédits*, vol. 1, 1740–1773 (Paris: Jean-Jacques Pauvert, 1982).

The Marquis de Sade's Correspondence

Papiers de Maurice Heine, tome 1, Bibliothèque Nationale de France, FR NOUV. ACQ NAF 24384-24397.

For Swinburne on Sade, see Donald S. Thomas above.

CHAPTER FOUR: SEVEN-HUNDRED-YEAR ITCH

Classen, Albrecht, *The Medieval Chastity Belt: A Myth-Making Process* (New York: Palgrave Macmillan, 2007).

Duvernoy, Jean, *Le Registre d'Inquisition de Jacques Fournier, 1318–1325,* 3 vol. (Paris: Mouton, 1976).

Duvernoy, Jean, *Inquisition à Pamiers* (Paris, 1966).

Le Roy Ladurie, Emmanuel, *Montaillou: Cathars and Catholics in a French Village, 1294–1324* (London: Penguin, 1980).

Weis, René, *The Yellow Cross: The Story of the Last Cathars, 1290–1329* (New York/London: Viking Penguin, 2000).

O'Shea, Stephen, *The Perfect Heresy: The Revolutionary Life and Death of the Medieval Cathars* (London: Viking Penguin, 2000).

CHAPTER FIVE: WILD AND CRAZY SWISS

Hay, Daisy, *Young Romantics: The Tangled Lives of English Poetry's Greatest Generation* (New York: Farrar, Straus & Giroux, 2010).

Dangerfield, Elma, *Byron and the Romantics in Switzerland* (London: Ascent Books, 1978).

Holmes, Richard, *Shelley: The Pursuit* (New York: NYRB Classics, 2003).

Marchand, Leslie A., *Byron: A Biography* (New York: Knopf, 1957).

O'Brien, Edna, *Byron in Love* (New York: Norton, 2009).

CHAPTER SIX: "LITTLE DEATH" IN VENICE

There are two general guides to the erotic history of the city by local historian Claudio Dell'Orso—the rather cheesy *Venezia Erotica* (Florence: Glittering Images, 1995) and the more restrained *Venezia Libertina: I Luoghi della Memoria Erotica* (Venice: Arsenale, 1999).

More academic background can be found in:

Le Cortigiane de Venezia, dal Trecento al Settecento exhibition catalogue, Casinò Municipale (Venice, 1990).

Lawner, Lynne, *Lives of the Courtesans: Portraits of the Renaissance* (New York: Rizzoli, 1987).

Casanova Biographies

Summers, Judith, *Casanova's Women* (New York/London: Bloomsbury, 2006).

Kelly, Ian, *Casanova: Actor, Lover, Priest, Spy* (New York: Tarcher/Penguin, 2008).

CHAPTER SEVEN: VATICAN VICE

Contardi, Bruno, *Quando Gli Dei Si Spogliano: Il bagno di Clemente VII a Castel Sant'Angelo e le Altre Stufe Romane del Primo Cinquecento* (Rome: Romana Società Editrice, 1984).

Dacos, Nicole, *La Découverte de la Domus Aurea et la Formation des Grotesques à la Renaissance* (London: Warburg Institute, 1969).

Deoclecio, Redig de Campos, *I Palazzi Vaticani* (Bologna: Cappelli, 1967).

Kertzer, David, *Prisoner of the Vatican: The Popes, the Kings and Garibaldi's Rebels in the Struggle to Rule Modern Italy* (New York: Houghton Mifflin, 2004).

Glaser, F.L., *Pope Alexander VI and His Court: Extracts from the Latin Diary of Johannes Burchardus* (New York: N. L. Brown, 1921).

Godwin, Joscelyn, *The Pagan Dream of the Renaissance* (Grand Rapids, MI: Phanes Press, 2002).

Rodocanachi, Emmanuel, *Histoire de Rome: Le Pontificat de Léon X* (Paris: Hachette, 1931).

Rowland, Ingrid D., *Giordano Bruno, Philosopher/Heretic* (New York: Farrar, Straus & Giroux, 2008).

Tinagli, Paola, *Women in Italian Renaissance Art: Gender, Representation, Identity* (New York/Manchester, UK: Manchester University Press, 1997).

I Modi

Lawner, Lynne, *I Modi, the Sixteen Pleasures: An Erotic Album of the Italian Renaissance* (Evanston, IL: Northwestern University Press, 1998).

The Vatican Archives

Blouin, Francis X. (general editor), *Vatican Archives: An Inventory and Guide to the Historical Documents of the Holy See* (New York: Oxford University Press, 1993).

Cifrese, Alejandro, and Marco Pizzo, *Rari e Preziosi: Documenti dell'età moderna e contemporanea dall'archivo del Sant'Uffizio* (Vatican City, 2006).

Fig Leaves

Prange, Peter, and Raimund Wünsche, *Das Feige(n)blatt* (Munich: Glyptothek, 2000).

CHAPTER EIGHT: RETURN OF THE PAGANS

Beard, Mary, *Pompeii: The Life of a Roman Town* (New York: Profile Books, 2008).

Clarke, John R., *Roman Sex: 100 B.C.–A.D. 250* (New York: Abrams, 2003).

Johns, Catherine, *Sex or Symbol: Erotic Images of Greece and Rome* (London: Routledge, 1989).

La Capria, Raffaele, *Capri and No Longer Capri* (New York: Nation Books, 2001).

Varone, Antonio, *Erotica Pompeiana: Love Inscriptions on the Walls of Pompeii*, tr. Ria P. Berg (Rome: L'Erma di Bretschneider, 2002).

Varone, Antonio, *Eroticism in Pompeii*, tr. Maureen Fant (Los Angeles: J. Paul Getty Museum, 2001).

ACKNOWLEDGMENTS

This book could never have been written without the kindness of many friends and strangers in Britain, France, and Italy. I'd particularly like to thank the staff in the department of prehistory and Europe in the British Museum for indulging my interest in the former Secretum and the very friendly curators at the Museum of St. Andrews University for helping me with the Beggar's Benison and Wig Club artifacts. In Paris, I could not have managed without the avid researches of Nicole Canet, owner of the gallery Au Bonheur du Jour, or the generosity of Louis Soubrier, who kindly opened up his family warehouse. In Provence, I'd like to thank Pierre Cardin for providing access to the Château Sade. In Rome, the staff of the Secret Archive in the Vatican were extremely helpful, as were the anonymous administrators who finally gave me access to the Stufetta del Bibbiena. In Capri, Ausilia and Ricardo Esposito, owners of the fine bookstore La Conchiglia, offered marvelous insider tips on the island's history.

In New York, thanks to my agent Henry Dunow, editor Charles Conrad and his assistants Jenna Ciongoli and Hallie Falquet, and to the friends who kindly read parts of the magnum opus in draft form, David Farley and Tom Downey.

The book would never have gotten off the ground without the encouragement and insight of June Thomas, foreign editor of *Slate* magazine, who supported the original idea of a series on lurid historical secrets, "The Pervert's Grand Tour."

I'd also like to thank my editors at the *New York Times*, Dannielle Maltoon and Stuart Emmrich, and my editors at the *Smithsonian* magazine, Carey Winfrey and Karen Larkins, for supporting various legs of the epic journey with assignments. Some parts of this book have appeared in different form in those publications.

And finally, my biggest thanks to Lesley Thelander, who contributed to the book at every stage—from plotting the journey itself to reading and editing the manuscript in its various incarnations and offering her support until the last full stop of composition.

ABOUT THE AUTHOR

The need for perpetual motion has always been Tony Perrottet's most obvious personality disorder. While studying history at Sydney University, the Australian-born Perrottet regularly disappeared to hitchhike through the Outback, sail the coast of Sumatra, and travel through rural India (enjoying a brief and inglorious career as a film extra in Rajasthan). After graduation, he moved to South America to work as a foreign correspondent, where he covered the Shining Path guerrilla war in Peru, drug running in Colombia, gold rushes in Bolivia, and several military rebellions in Argentina. A brief visit to Manhattan twenty years ago convinced him that New York was the ideal place for a rootless wanderer to be based. From his current home in the East Village of Manhattan, he has continued to commute to Fiji, Iceland, Tierra del Fuego, and Zanzibar, while contributing to the *New York Times, Smithsonian Magazine, Condé Nast Traveler, Slate, Outside, The Believer,* the *Village Voice,* and the *London Sunday Times.* His work has been selected for the Best American Travel Writing series four times.

Perrottet is the author of four previous books, which have been translated into eight languages—*Off the Deep End: Travels in Forgotten Frontiers* (1997); *Pagan Holiday: On the Trail of Ancient Roman Tourists* (2002); *The Naked Olympics: The True Story of the Ancient Games* (2004); and *Napoleon's Privates: 2,500 Years of History Unzipped* (2008). *The Sinner's Grand Tour* began as an award-winning series for *Slate* magazine on the salacious historical secrets of Britain, France, and Italy.

Perrottet is also a regular guest on NPR Radio and the History Channel, where he has spoken about everything from the Crusades to the birth of disco.

Further information on the author's books and magazine pieces can be found on his website, www.tonyperrottet.com.